History of Tripura:
As Reflected in the Manuscripts

The National Mission for Manuscripts was established in February 2003 by the Ministry of Culture. Its purpose is to locate, document, preserve and disseminate the knowledge content of Indian manuscripts. While looking ahead to reconnect with the knowledge of the past, the Mission is in the process of trying to re-contextualize the knowledge contained in manuscripts for the present and the future generations. The Mission organizes seminars on various subjects related to Indian knowledge in different locations of India. The papers presented in the seminar are collected and published under the Samiksika series.

This Samiksika series brings forth the papers presented at the seminar "History of Tripura: As reflected in the Manuscripts". The Seminar was organised in collaboration with Tripura University and Prof Satya Deo Poddar was the Coordinator of the seminar. The book aims at exploring the resources for the reconstruction of the history of Tripura utilizing manuscripts as a source materials. While going through the contents of papers, there emerged a fresh look about the history of Chakma and Mogs in Tripura. The social practices, rituals and traditions of Tripura have been comprehensively described in this book.

Samīkṣikā Series No. 10

General Editor
VEENA JOSHI

The Samīkṣikā Series is aimed at compiling the papers presented by the various scholars during the seminars organized by the National Mission for Manuscripts. The seminars provide an interactive forum for scholars to present to a large audience, ideas related to the knowledge contained in India's textual heritage.

In keeping with the title, the Samīkṣikā (research) Series is concerned with research papers of distinguished scholars and specialists in different intellectual disciplines of India.

History of Tripura:
As Reflected in the Manuscripts

Editor

Satyadeo Poddar

राष्ट्रीय पाण्डुलिपि मिशन
॥ विज्ञानमुपास्व ॥

National Mission for Manuscripts

Dev Publishers & Distributors

Published by:
National Mission for Manuscripts
Indira Gandhi National Centre for the Arts
11 Man Singh Road
New Delhi 110 001
Phone: 91 11 2307 3387
E-mail: directornamami@nic.in
Website: www.namami.nic.in

and Co-published by:
Dev Publishers & Distributors
2nd Floor, Prakash Deep,
22, Delhi Medical Association Road,
Darya Ganj,
New Delhi-110 002
Phone: 011 43572647
E-mail: devbooks@hotmail.com
Website: www.devbooks.co.in

ISBN 81–904029–6–X (Series)
ISBN 978–93–80829–39–5 (Vol. 10)
First published 2016

Price : ₹ 450

CONTENTS

Foreword

One of the major objectives of the National Mission for Muniscripts (NMM) is to provide ready access to the manuscripts or related informations through publication. Scholars specializing in various fields are invited to present research papers in the seminars which are eventually published by the Mission under its title Samkshika series. The Mision had organized one such seminar on 'History of Tripura as Reflected in the Manuscripts' in collaboration with Tripura Unniversity.

Tripura has a treasure of more than two thousand unique manuscripts of various communities spread out all over the state. The manuscripts were written mostly in Bengali and Sanskrit. Recently a good number of Mog and Chakma manuscripts written in Brahmi and Chakma scripts are found from Sabroom and Pencharthal areas respectively. The manuscripts deal with the history of ethnic tribes, their culture, music and herbal medicine practices.

Research papers in the seminar are presented by the eminent scholars and academicians. Most of them have come from different states of India, but there are contributions from Bengladesh as well. Large number of participants including the Research Scholars of various departments of Tripura University attended the seminar. The Research-articles in this volume contain varied aspects of the history of the region as emerged from the available manuscripts along with the interpretation of the scholars.

Our special thanks are due to Prof. Satyadeo Poddar for taking an active role in organizinig the Seminar in Tripura University. But for his wholehearted support and involvement we would not have been able to publish this volume.

I do hope this publication will with facilitate a deeper study of the manuscripts of Tripura.

VEENA JOSHI
Director and Joint-Secretary

Introduction

North East India stands in near oblivion in the cultural contour of India because we do not have any written records. Identification, documentation and editing of manuscripts can help the scholars for reconstructing the cultural mapping of the region. Cultural mapping of India will remain incomplete without Tripura in particular. Ancient and Medieval history of Tripura is bleak in terms of source materials and modem history of the state is also based on chronicles and mostly on English sources. Rajmala is the only written chronicle where the idea of monarchial structure can be deciphered. We do not have the social, cultural and economic contour of ancient and medieval Tripura in absence of ready reference. We construct some history from Persian source materials during the time of Samser Gazi but that too is not sufficient. The study of history is a continuous process and the continuity of medieval history of India has been lost in the land of Tripura. We do not have ample information of the history of Chakma and Mog tribes. More than two thousand Chakma and Mog Manuscripts have been identified so far and around a thousand manuscripts are left with non-tribal communities, say Manipuri and Bengalee of Tripura.

It is expected from the scholars that the study of the region be analyzed in tune with the contemporary source materials. While dealing with the ancient and medieval history of North East India in general and Tripura in particular, we find lots of problem to link the history of the region, with the rest of India due to dearth of archival and other source materials.Manuscripts are spread in both private and public custody. The main objective of the current volume is to explore the manuscripts of the region and depict various aspects of social, economic, political, religion, medicine, technology, environment, etc as reflected in those manuscripts. Sincere efforts have been made to identify the manuscripts that are related to the topic and accordingly it has been incorporated in the presentation. While exercising such effort, there is enough possibility of the interpretation of the content on the basis of known source materials. The connotation of manuscripts of other region has also been utilized in order to understand the continuity and change of history of the region. So the present volume aims at establishing and strengthening the missing link between ancient, medieval and modem history of Tripura and its relation with the neighboring states and countries as reflected in various manuscripts. **Prof. I. Sarkar** in his keynote address made an attempt to portray a fact that there are various documents and manuscripts on Tripura, which have already been studied or are being handled by the scholars, but there is a need to look at these documents afresh or to find out new manuscripts in order to trace the "missing link" of the history of this region. **Dr. Juthika Basu Bhowmik** in her paper brings to the fore some important tales of history based on the manuscripts of Tripura. This paper is just a snapshot view of some of the historical facts and would call for greater investigation by other scholars of the present time to dig out the several untold stories of the bygone era. **Bikach Chaudhuri** in his paper throws a new light on the structural history of Tripura. He discusses the relationship of the Manikya Kings with the Mughals. **Dr. Chiranjivi Chaubey** in his paper studied the similarities of Bhairava worship in Tripura and Varanasi. **Dr. Rabindranath Das Shastri** observes that the manuscripts of Tripura definitely can explore the social aspects, economic and political developments, religious and cultural heritage, and may be the traditional medicinal practices and environment. **Ashok Kumar Nath** through his paper eloquently brings out the significance of Digital Preservation of manuscripts, Counterfeiting of intellectual property and its digit-micro-photo remedies, to ensure archival conservation of intellectual property for posterity. **Bihari Jha** in his paper tries to find out the importance of Border management in Tripura. He argues that a large number of manuscripts are lying in the border areas which will play a vital role to reconstruct the history of Tripura. **Dr. Kalpana Haldar Bhowmik** elaborately narrated the Collection and Preservation of Manuscripts in Bangladesh. The paper also discusses the various dimensions of Manuscript collection in different parts of Bangladesh. **Naresh Ch. Dev Varma** discusses about the Kokborok manuscripts lying in Tripura and traces the evidence of manuscripts written in tribal languages of the State. Numerous folk-tales and folk-songs which are in vogue amongst the Kokborok, speaking tribes have been orally transmitted from the remote past. **Dr. Neeru Wahal** in her paper made an attempt to justify the 'royal' and 'public"—efforts of social and religious reforms that paved the path of progress for tribal state of Tripura. **Ng. Kangiia Mangang** is of opinion that both Tripuri and Meetei Manipuris are mongoids. Their appearance, facial cuts and skull forms are the same. Therefore, assimilation and adaptation process is quick and speedy and that is why indigenous Tripuris are all bonafide Meeteis in Manipur. They are never mentioned as Tripuris in the manuscripts of Manipur which are written in Meetei script. **Dr. Nirmal Bhadra** makes an enlightening study on the role of incantation and superstition in connection with the medical treatment in Tripura during the second half of the twentieth century. It also attempts to focus on the social-religious condition of the then Tripura. **Dr. Pradeep Kumar Deepak** in his paper attempts to explore the historical background of Tripura Sundari Temple in the light of several literary sources, manuscript, inscription, oral records and traditional findings. Tripura Sundari Temple is considered as one of the Pithas of Indian Cultural History. **Rupak Debnath** in his article analyses, within a comparative frame, the southward migration of the Tipperas as recorded in the Rajmala and in one oral tradition and shows how vital it is sometimes to sieve out fabrications that have penetrated deep into the commissioned documents of culturally assimilated peoples of the Northeast. **Sanjukta Mandal** in her paper, brings into the light Tripura's role in literary life of Rabindranath Tagore and also tried to narrate the literary history of Tripura which was related to Rabindranath Tagore. **Soma Basu** tried to cast a brief glance on the princely state that is Tripura with relation to Tagore's writings, i.e., how Tripura has come in his writing or how it has cast its spell on Tagore's mind so much so that he was inspired to take up his pen. **Dr. Chandan Kumar Chakraborty** in his paper highlights how Sanskritic culture was eagerly embraced by the princely state of Tripura in the past. He also argues that the cultural history of Tripura would have been written in a different manner if there was no favorable attitude of the tribal kings towards Sanskrit. **Prof. Satyadeo Poddar and Nirmalya Karmakar** in their joint paper have tried to focus on socio-cultural as well as historical facts about the Mog people in the light of manuscripts and decipher the several unwritten history of the Mog tribe. Further, a deep and serious study of these Mog manuscripts may open a new chapter of historical research on Tripura and adjoining regions. **Prof. Sitanath Dey** gives a bird's eye view of the history of Tripura specially in the ancient and medieval period as reflected in the manuscripts. **Rajib Ch. Paul** in his paper has tried to analyze the ancient heritage of the manuscripts of Tripura under the light of Bhavaninath's Ramayana. **Sri Jahar Acharjee** in his paper argues that besides the study of manuscripts, ancient history of Tripura and parts of neighbouring Bangladesh may have been rewritten after a detailed study of the coin inscription, stone inscription and copper plate inscription. The article of **Samhita Das** gives an account of the royal patronage to the writing of manuscripts and other allied documents which promoted the cultural development of Tripura. **Priyanku Chakraborty's** paper attempts to explore marvelous rock carvings and the stone images of Unakoti as reflected in the manuscripts. **Dr. Harekrishna Acharjee** has discussed the long history of manuscripts found in different corners of Tripura which narrate the phases of its development The paper also tries to attempt the importance of preservation and conservation of this age-old heritage of Tripura.

It is for this reason that this volume has emerged in the shape of book and we do hope it will facilitate a deeper study of the manuscripts of this region. The materials published in this book consists of twenty-four research papers Presented in the three days' National Seminar on History of Tripura as reflected in the Manuscripts from 19th to 21st January, 2012, organized by the Tripura University in collaboration with National Mission for Manuscripts, New Delhi. Despite many limitations, we hope that the book will be welcomed by the readers as a reliable source of information of Tripura. My warmest thanks and gratefulness go to our esteemed contributors, the publisher and the National Mission for Manuscripts, who had sponsored the seminar and has published the proceedings in its Samīkṣikā Series.

SATYADEO PODDAR

Key to Transliteration

VOWELS

अ a	आ ā	इ i	ई ī	उ u	ऊ ū
(but)	(palm)	(it)	(beet)	(put)	(pool)
ऋ ṛ	ए e	ऐ ai	ओ o	औ au	
(rhythm)	(play)	(air)	(toe)	(loud)	

CONSONANTS

Guttural	क ka	ख* kha	ग ga	घ gha	ङ ṅa
	(skate)	(blockhead)	(gate)	(ghost)	(sing)
Palatal	च ca	छ cha	ज ja	झ jha	ञ ña
	(chunk)	(catchhim)	(john)	(hedgehog)	(bunch)
Cerebral	ट ṭa	ठ* ṭha	ड/ड़ ḍa	ढ*/ढ़ ḍha	ण* ṇa
	(start)	(anthill)	(dart)	(godhead)	(under)
Dental	त ta	थ tha	द da	ध dha	न na
	(tomato)	(thunder)	(that)	(breathe)	(numb)
Labial	प pa	फ* pha	ब ba	भ bha	म ma
	(spin)	(philosophy)	(bin)	(abhor)	(much)
Semi-vowels	य ya	र ra	ल la	व va	
	(young)	(drama)	(luck)	(vile)	
Sibilants	श śa	ष ṣa	स sa	ह ha	
	(shove)	(bushel)	(so)	(hum)	
Others	क्ष kṣa	त्र tra	ज्ञ jña	ळ* l	ॠ* ṝ
	(*kṣatriya*)	(*triśūla*)	(*jñānī*)	(play)	

अं (—) *ṁ* or *ṃ* *anusvāra* (nasalisation of preceding vowel) like *saṁskṛti/saṃskṛti*

अः *visarga* = *ḥ* [aspiration of preceding vowel like (*prātaḥ*)]

ऽ *Avagraha,* consonant (like *ime' vasthitā*)

[*Note: Anusvāra* at the end of a line should be presented by *m* (म्), not *ṁ*.]

*No exact English equivalents for these letters.

1

MANUSCRIPTS AND HISTORY

I. SARKAR

In view of the recent trend of historical studies and research, investigating and interrogating history from various dimensions and perspectives, have drawn the attention of the modern scholars over the decades. Among the reasons, the most vital one may be a timely need to set courses and events of history in a new framework with the help of documents and sources already explored or being investigated. It is inspiring that some historians of our time have understood the importance of such a model of historical research studies and have been successfully setting examples in interpreting history devoid of many outdated ideas and perceptions. This trend has not only changed the nature of historical research but also opened a new horizon of historiography. While this is acknowledged in the practice of research, the present three days National Seminar of history of Tripura as reflected in the manuscripts (from 19–21 January, 2012) is a unique effort to study and highlight the history of Tripura in a new perspective. It is a fact that there are various documents and manuscripts on Tripura, which have already been studied or are being handled by the scholars, but there is a need to look at these documents afresh or to find out new manuscripts in order to trace the "missing link" of the history of this region.

It may be noted that initiative for the compilation of manuscripts on Assam was taken up by Hemchandra Goswami in the beginning of' the last century and his efforts took the shape of a book titled *Descriptive Catalogue of Assamese Manascripts*, published in 1930, by the University of Calcutta. It is interesting that there were no effective steps to compile or study the manuscripts and documents of Tripura history over the few last decades. The Institute of Historical Studies, Calcutta, had taken up to make a comprehensive study on the sources of the history of India. Only in volume IV of these series two articles have been incorporated, but the academic values of these two articles are not up to mark. In the same way the research based work taken up under the auspices of the ICHR, New Delhi, to study the sources of history of North East India is not helpful. Only an article on Tripura has got a place in this book *(North East India, Interpreting the sources of its history)* and this is on pre colonial Tripura. So we can understand the gaps in the writing of the history of Tripura both during colonial and post colonial period.

It is known to all that the *Rajmala* or the chronicles of the royal family of Tripura occupies an important place in the history of Tripura. This *Rajmala* is said to have been composed during the reign of Dharma Manikya (1431 AD) who engaged two Brahmin pundits named Sukreswar and Baneshwar for this great task. It is however noteworthy that the oldest *Rajmala* written by those two Brahmin pundits are rare and the opinion of Kailash Chandra Singha is not always acceptedby the scholars, it is perhaps a time to look at the Rajmala by Kailash Chandra Singha seriously and to avoid controversies of this work being a pioneer one. Another editor of the *Rajmala*, Kali Prasanna Sengupta says that the lost manuscripts of the Rajamala was discovered from Ujirbari of Agartala after the death of Birchandra. Kali Prasanna Sengupta (Vidhva is also of the opinion that Rajmala or Sri Rajmala was complied six times.[3] Whatever may be the fact the historical value of the Rajmala is above question. We may refer here a reputed scholar named Rama Prasad Duna who in his book *Tripurar Prachin Furthi Prasange* has stated how he could discover four manuscripts from Rajmala office, Tripura.[4] In addition to Rajmala he found out three more manuscripts namely *Krishnamala, Chompak Vijaya* and *Gazinama.* Apart from the Rajmala the historical importances of these three manuscripts have been studied by the scholars.

The hero of this Krishnamala is Krishna Manikya who is said to have been the fifth king of the Tripura Raj. The Krishnamala covers an episode of the heroism of Krishna Manikya who could recapture the throne of Tripura in 1760 AD. It is likely that this Krishnamala was written during the time of Rajdhar Manikya and the time is stated to be in between 1785 AD to 1803 AD. There are many information about the reign period of Krishna Manikya and his relation with the English East India Company and the Nawab of Murshidabad have been discussed here in detail.[6] It is said that as there were interaction and warfare with the Muslim power of Bengal, many terms of Arabic, Urdu and Persian are used in the Krishnamala,[7] and this may open another dimension of studying the development of contemporary literature. The most important aspect of the Krishnamala is the history of the Kukis who were said to have been the hill tribes of the East and North East Tripura.

The Champak Vijaya is a historical poem and the name of the composer is Sheikh Mahaddin. The story of this work is about the recapture of the throne by one Champak Roy who is said to have enjoyed political help from one Mirkhai of Chittagong. Infact this period was full of political crisis and it is likely that sometime during the reign of Ratna Manikya (1681–1712 AD) this Kavya was written by Sheikh Mahaddin. It may be known to us that Champak Roy was driven out from Tripura by the rival King Narendra Manikya and the situation was such that he took the helping hand of Mirkhai to help Ratna Manikya, the ruling king of Tripura. Incidentally Mirkhai was an army man and his brilliant activities have been stated in the Champak Vijaya.[10] Champak Vijaya is a historical episode in the poetic style, but its historicity and literary value are above the question. Many new information may be available after an indepth study of this document.

The *Gazinama* is another important source material for the reconstruction of Tripura history. The author of this work is Sheikh Manur Ali. It is said that Nasir Muhammad, a zamindar of present Belonia (Dakshinsik) and he had a ryot named Pir Muhammad. The son of Pir Muhammad was Shamsher Ghazi. From his childhood Shamsher Ghazi has been described as one of the brilliant boy and the zamindar took the responsibility to look after him. But within a short time a conflict started when Shamsher Ghazi wanted to get married to Daiya Bibi, daughter of the zamindar of Belonia or Dakshinsik. After some historical development Shamsher Ghazi declared himself the zamindar of Dakshinsik. The next phase starts with the conflict and confrontation of Shamsher Ghazi with the Tripura king.

The Ghazinama is also a historical poem. Various incidents have been incorporated in this work. The significant aspect of this Kavya is the statement of Tripura Kingdom at a time when it was passing through various political crisis. We come across another document named Srenimala another historical work and is considered to be a Rajmala. Kali Krishna Sengupta is said to have written his Rajmala. in the light of this Srenimala.[11] The uniqueness of this Rajamala is that one may come across a systematic list of the reigning kings of Tripura[12]. Although there is no specific date of the composition of Srenimala yet it has been accepted that it was composed sometime during the reign period of Kashi Chandra Manikya.

Fact remains that there are more than one Rajmalas and there is a need to make a comprehensive study of all the Rajmalas and it is very likely that after such an attempt a new history of Tripura may be written. Kaliprasana Sengupta himself has raised many controversial points as to the origin[13] of the Tripura kings and also the reign period of the different kings[14] and these deserve to be sorted out. The initiative of the Manuscript Research Centre and Manuscript Conservation Centre, Tripura University may be a significant step to this effect.

In the long run it is important to note that Rajamala is a document of the kings, if not the history of the people of Tripura. Again it is not out of question that the composition of Rajmala may be taken as the beginning of writing history in Bengali language.' Apart from the Rajmala there are huge number of medieval sources right from the Ain-i-Akbari to Tarikh-i-Bangla and Riyaz-us-Salatin. We have another medieval document Baharistan-i-Ghayebi and all these sources provide us with historical information about Tripura.

The history of North East India is primarily based on a valuable document known as Buranjis. The historicity of the Buranjis cannot be underestimated. Tripura Buranji popularly known as Tripura Desar Kathar Lekha, the name by which the original manuscript is known bears testimony about the history of the region of a crucial period. We are fortunate that there is a Tripura Buranji written by Ratna Kandali and Arjundas Kataki. It has been edited by S.K. Bhuyan and published from historical and antiquarian studies Gauhati 1990. In the introduction of this Buranji S.K. Bhuyan says that Tripura Buranji has been reproduced from an old manuscript in the British Museum, London. A photostate copy which was obtained in January 1936 through the courtesy of Dr. Lionel. D.

Barnett, the then keeper of Oriental Books and Manuscripts. The Tripura Buranji is no doubt a valuable document to study Assam Tripura relation vis-à-vis their relation with the Nawab of Bengal during Maharaja Rudra Shinga of Assam and Ratna Manikya of Tripura. It is interesting that some diplomatic relation was established between Assam and Tripura and the story runs as how Ratna Kandoli, and Arun Das Kataki played the role behind the screen.

Incidentally we come across one interesting document of Gobinda Manikya's period and his relation with Mughal Emperor Aurangzeb. There is a letter from Aurangzeb to Gobinda Manikya. And the content of the letter is how Shuja the standing enemy of Aurangzeb had taken shelter somewhere in the kingdom of Govinda Manikya. The letter was written with an approach of getting help from the king of Tripura. Infact such type of documents are lying in the archives and we are fortunate that about 58 such valuable documents have been collected in a book titled *Tripura Historical Documents* compiled by Maharaja Kumar Sahadev, Bikram Kishore and Dr. Jagadis Gan-Chaudhuri. This book contains many documents in addition to that of Aurangzeb, from Warren Hastings down to 3.7.1947 in which we come across a notification containing Mr. Girija Shankar Guha, M.A., Barrister in Law, Minister Government of Tripura had been duly chosen as representative of Tripura, Manipur and Khasi states group in the Constituent Assemble of India. Another interesting document is a notification dated Agartala, the 11th June, 1947. It is hereby notified that the late Colonel, His Highness Maharaja Manikya Sri Bir Bikrani Kishore Deb Barman, G.B.E., K.C.S.I. ruler of Tripura state, having decided to join the existing Constituent Assembly, nominated on the 29th April, 1947, Mr. U.S. Guha M.A., B.L., Bar-at-Law, Minister, Government of Tripura, as the representative of Tripura state to the said Constituent

Assembly, which was duly communicated to the Secretary, Constituent Assembly, New Delhi, by a telegram of the same date.[17]

Administrative reports and documents are important. History of Tripura especially that of modern period vis-a-vis the colonial era is intimately connected with such reports. Very recently one such report has come down to our notice and fortunately it has been published by the Tribal Research and Cultural Institute, Government of Tripura, Agartala, 2004. We come to learn that a manuscript of this report was lying with Rama Prasad Datta, an eminent scholar of Tripura and the report covers the administration state of Tripura from 13th April 1890–12th April 1921. This is a document which contains valuable information about the history, culture, administrative set up and some other details useful for understanding the cultural demography of Tripura. Incidentally the Administrative Reports of Tripura State since 1902 to 1943 edited by Professor Mahadev Chakraborty are valuable documents which may bring to light many unknown facts and history of Tripura.

The importance of Memoirs, Biographies and Diaries can hardly be ignored for the purpose of history writing. In fact a major part of Indian history has been written on the basis of these documents and a few Mughal rulers may be taken as the path-finder of this discipline. Incidentally we come across such type of memoirs and biographies about Tripura. Mention may be made of *Tripura Smriti* by Samarendra Chandra Deb Barman, Nepal Nag's *Smriti Charana.*

Bidrohi Sachindra Lal by Sakti Haldar, *Tripurar Sivadinla Samgramer Smriti* by Tarn Mohan Dasgupta. In fact these are published works but many historical information may be seen to link up the missing history of Tripura. The rise of Ganamukti Parisad, Peasant Movement, pre-historic sites and antiquities are someway or rather have been incorporated in these works.

The relation of Rabindranath Tagore and the Tripura Raj family is a known history. The letters written by Tagore to Mahraja Bir Chandra Manikya and Radha Kishore Manikya are not only valuable to highlight the contemporary history and society of Bengal and Tripura but also give hints to think about Tagore's involvement in many affairs of the *Tripura Raj.* Fortunately some of the documents are compiled in a book *Tripura's Ties* with Tagore by *Sri S. Thnerjee.*

The work and reference to Rabindranath Tagore by Bikach Chaudhary[19] through his book *Tripurar Rabindranath.* The most important aspect of this book is to trace a familiar relation of the Manikya family of Tripura (i.e. Maharaja Kishore Manikya) with Dwarkanath Tagore. It is said that in 1293 B.S. 123rd Baisakh) Rabindranath Tagore wrote a letter to Maharaja Birchandra of Tripura for some historical information for his proposed novel *Rajarshi*[20]. Infact Bikach Chaudhury has incorporated a number of letters of Rabindranath Tagore addressed to Maharajas of Tripura and all of them are valuable to look at the history of Tripura in a new dimension.[21] In this respect we must recall here the recent work by Professor Arunoday Saha, Honourable Vice-Chancellor of Tripura university on the letter correspondences between Rabindranath Tagore and Maharaja Bir Chandra Manikya, Maharaja Radha Kishore Manikya of the Tripura Royal family. This work titled Raja O Kavi has opened some new dialogues and discussions on the relation between the Tripura royal family and the Tagore family of Jorasalko, Calcutta with special reference to Rabindranath Tagore.

The study of manuscripts and documents will remain incomplete without referring the documents of Tripura highlighting the role played by the people of Tripura and the documents available to us for the study of the same. Dr. Sukumar Biswas has compiled a huge number of documents on the liberation war and its relation with

Tripura and its people. A thorough study of this documents or dalil may open a new phase of Indo-Bangladesh history in the days to come. There are still huge documents lying in some areas of Bangladesh which may throw light on the history of Tripura down the ages.

Apart from the primary sources, we have discussed some secondary documents which were initially in the manuscript form but they are now in a published document. The historical value of these manuscripts-cum-documents are unquestionable. Careful patience and meticulous analysis are needed to study these documents in order to write the history of Tripura from the new perspective.

Let me conclude with a hope that the investigation and study of the manuscripts under the able guidance of this Centre may open a new chapter or historical research on Tripura and a new historiography is to born in near future.

References

1. *Analysis of the Rajmala or Chronicles of Tripura* by the Rev. James Long, published from Tribal Research Instittute and Museum, Government of Tripura, (Reprint), 2008, introduction.
2. *Tripurar Prachin Punthi* (Bengali) by Rama Prasad Dutta, Agartala, Tripura, 1998, p. 8, infact there are four Lahars (parts) of the Sri Rajmala, edited by Sri Kali Prasanna Sengupta, Agartala, 2003.
3. Sri Prasanna Sengupta, op. cit., Lahar 1, p. LII (Purvabhas).
4. Rama Prasad Dutta, *Tripurar Prachin Purva Katha,* Rama Prasad Dutta-Tripurar Prachin, p. 24.
5. LOC., cit.
6. For details see "Tripurar Raj Amalar Bangla Sahitya" by Dr. Ranjit Chandra Bhattacharyya, Tripura, 2003, p. 58.
7. LOC., cit.
8. Dr. Ranjit Chandra Bhattacharyya, op. cit., p. 47.
9. Dr. Ranjit Chandra Bhattacharyya, op. cit., pp. 60f.
10. Ibid., op.cit, p. 89.
11. LOC.cit.
12. Sri Kali Prasanna Sengupta, op. cit., Lahar 1, p. LIII.
13. Ibid., p. 81.
14. Ibid., p. 82.

15. *Tripura Historical Documents* by Maharaja Kumar Sahadev Bikram Kishore and Dr. Jagadis.
16. Ganchoudhury, Calcutta, 1994, pp. 1–2.
17. Ibid., pp. 174–75.
18. Published by the State Council for Educational Research and Training, Government of Tripura, repr., 1999.
19. Published by Smriti Poddar, Agartala, 2001.
20. Bikach Choudhury.
21. Bikach Choudhury, Patra Malay Tripura O Rabindranath.

2

TALES OF HISTORY FROM THE MANUSCRIPTS OF TRIPURA

JUTHIKA BASU BHOWMIK

Tripura is a land of multi-ethnic diversity as a result; various languages have been and are in vogue for long. However, Bangla had emerged as the medium of literature, culture and social exchange under the patronage of the erstwhile princely rulers of the land. The tutelage to 'Bangla' from the Royal court is evident in the numerous copper plates, rock inscriptions, stamps and coins of the period. However, the most prominent of these have been the several manuscripts (mss) whose historical importance has been growing over the years. It should be noted that the National Manuscript Mission states that 'Manuscript is a handwritten composition on paper, bark, cloth, metal, palm leaf or any other material dating back at least seventy-five years that has significant scientific, historical or aesthetic value. Interesting to note here that in Tripura, though primarily written in Bangla, these mss often included sections written in Sanskrit and had substantial usage prior to the advent of printing in a mass form. As a result, the hand written mss remained the foremost medium of literary and cultural pursuits in the state.

It has been observed that the Puranic traditions and the epics were the mainstay of these mss but these handwritten treatises had a different dimension owing to the incorporation of the contemporary events, particularly royal, in the process. However, it was not always that the mss were written only at the instructions of the royal families, rather these were often written at the initiative of many private individuals or families. The absence of the knowledge of printing had made the mss as the most important means of documentation during the time. Even though, the publication of Halhed's 'Bengali Grammar' marks the beginning of the printed Bengali books, the use of mss continued even later not only to suffice the orders or desires of the rulers but also as a means of expression and creation. Thus, today mss remain as the source of social, political, religious and literary history.

The exact number of mss found in Tripura is yet to be determined but whatever has been found appears to be originated between the seventh and the nineteenth century. Tripura here obviously refers to the present state as well as the Tripura district of the British period. Generally, the mss. writers or scribes began or ended their narrative with a eulogy to the king, ruler or the sponsor, but in course of the narrative also details out their individual profile in terms of names, genealogy, habitations, occupations, hobbies, religion and social preferences which certainly are important ingredients for the reconstruction of history of the time. Thus, hand-written mss. like 'Rajmala', 'Krishnamala', 'Champakvijay', 'Gazinama', etc have emerged as the reference books of history in later periods. It should be noted here that the earliest historical text of Tripura, 'Rajabali' has also been accepted as one of the earliest texts of the Bengali prose, but unfortunately, the book is no longer traceable.

The chronicle of Tripura's royal history, 'Rajmala' was edited by Kaliprasanna Vidya Bhusan on the basis of the hand written mss of Durgamani Ujir which is preserved at the Government Museum Agartala. The ms. belongs to 1238 T.E, 1838 AD and comprises of 149 pages made of cotton pulp measuring 41.5 cm by 13.5 cm. The author identifies himself as the son of Maharaja Ram Ganga Manikya and narrates the history for the period beginning with Maharaja Daitya to that of his uncle, Maharaja Kasichandra Manikya, who was at the throne during that time.

'Champaka Vijaya' written during the reign of Maharaja Ratna Manikya II, 1682–1711 AD narrates the events of the king's recapture of the throne after being removed from power by his uncle Narendra Manikya. Sheikh Mohuddin authored this narrative on the directives of the Mir Khan Gazi, the general of the king.

> *"Sri Mir Khan Gazi Bhuban Durjoy /*
> *Tahan Aadeshe Dhori Mohuddiye Koy //"*
> ....
> *'Champak Bijoy Kotha Madhu Ros Bani/*
> *Sheikh Mohuddiye kohe Yuddher Kahani'* //
>
> (Govt., 1977, p. 61)

This ms has a lot of Arabic and Persian words possibly because the author is a Muslim, but it also incorporates events related to Hindu gods and goddesses attesting the secular relation of the time and place. A copy of the same has been made by Ramnarayan Deb resident of Vidyakut village in the Nurnagar Pargana. The referred village, presently in the Brahmanbariya district of Bangladesh is credited to be the residence of several learned men and scholars. Interestingly, the same person comes to the fore as the copyist of the Rajmala ms which is preserved at the Bangiya Sahitya Parishad and later published in a printed book format by the Education Department of the Government of Tripura in 1967. In this context one may infer that *Manuscript copying and compiling* might have been a *prevalent vocation* during the time.

It should be noted that Nurnagar was one of the most distinguished parganas of Chakla Roshanabad. Chakla

Roshanabad as the plains of Tripura were commonly referred had 24 sub-divisions. It is said that a Mughal Feudal lord, Nurbulla Khan annexed the three provinces of Heuing, Beuing and Kailargarh and combined them as a unit naming the new region in his name. It is further observed that a custom had emerged whereby many of the royal officials and servants used to rename certain portions of the subdivision in their name. A similar reference can be made about Champaknagar as referred in the Chaitanya-mangal. The origin of Champaknagar is credited to Yuvaraj Champak Manikya, who was at the helm of Nurnagar during the reign of Ratna Manikya II (Singha, 1984; pp, 199).

We may recall here that presently, there is a place called Champaknagar at a distance of 28–29 kms from Agartala on the National Highway 44, which has a very interesting historical fact attached though of a different dimension. During a visit to the state in 1948, the Chief Minister of West Bengal, Dr. Prafulla Ghosh offered Rs. 10000 for the construction of a school for the Tribes of the state of Tripura. Accordingly, Tripura Lok Shikshalaya, a school exclusively for the tribals of Tripura, was set up at Champaknagar on 7th May, 1949 with the internationally famed painter Dhiren Krishna Debbarman as the Director. The faculties included Gopal Chandra Bhattacharya, Tarit Mohan Dasgupta and Ajit Bandhu Debbarma while Phanibhusan Debbarma and Durga Mohan Debbarma joined as Mechanical Instructor and Teacher in Smithy class (learnt from the eminent painter of Bengal School Dhiren Krishna Debbarman in 1977).

On the other hand, we find that the date and time mentioned in the mss generally provided links to the reign of the kings as is seen in the Kriya-jog-sar ms Maharaj Jagat Manikya directed the Brahmins to copy and transcribe the Padmapurana to facilitate noble thoughts among his subjects. The author Mukunda Brahmin also says that the king offered five coins as honorarium for each chapter which is a proof of the benevolent nature of the ruler as well as gives an impression that there were a sizeable number of manuscript writers in the kingdom. We quote–

> *"Basu veda rasa Arka saka Pariman,*
> *Baishakh masher dasadin abasan,*
> *shombar amabassya punya tithi jani*
> *karila dharmer chinta bipragana ani"*

The period can be identified as 1648 saka era (1826 AD), because basu = 8; veda = 4, rasa = 6, arka = 1; which corresponds to the reign of Maharaja Jagat Manikya on the throne of Tripura.

In the later day ms of '*Ramayana* (Uttarakanda)' reference to Rajdhar Manikya is made in the post colophone statements along with the mention of 'Rajdhani Hastinapur', 'Sarkar Udaipur' and 'Chakla Roshanabad' similar to that of the copper plate inscriptions. Interestingly, the kings of Tripura claimed to be descendent the mythological king Yayati of Hastinapur, thus naturally, their capital was also referred as Hastinapur. Udaipur had been the traditional capital of the kings of Tripura for long, however, during the Mughal period much of the plains of Tripura were annexed by them. The lost land was initially called as Sarkar Udaipur and later renamed as Chakla Roshanabad and it was during the rule of Nawab Shujauddin (1727–37 AD) that Maharaj Dharma Manikya obtained the *zamindari* rights for the place.

Interestingly, the periods quoted in the ms of Ramayana are 1203 BE, 1206 TE and 1718 AD. Moreover, Rajdhar Manikya is at times refered as the Zamindar King definitely suggesting that the King of Tripura was the Zamindar of Chakla Roshanabad and that area was also known as Sarkar Udaipur. Rajdhar Manikya II who reigned from 1785 to 1804 AD was the nephew and inheritor of Maharaj Krishna Manikya and it was on his directives that the book 'Krishnamala' was written. The book written by Ram Ganga Bisharad in a prose format depicts the life and times of Maharaj Krishna Manikya and accounts rare and unknown facets of the time.

Another important historical ms. from Tripura is the Gazinama written by the poet Manohar Ali from Dakshin Shik. The ms tells the war between Samsher Gazi and Tripura represented by the King Indra Manikya and prince Krishna Manikya. Moreover, we also have reference of another historical chronicle of the royal family in 'Srenimala' written by Durgamani Ujir.

During the time of Rajdhar II, copies of Sanjoy's Mahabharata and Bharat Sabitri were also made. We find that these two mss along with that of Ramayana were copied by Gangagovinda Bardhan, a resident of Maniyanda. This corroborates our proposition of the existence of the vocation of copyists. On the other hand, Maniyanda is a village in the Kamalasagar region of the present day Bangladesh. The Bardhans of the region were an illustrious family. An inscription of Maharaja Ram Manikya, the son of Maharaja Gobinda Manikya dated 1093 TE, (1683 AD) refers to the event that 'Sri Sangram Choudhuri has been granted a tax free grant of 51 Dronas in the Muni Yando village' (Singha, 1984). Over time, Muni Yando transformed as Muniyando (narrated by Dwijendra Chandra Dutta in 1976).

After the demise of Rajdhar II, Prince Durgamani inherited the Chakla Roshanabad region in 1809 AD. The script of 'Sri Ramayan Lankakanda' copied by Haragobinda Das Baishnab in 1812 AD refers to Roshanabad, 'Rajdhani Hastinapur' and 'Sarkar Udaipur'. It also mentions about Gopinathpur, a place between Kasba and Mogra in the present-day Bangladesh. The culture of manuscript writing and copying continued also during the reign of Maharaja Krishna Kishore Manikya. The focus of the period however was Baishnav literature as many such pieces have been compiled during that time. The 'Geetkalpataru' written in 1835 AD is pictorial in nature with illustrations from the famous Muslim artist Alam Karigar. The said manuscript attests to the cultural insight of the rulers of Tripura making is a unique creation. Maharaja Ishan Chandra Manikya ascended the throne after Maharaj Krishna Kishore Manikya in 1850 which is evident in the eulogies of the King.

Tripura's history characterises well documented evidences of proficiency of Bengali language particularly among the women of the royal families. Moreover, we also find reference of Subhadra Baishnabi as the compiler of the 'Prembhakti Chandrika' ms. A resident of Agartala, her mss. dates to 1244 TE (1834 AD), a time when the ruler of the state Maharaja Krishnakishore Manikya had shifted the capital to Agartala. It is true that education and learning did spread through Tolls, Chatuspatis, etc but the number of females in such institutions was very limited. No doubts, that manuscript copying had emerged as a vocation by then but such employment opportunities for females were certainly very limited. It is not certain whether Subhadra Baishnabi was a professional or not, but her case certainly deserves special mention. However, during the same time, we have references of Sanskrit proficient women like Hati Vidyalankar, Priyambada Devi, Anandamayi Devi, etc at various other places. The queen, princess and other royal females of Bishnupur used to read and write mss, as is evident in their own hand written books. However, the fact that Subhadra Baishnabi took up the task around 177 years ago in Agartala is a big event for the state and its history.

Nevertheless, it can be said that mss, particularly, the Bengali mss do tell us a lot of events and provides us significant narratives of the period. However, on the basis of the above discussion it should be reiterated that the mss of Tripura allows us to make two major observations which deserves special merit and acknowledgement. These two are:

- Prevalence of Manuscript copying and compiling as a

profession, and

- Existence of lady manuscript copyist in Agartala, Tripura.

However, it should be noted that the present paper is just a snapshot view of some of the historical facts and would call for greater investigation by other scholars of the present time to decipher the several untold stories of the bygone era.

Bibliography

- Government of Tripura, 1977, 'A Descriptive Catalogue of Manuscripts in the Library of the Government Museum, Agartala.
- Chakraborti, Bhupendra Chandra, 1941, 'Rajmala', Indian Photo Engraving Co., Kolkata
- Singha, Kailash Chandra, 1984, '*Rajmala or Tripurar Itibrityo*' Ed (Chakraborty, et al); Barnamala Prakashani, Agartalae.
- Government of Tripura, 1967, 'Rajmala'; Education Department, Agartala
- Bhowmik, Juthika Basu, 1999, 'Bangla Puthir Pushpika', Subarnarekha, Kolkata.

*Former Publication Officer, Department of Education, Government of Tripura; Pursued her doctoral research on the Post-colophone Statements of Bengali Manuscripts from Visva Bharati University.

3

TRIPURA: A PEEP INTO THE PAST

Bikach Chaudhuri

Tripura—a hilly state is proverbially known as 'Paandava Barjita Desha' a land despised by the Pandavas. As a sequestered land in the north-eastern corner of India covered by thick foliage and crisscrossed by number of hill ranges, buttressed by meandering rivers and rivulets, we in our tiny hamlets beneath the sylvan shadows were far away from the lime light of the so called modern civilisation for too long indeed! Thus the everlengthening shadows of tragedies engulfed us and we were entrapped forever in the catacomb of history beneath the horrors of cimmerian darkness. And yet we had our own proud history and lofty cultural traditions.

It was our grave misfortune that the Mughals plundered us time and again, the British stigmatised us by putting our fellow brethren behind the forbidden iron curtain of 'Excluded Area.' And finally when the nation at large, after a long slumber awoke to the new dawn of freedom, we continued, as a matter of ill-fated decree, to languish in utter isolation for nearly half a century after Independence behind the stonewall of so called 'Restricted Area' The stigma was finally removed after a long struggle only in 1992.

Friends, it has been a great tragedy that colonial hangover still haunts us even after sixty-five years of Independence. The very mention of the North Eastern Region conjures up in the minds of the millions of our countrymen a strange feeling of mystery and utter disbelief. Few years ago in a seminar entitled 'Resurgent India' held in Kolkata, Toki Blab a former buraucrat from this region aptly described the curious feelings of the people in some parts of the country about us in the land of Seven Sisters called North East. "To some the region continues to remain the land of mystery, eternally shrouded in the mist of upland tribal legends and folklores. For many others, it is the region that some how always finds mention in the front page coloumns of Indian Newspapers, usually for all the wrong reasons"[1] He went further to say. "There is an adage that says - "We hate the people (of the north east) because we don't know them and we don't know them because we hate them."[2]

This utter disregard and callous attitude had their origin in the colonial mind set of the British Historians. (It has however, to be admitted with due respect that there were noble exceptions too). Alexzander Mackenzie in his book - "History of the Relationship of Government with Hill Tribes of North East Frontier of Bengal", 1884, described Tripura in the following words—"Covered with jungles and inhabited by tribes of whom nothing was known, save they were uncouth and not particular as to clothing, the hills were looked upon as something apart. The Rajash claimed to exercise authority with them, but did not as it seemed derive much profit from them."[3]

It is interesting to note that this striking remark became public at a time when Maharaja Birchandra Manikya the most enlightened ruler of Tripura who was credited with many far reaching reforms and who himself was an accomplished scholar of distinction, was in the seat of power. The eminent historian Dr. Surendranath Sen had said about Birchandra—

"Birchandra Manikya earned from the grateful people of

Bengal the covetable but appropriate title 'Vikramaditya' of present age."[4]

A Peep into the Past

The Tripura ruling house was traditionally believed to be the oldest Princely dynasty in the country and claim their discent from Yajati, the sixth discendent of the Lunar Dynasty. According to traditional belief Prince Druhya being exiled by his father embarked upon a career of conquest and political adventurism and in the process defeated and overthrew the king of Kiratas and had set up a new dynasty in North–Eastern India. The same sources further go on to suggest that king Trilochana of the dynasty attended the 'Rajsua Sacrifice' performed by king Yudhisthira and was greatly honoured by him.

Dr. H.L. Chatterjee a very distinguished historian who spent long years in Tripura and closely studied its history, had a different opinion. He said.

> "Sober history is however, inclined to treat accounts such as these as legendary and dismisses as fictitious the claims of the Kings of Tripura as being scions of the Lunar race. Undoubtedly, they are a Hinduised Indo-Mongoloid people significantly termed 'Kiratas' by the great linguist Dr. Suniti Kumar Chattopadhay, JASB vol-vi, no. 2, 1950, p. 216, having close affinity and kinship with races of outlying tribal areas widely scattered over the entire North-Eastern frontier of our country."[5]

'Rajmala' the royal chronicle of Tripura ruling dynasty created more problems and confusions in determining the authentic history of Tripura. The Royalist school as ardent followers of Rajmala and other mythological evedences, strongly believe that 'Druhya' as the first formal Ruler of Tripura Kingdom claiming his descent from Yajati had established his independent empire at a Tribeg near the river Kapili flowing down the Kamakshya hills of Assam. Thus the claim of discent from Lunar race, according to them, is justified. Further in all royal proclamations of Princely Tripura, till the time of the last independent ruler the state capital had always been mentioned as 'Rajdhani Hastinapura'-which in fact was the capital of Kauravas and Pandavas.

EF Sandys a British official in the Tripura royal court in his book entitled. 'History of Tripura' claimed that Tripura finds a mention in the 153rd chapter of 'Vanaparva' of Mahabharata and according to him Tripura kingdom existed far before the beginning of Christian era. In the absence of any concrete historical evedence numismatic, epigraphical or archaeological such claim can hardly be entertained. But the mention of 'Tripura Kingdom' in the Ashokan Piller dating back to 400 BC and Allahabad Stone Inscription of Samudra Gupta, *c.* 350 AD again make the claim of the royalist school about their ancient heritage rather stronger, for the Allahabad inscription clearly mentions— Rulers of neighbouring states which include Kamarupa, Nepalaka and Tripura.' This Tripura is certainly not the Mahabharatan 'Tripura' which was located near Jabbalpur of Madhyapradesh adjacent to ancient 'Koshaldesha'. The very geographical proximity of Tripura to the Kingdoms of Kamrupa, Nepalaka etc obviously refers to Tripura of Manikya Dynasty.

Although 'Rajmala' has been often disproportionately blamed for many of the confusions of Tripura's history particularly its genealogy of Tripura Kings, geographical area under their command etc. Eminent historian Dr. D.C. Sirkar observed that—

> "There is no doubt that the accounts of Rajmala have an historical basis and are fairly reliable in regard to the period witnessed by the compilers." [6]

He was also of the opinion that facts provided by Rajmala down to the 18th century needs further verification.

It is again curious that Rajamala is quite silent about the presence of Buddhist Rulers in some parts of Tripura. Whereas the seventh–eighth century archaeological findings of Mainamati (now in Bangladesh) Complex near Comilla a few Kilometres away from Tripura's State Capital Agartala, bear striking similarity with the findings of Pilak and Deotamura in South Tripura. Samatata was once ruled by very powerful Buddhist Rulers and held in their sway a vast area extending from Arakan to Kamrupa. It, therefore looks most improbable that Tripura could survive that powerful onslaught. Even T.H. Lewin in his book" The Hill tracts of Chittagong and Dwellers therein", 1869 mentioned about 'Buddhist King of Amarpur in South Tripura - once capital of the Kingdom of Tripura. A German scholar visited Tripura around 1967–68 and he was of the firm opinion that Tripura's southern portion was under the sovereighn authority of Buddhist rulers atleast from seventh century.[7]

Out of the dark lanes

Let us now come out of the dark lanes and try to embark upon the more illumined zone of our glorious history. we too had our delightful days of valour, generosity, courage, compassion and convictions as well as unparalled creative visions. It is a fact that here in this land, blood was spilled again and again by the marauding hoards of invaders, but nothing could deter the people from their creative urges. Tripura the docile daughter of the verdure forests is never known to the historians for any loud notes. Tripura always extended unreserved hospitality to whoever came to settle here, as a result of which there had been drastic changes in the demographic composition of the population mix in the state. People speaking different languages and dilects, practising different languages and dilects, retain in this land a unique mosaic of social and cultural milieu, which great travellers like Huen Tsang, Tavernier, Abul Fazal and lately the world famous poet Rabindranath Tagore spoke eloquently about In fact Tagore's first public rcognition as a great poet in the making came from Maharaja Birchandra in 1882 when the fame of the poet was none too loud.

A Historic letter from Aurangzeb to Govinda Manikya

There was a priceless treasure in the Mahafezkhana' of Tripura royal family a letter from Badsha Alamgir (Aurangzeb) to Govinda Manikya the then ruller of Tripura (Annexure–'A'). After being dismissed by his Emperor brother Aurabgzeb from the Governorship of Bengal, Shah Shujah reportedly fled from Dacca, May 1660 AD and sought shelter and protection from Govinda Manikya.

On learning about this Badsha Aurangzeb sent this historic letter to Govinda Manikya with a request to capture Shujah and return him immediately to him under military escort or face the consequences of defiance. Govinda Manikya then himself in exile living in the deep jungles of Chittagong where he had built up a spacious manson for himself.[8] Traditional history has it that Govinda Manikya, true to his heriditory generosity, spared his own mansion for the valued guest prince Shujah and attended unreserved hospitality to him. Shujah in return presented his precious sword and a diamond ring to Govnda Manikya.[9]

Unfortunately no account of this historic meeting between the two royals in exile have been recorded in history. But the sword presented by Shujah as a proud possesion was in display in the Royal palace of Agartala till their last days.

Tradition also has it that Govinda Manikya (probably during his second tenure) built a huge mosque at Comilla (Annexure–'B') known as 'Shujah Masjid' as a mark of love and respect for the prince in exile.[10]

Kailash Chandra Singha however believed that the mosque was built by Shujah himself after his earlier victory over Tripura."[11]

Barathakur Samarendra Chandra a scion of Tripura Raj family was a scholar and celebrity in his own right and had deep interest in the ancient history of Tripura. He translated the historic letter of Aurangzeb from original persian into Bengali and incorporated the same in his famous book 'Tripura Smriti' (Memories of Tripura). He also mentioned that expenditure towards the maintenance of Shujah Masjid was always charged to the Zamindary Budget of Chakla Roshnabad which was under the possesion of the rulers of Tripura.[12]

Legitimate question therefore, arises as to why Shujah Masjid continued to be charged to the royal estate of Tripura for nearly three centuries, unless it was built by one of its past rulers?

It may be mentioned here that Tripura at least enjoyed a de facto independent status in respect of hill areas at that time, otherwise Emperor Aurangzeb would not have addressed that letter to Govinda Manikya. The letter started in a most courteois language recalling the past happy relationship between the two royal families, but curiously enough ended with a strong ultimatium. The concluding part of the letter read as follows:

> "I hope you will capture him and send him carefully under the surveillence of your army officers and thereby oblige me, so that the age old friendship may continue to exist. Otherwise, you will take it for certain that as a result of the stay of that imprudent rush in your territory, our happy relationship will be breached by conflicts. I do believe that things will be done in accordance with my letter."[13]

There is no evidence to show that Govinda Manikya obliged Aurangzeb defying his heriditory tradition of 'Athithi Deva Bhava. History has it that Shujah left for Arracan finally on 12 May, 1660 with his family and less than 40 followers to take refugee under the protection of the king of Arrakan.[14]

Tripura Deshor Kathar Lekha

We now would like to share with you another startling story regarding our glorious history.

The Library of British Museum preserves a manuscrit since January 8, 1842 written on Sanchi-Pat made of the bark of aloes wood. It was written in Assamese language by two emissaries of Ahomraj Maharaja Rudra Singha (1696–1714 AD) namely Ratna Kandali Sarma Kataki and Arjun Das Bairagi Kataki who were sent to the court of Maharaj Ratna Manikya, 1698–1772 AD of Tripura. They visited Tripura on three occasions between 1709 and 1715 . King Rudra Singha was extremely annoyed with the Governor of Bengal, Nawab Murshid Kuli Khan who used to send 'Khelats' to Sargadeo Rudra Singh 'insinuating' thereby that the Ahom Monarch was subordinate to the government of Moghuls. Rudra Singh was 'therefore' keen on organising a formidable confederacy against the Moghuls whom he described as 'enemies of Hinduism'. He despatched his envoys to the Rajas of Morang, Bana-Vishnupur, Nadiya, Cooch Behar, Burdwan, Barahanagar and Tripura seeking their support and cooperation in the fight against the invaders.

The account of the visits to Tripura by the two emissaries was recorded by them in 146 folios incorporated at the end of the manuscript there was a table of contents. The name of the manuscript was "Tripura Deshor Kathar Lekha". It was completed in 1724.

Dr. Surjya Kumar Bhuyan an eminent historian of Assam closely studied this manuscript at the British Museum London in the year 1937 and edited the Chronicle and published it in the year 1938.

This 300 years old manuscript is an unique document that provides not only the account of three diplomatic missions but also incorporates unique description of places, ceremonies and customs so keenly observed by the two author ambassadors'.

Apart from being a highly valuable document of history it

is also an unique piece of ancient Assamese literature written in lucid language.

The small book though little known now-a-days, is a treasure house of information vividly depicting the contemporary social, economic, cultural and political tradition prevailing in the region in the first and second decades of eighteenth century.

Dr. Surjya Kumar Bhuyan described the book in the following words "on the whole 'Tripura 'Buranji' constitutes a distinct landmark in the history of Assamese prose and Assamese historical literature with regard both to its contents and expression, occupying a position far above the average Buranji". It also reveals significantly about the contemporary socio-political history of Tripura as well .

Let us take for example the confidential letter of Sargadeo Rudra Singha Ruler of Assam had sent to the Tripura King Ratna Manikya which will show the highest standard of protocol being maintained in sending diplomatic missions at a time when the rules of international law were just taking shape and the work of Hugo Grotius was to receive the wide publicity that it afterwards came to have.[12] In order to present this letter, full-fledged diplomatic formalities were scrupulously followed. The envoys on their arrival at the capital first called on Barbaruah who was some sort of a foreign minister, before they could present their credentials before the monarch. The letter also begins with formal norms of addressing a Head of the State. The gist of the letter is that the Ahom King Rudra Singha invited the king of Tripura to join a confederation along with other neighbouring Kings in order to foil the evil designs of the Mughals. The letter was dated 5 Kartika, 1633 Shoka, vide page 15, 6th chap. "Tripura, Buranji", Dr. S.K. Bhuyan, 1938.

It is interesting to note that due care was taken by the Ahomraj to make the language understandable to the Raj of Tripura where Bengali was the court language.

The book provides interesting clue about the ancient history of Tripura along with an intimate account of life, culture and economy of the people in minutest details. The power of observation and the skill of presentation of the narrators are remarkable indeed!

Dr. H.L. Chatterjjee one of the eminent historians of Tripura eloquently praised the skill of history writing of these two Assamese Envoys. In chap. XII of the manuscript they provided an interesting Genealogical clue of the Tripura ruling house.

> "Purva Ihatar Rajanaam naikachil Omuk Fa tamuk Fa Ene naam achil"

According to Dr. Chatterjee this statement deserve more than mere passing notice, giving a lie direct to the traditional belief that kings of Tripura belong to the. Lunar dynasty. It confirms that Tripuries like other people of non aryan descent living in different parts of the region belonged to the invading Mongoloid groups. (Prachi—the annual magazine of MBB College. Agartala 1954–55).

The Spring Festival

The document provides a very interesting account of the Spring festival in Tripura in those days.

The Assamese envoys reported that the spring Festival had all its regal splendour around it. The King himself in a ceremonial procession used to go to river Gomati with ten thousand followers and ceremonially dressed royal officials and enjoyed the festival of colours with heart's content, 'Tripura Buranji, chap. vi, pp. 15–16.

Thereafter the colour festival started. 'On this occasion the state capital was converted into a veritable rendezvous and all manner of people from far and near made it a point to attend these festivities in their multi-coloured costumes. 'Dr. H.L. Chatterjee, described this festival as a national festival in our sense of the term.

The great poet Rabindranath Tagore paid several visits to

Tripura as the honoured guest of the rulers of Tripura. Every time the poet was received with traditional cultural offerings which invariably included the colourful Manipuri 'Ras Nriyta' with its unmistakable essence of the season of spring. He was so greatly impressed by the superb cultural ethos of Tripura and particularly by festivities of the Spring, that he not only arranged for Manipuri dance tutors from Tripura at Viswa Bharati but also introduced the 'Spring Festival' at Shantiniketan in the year 1923. This is a fact which some people in Bengal find it difficult to believe.

References

1. India's Eastern Neighbourhood—Challenges in our Relationship and the 'Look East Policy'—Toki Blab, 'Rsurgent India', 2007, ed., Dr. B.B. Datta, p. 56.
2. Ibid., p. 57.
3. *History of the Relationship of Government with the Hill Tribes of North -East Frontier of Bengal,* 1884, Mackenzie, p. 274.
4. *Rulers of Tripura* (in Bengali), Dr. S.N. Sen Chunta Prakash, Now defunct, Extraordinary, issue published from Chunta (now in Bangladesh), January, 6, 1929.
5. *Glimpses of Tripura's History,* 'Tripura Review' a Periodical Journal of Tripura Government, 15 August, 1972, p. 6.
6. JASB, vol. XVIII, 1951, no. 21, p. 76.
7. 'Educational Miscelliny'—an annual journal of Education Department Tripura (now deffunct) Combined 1967–68 edition. The essay of Dr. Heinz Beshart entitled 'Contemporary Buddhism-Bengal and Tripura translated by Bijankrishna Choudhuri, Tripura Prasanga a literary journal of Government of Tripua, 1975, pp. 53–56.
8. 'The Hill Tracts of Chittagong and the Dwellers Therein' T.H. Lewin as quoted in Tripura District Gazetteers, 1974, p. 90.
9. Ibid., p. 90.
10. Rajmala, Kailash Chandra Singha, vol. II, chap. 7, p. 94.
11. Ibid., p. 94.
12. 'Tripua Smriti', 1927, pp. 209–10.
13. Ibid. English rendering of the protion of the letter from Tripura District Gazetters, 1914, p. 89.
14. A short History of Auranzeb, 1962, Sir Jadunath Sarkar, p. 92–93.

Annexure— "A"

Letter from Aurangzib to Maharaja Govinda Manikya of Tripura.

The history of Tripura (ancient & medieval period)
as reflected in the Manuscripts : A birds eye -view.

* Copy of the letter addressed to the Maharaja Govinda Manikya by Aurangzib as contained in File no. 1 of State Archives, Tripura written tentetively in May 1660

Annexure—"B"

Shujah Masjit at Comilla built by Yaharaja Govinda Manikya

'Sujah Masjid' in Commilla built by Maharaja Govinda Manikya of Tripura.
–Courtesy J.M.Acharjee

Annexure —"C"

An Official Note on Aurangzeb's letter by senior court official of Tripura.

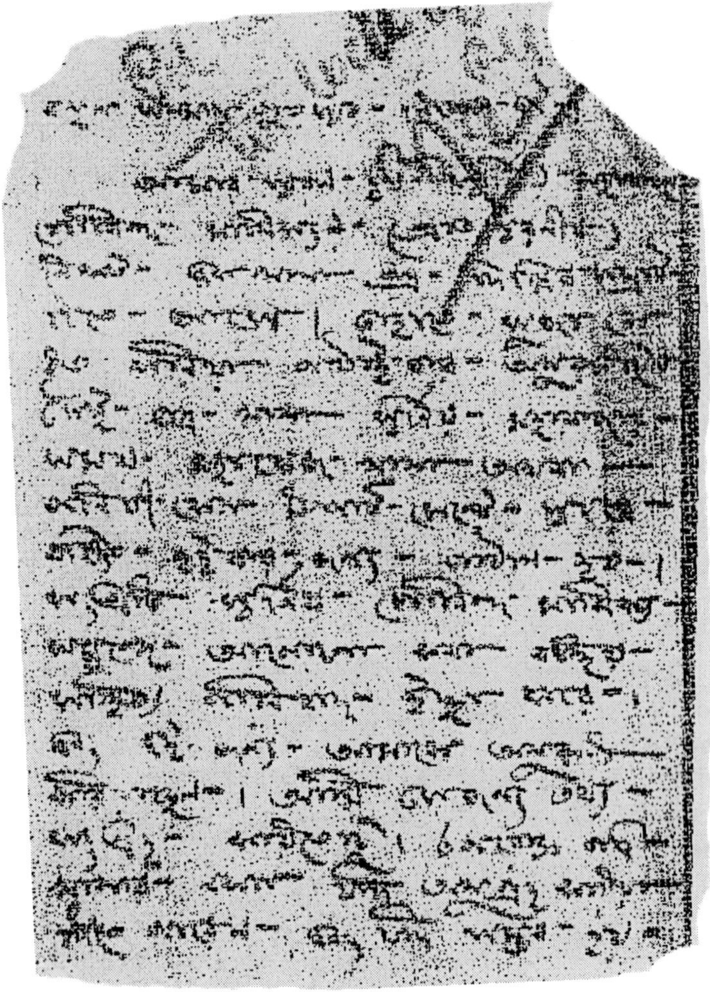

Authenticity of the letter of Aurangzib to Maharaja Govinda Manikya has been confirmed by Col Mahim Chandra Debbarman ADC to Maharaja Birchandra in the above note to the Minister-in-charge of Political Department dated 3 February 1918. Unfortunately, the original letter of Aurangzib written in Golden ink on special court paper is no longer traceble in the state archives.

4

BHAIRAVA WORSHIP IN TRIPURA AND VARANASI—SOME SIMILARITIES

CHIRANJIVI CHAUBEY

The word Tripura is a combination of two word; tri (three) and pura that is three cities. It is a name of Lord Shiva who is believed to have destroyed three cities of Asuras, that is demons. In local language of Tripura it has become Tuipra but here its meaning has changed. Tui in tipuri language means water and the word Pra means mouth of river. Thus it means mouth of river.

The religious history of Tripura is related with neighbouring state of Samatata whose kings ruled Tripura up to the twelfth century AD.[1] Samatata is mentioned in the Allahabad inscription of Samudragupta in the fourth century AD. In the Pala period an acharya named Virupa is mentioned in Buddhist Tantric work who belongs to Tripura (Tippera).[2] Hinduism is the earliest religion of Tripura and its various sects in their full fledged form flourished for long.

The kings of Tripura were Saivaites, Sakta and later became Vaishnava. After the kings became Vaishnava they never abandoned their interest for Shiva. Though religious allegiance of King's oscillated between the Hindu and the tribal Gods, yet it (Tippera) had been chosen abode of Saivism.

The copper plate inscription of Gunaighar in Comilla (at

present it as a district and part of Bangladesh) also informs that the cult of Shiva had secured royal patronage in Tripura region. Saivism as identified in the above inscription is a federation of cult which had combined in its various forms of Rudra, Soumya and Linga.[3] So for as Tripura is concerned a collection of Shiva antiquities, attributed to the period from 700 AD to 1200 AD has come to the light from Unakoti, Pilak and from some other parts of Tripura.

An image of Uma-Maheshwar made of black stone has been found from Udaipur in which Shiva is shown in Sukhasana pose with his consort Uma.[4] The god and goddess are represented embracing each other. Shiva has utpala in his upper right hand while the normal right hand is placed on the right breast of Uma. The left normal hand embraces the goddess's waist below her left breast. The other hand holds the trident. The right hand of the goddess embraces the neck of the god and left hand holds a mirror. This image is of twelfth century AD.[5]

Vaivahika or Kalyansundara type of composite Shiva icon indicates Shiva's marriage with Uma. A broken Kalyansundara murti made of sandstone has been found at Unakoti. The image is badly mutilated and the lower portion of the god along with the figure of goddess is damaged. The god stands on the padmapitha in the middle of a stele. The goddess stand in front of Shiva; her feet partly rest on two feet of god. Near the waist of god on its left side stand the figure of a male and a female representing Himavat and Menaka pouring water; this illustrates the *Abhiseka kriya*. This image is also of twelfth century AD.[6]

Shiva's image of both Ugra and soumya type has been illustrated in icons. The god Aghore Rudra has been represented in a medieval sculpture of Tripura. It is not possible to do the justice with all forms of Shiva. So here I have concentrated only on Bhairava form.

A unique colossal head image of Aghore Rudra is carved on the rock wall of Unakoti hills and the decanting head bears the terrific aspect of Shiva. It has vertically set third eye marked on the forehead. It wears an ornamental conical crown and earring. The right half of moustache is prominent while the left half is missing. The upper lip and the lower lip are indicated by the two horizontal lines only. The face bears the double contour lines while the brows are absent. The image belongs to the eleventh and twelfth century. Shiva as Bhairava represents himself in a terrible form of healer of all evils. The image of the Bhairava with his consort Bhairavi is seen on the stone wall of the Unakoti hills facing the stream Unakoti chaua. The colossal panel of the god measure 12m* 10m* 70cm* 25cm.[7] The three eyed god presses the rosary against his breast with his left hand while his right hand is missing. He wears the decorated crown, hearing and a pectorals round the neck. He bears the garland of skulls. Bhairavi is also sitting cross legged in a padmasan posture on the left side of Bhairava. She has a mirror in her right hand.[8]

In Varanasi, the centre of Hindu culture, Bhairava is known as chief god (kotwal). In Hindi Sabdsagar, it is given as Kotwar, Kotavala and explained as a police ka pradhan karmachari.[9] The meaning contributes to a better understanding of the official status of kal Bhairava in this city. He is a typical protector or guardian of territorial limits (Kshetrapala) for more socio-centrally located pure divinities like Viswanatha in Kashi and also functions as doorkeeper (dwarpala) at the temple of such, even Jaina divinities. His public worship in the Indian temples is now-a-days conducted in a purely innocuous brahmnical mode. His major temple festival of Bhairavashtmi is wholely derived from the above brahminicide myth, all of whose symbolism is strikingly retained in his iconography.[10] His vehicle the dog with which he is identified is the impure creature in the Hindu bestiary. The independent temple of Kal Bhairava, popularly known as Bhaironath is now located between chaukhamba Lane the main street of modern

Varanasi and Maidagini Park, the temple is a spiritual centre for the most severe of shaiva ascetics like kapalikas and Gorakhnathis. These ascetic groups take as their model the ascetic and fearsome Bhairava, whose way run counter to the ordinary cast society.

The most important festival dedicated to this guardian policeman is Bhairvashtami, which instead of deliberating his investure with the office of kotwal, on the contrary celebrates the birth of Bhairava, born only to perpetrate his brahminicide immediately. "On this day alone, the cloth apron that covers all but kal Bhairava face is removed. He is garlanded with necklace of solid silver skulls. People shout for full darshan on this day.[11] Not only officiating priest at the temple know the original myth of brahminicide Bhairava by heart, it is also inscribed in Hindi on a marble slab on the walls[12] and forms of Bhairava are painted on the temple walls bearing the bleeding head of Brahmā. One is never sure it is kotwal that is worshipped or rater the Brahminicide kapalika-Bhairava. The myth and along with it the ordinary worshipper seeks to rationalize and minimize these two incompatible identities of Bhairava by inserting a dichotomy between them. Bhairava becomes kotwal of kashi only after he purified himself from the crime of brahminicide at kapalmochana Tirth at kashi. The god of the great temple of pilgrimage is-whatever be his name and his myth—the pure god (the chief god), withdrawn into himself, the god of ultimate salvation.

References

1. N.R. Roy, *Bangali Itihasa; Adirparva,* repr., ed., Calcutta, p. 446, 1959.
2. *History of Bengal,* vol. 1, R. C. Majumdar, Calcutta, 1971.
3. Ibid., p. 404.
4. From Museum of Agartala, Tripura.
5. Ibid.

6. R.C. Majumda, ibid., pp.. 445–56.
7. Saigal, Omesh, *Tripura its history and culture,* Delhi: Concept Publication, 1978.
8. R.C. Majumdar, ibid., p. 407.
9. In Jaina temples of Varanasi, Ujjain and Rajasthan he is sometimes simply called protector of the territory (Lshetrapala) or given a new name, Manbhadra. There are Jaina texts like the Bhairava Padmavati-Kalpa which deal with worship of Bhairava.
10. There are three basic iconography representation of Bhairava which derive from this myth; as Brahma Sira S chhedaka he grasp by its hair the severed head whose dripping blood is greedily lapped up by dog, as Kankalmurti spesring aman or already bearing the letter's corpse (or skeleton) on his shoulder. In both cases either naked or earing a tiger or elephant skin, a garland of human skulls, snakes around his necks and arms and in grosteque with dark skin and two monostrons fangs. Ass the milder Bhikshamurti, he is depicted roaming to beg for alms.teztual and Iconography reference may also be found in M. Adiceam," The Images of Shiva in India Bhairava, Arts Sagittarius, volumed, 1965. pp. 23–24.
11. D.L.Eck, *Banaras: City of Light,* London: Routledge & Kegan Paul, 1983, p. 274.
12. Ibid., pp. 194–95.

5

SOCIAL HISTORY AS REVEALED IN THE MANUSCRIPTS OF TRIPURA

Rabindranath Das Shastri

Social history of the people of Tripura is authentic and again marvelous when it is reconstructed from the manuscripts of the state itself. It has a special effulgence and affiliation of the elites as well as the patriots of the country. Study of the manuscripts remains tough and troublesome but becomes easy and appreciating as you go on deciphering its script to the extent of their enchanted essence. The manuscripts of Tripura definitely can explore the social aspects, economic and political developments, religious and cultural heritage, and may be the traditional medicinal practices and environment.

Rajmala, the historical chronicle of the kings of Tripura compiled in the beginning of the fifteenth century AD is perhaps the first known manuscript of the state.

Government of Tripura entrusted me with the study of the manuscripts, paleography, epigraphy, numismatics, iconography of the available exhibits in the Tripura Govt. Museum in the year 1973–74. I could decipher the colophon or post-colophon of the manuscripts of Tripura which are the treasure-house for the investigation of the various elements, so as to frame the social environment of the then period.

Extensive research work can still be undertaken following the correct methodology of the study of manuscripts and again the new generation is fortitied with electronic gadgets like digital cameras, computers and scanners. I intend to discuss the social history as revealed in the manuscripts of Tripura under the following heads:

1. Composite nature of the society
2. Social welfare
3. Faiths and religion
4. Rituals and practices
5. Materials and paintings

Composite nature of the society

The royal leaders and the ruled had great intellectual acumen, the marks of which can be traced from the multifarious manuscripts of the state.

The manuscript of Rajmala, mentioned earlier, was prepared by the royal priests to delineate the history of the lunar dynasty of the Tripura monarchs to its subjects six centuries back. Rev. James Long remarked that "We may consider this as the most ancient work in Bengali that has come down to us, as the Chaitanya Charitamrita was not written before 1557, and Kirtibasa subsequently translated the Ramayana." (Analysis of the Rajmala, p. 4)

The manuscripts of the state were mostly written in Bengali and Sanskrit. We could however trace the evidence of a manuscript written in Kok-Borok, the language of the tribal community title "Surchya Pujar Klaanaimani" of 'Durga Prasad Narayan Tripurasya' was copied by Sri Krishna Ballav Debsharma during the reign of Maharaja Mahendra Manikya in 1621, S.E. (1699 AD) as mentioned "*eti senga* 16 *21//tang 28//Bhadra*". Bengali script was used in this Kok-Borok mss a testimony of the long drawn heritage of socio-cultural blending among tribals and Bengalees.

Although ruled by the tribal monarchs, Tripura had always been with the mainstream Indian thoughts and intellect. People irrespective of caste, creed, credence, religion and mother-tongue were free and harmonious. Not only the pandits, brahmins and jyotish but also the *vaisya, kayastha, kapali, vaisnavi, muslim,* professional, military personal, dwellers in hermitage and sannyasins were among the copyists of the manuscripts.

Several evidences of the high status of the women in the community and female education are convincing. The copying of the Narottam Das's Premabhakti Chandrika in 1244 T.E. (1834 AD) by Subhadra Baisnabi, not only testifies the participation of females, must be an educated devotee, in the preparation of the manuscripts but also the popularity of the Vaisnavism at least 255 years back in Tripura.

Social welfare

Many of the manuscripts and the copies thereof were written for the welfare of the members of the community. The benevolent and lofty thinking of the copyist expressed in the colophon and post-colophon attests the proof of such social welfare activites. Some of them obviously devoted to do good to the inhabitants of the region. The post-colophon of the manuscript titled 'Paribhasa' speaks:

> *"likhitam Ramatattamaja-karuna-Samkarena . . . Paro-pakārartham"*

Karunasamkara, the son of Ramadatta copied the book Paribhasa for the welfare of all. The similiar idea runs in the post-colophon of the manuscript 'Subhasita— Muktavali' as *paropakaraya.*

Ramsharan Sharma copied a ms titled Visnu Puranam in

1729 S.E. (1807 AD) aiming at the well-being of his disciples (*shisyanam hitartham*).

As part of social welfare activities, the royal rulers as well as the educated persons have given proper impetus to the preparation of the manuscripts. In order to propagate the knowledge embedded in the manuscripts they were copied. This may be the only way, at that time, the works of the elites to be disseminated among the disciples, devotees and fellow brethren of the community.

In many a manuscripts it is noted that the ms is written with great difficulty ('kastena *likhitam')*—still Gopinath Sharma copied a manuscript on Shastra on the bark of tree in 1577 S.E. (356 years back) so that the people can be benifitted with morals of the Shastra.

In 1808 AD Sri Vishnudas Bairagi copied the Padavali of the celebrated visnuite poet Chandidasa. Sri Bairagi confessed that he copied the book for *nija pathanarthe.* The said person copied the *Gita* for his mental wellbeing—such was the noble belief.

I came across a manuscript Uttamanushasanik parva wherein the copist Kirtichandra Sharma in 1730 S.E. wrote the post-colophon as *patu nityam saputrakam*—he desires to attain surakshanam along with his son for such prestigious activity of manuscript writing.

One aged copist of Kalidasa's Raghuvamsam mentioned: '*bhagnadristi kati griva-badhamusti-adhomukham,* still he is engaged in the copying of manuscript as it was an honourable means to accumulate his bread and butter—a great sense of values.

Gangagobinda Bardhan Das, copyist of the Mahabharata lamented that he is copying the manuscript to mitigate his financial constraint ('*arthacintaya*') thus keeping himself engaged in such welfare activities. This reminds us an obscure sloka of the great poet Kalidasa—"*Annacinta chamatkara kutah kavita daridra sutah.*"

The intentions expressed by all these copyists definitely prove that people were mentally, socially and spiritually (*atmik swastha*) healthy at that period in this state.

Faiths and Religion

The manuscripts—their subject matter as well as colophon or post-colophon therein correlates to the prevalent faiths and religion of the people. In 1726 AD Kriyayogasara, a fragment of Padmapurana copied by Mukunda Brahmana reflects his faith in the recipe for success:

"Sri Hari sharanah satatam mama//
Sri Radha-Krishnahsharanam satatam mama//
Sri gurusharanam//
Sri Saraswaticharane mama bhaktirastu//
Sri Harih// Sri Ramah//Sri Krishnah//"

Several manuscripts belonging to the Bhakti Cult were prepared by their copyist viz., Bhaktishastra (1849 AD) by Badandas, Chaitanya-mangal (1805 AD) by Lochandas, Gitagobindam (1831 AD) by Rasamoy, Naradiya-puranam (1827 AD) by Rudreswar Debsharma and so on. One of the monarchs Maharaja Birchandra Manikya (1862–96 AD) embraced Vainavism and is till date prevalent among the tribal population.

The Ramayana and Mahabharata, the two great epics were copied by many a copyists. Kirti Sarman copied a portion of the Mahabharata 203 years back wherein he prayed to the Almighty to save his country from 'Dharmasankatat'.

"Ashudha haile pad shudha kare diva/
balaker aparadh sakal kshiuva//
Ramachandrapade ami rikta haiya lagi/
laiya Ramer nam antakale mari//"

—the copyist undoubtedly a staunch devotee of Sri Rama

was none but Gangagobinda Das of Maniyand who copied Valmiki Ramayana in 1796 T.E.

The colophon of Ramayana, the manuscript copied by Sri Haragobinda Das Bairagi in 1222 B.S. relates the will of the copyist as:

"Ramah Ramah Ramah
Ram nam balo bhai sabe badana bhari/
Haragobinda bole Rama Rama laiya mari//"

The Kok-Borok manuscript belonging to the chief priest Sri Durga Prasad Narayan delineates the worship of deities like Sangrama, Kamasri, Naka, Chaturdas devata besides Surchya the Sun God among the tribal population of Tripura. The very first sloka of the forty slokas in the manuscript mentions their faith in the worship of the Bamboo *(oanao namananih)*.This Vedic origin of worship is also traced in the Bamboo worship where majority of the tribal people bow their heads to the feet of this tree-god. (Ref: A peep into the foundation of tribal culture in Tripura, Lectures on Indology, Dr. R.N. Das Shastri, p. 118).

Rituals and practices

The copyist Gopinath Sharma copied a manuscript titled Vajasaneyi Upanayana Paddhatih in Sanskrit in 1577 S.E. The Upanayana is a ritualistic ceremony of the Hindu Brahmins as mentioned in Smriti Shastra.

In this context we may cite a manuscript titled Shradha-Tattvam of Raghunath Bhattacharya copied by Sri Dwija Ramamohana.

Astrological practices were very much in vogue. Reference can be given of the two manuscripts Dwadashbhava Phala copied by Umakantacharya (1768 AD) and Vairava stavarajir Punthi Copied by Kailashchandracharya (1894 AD) relating to the practice of astrology. Recovery of the ms titled Rajmala punthi from Vangiya Sahitya Parishad Granthasala in 1949 revealed that the ms was copied by Ram Narayan Deb. The Horoscope of Maharaja Kalyan Manikya (1625–60 AD) was casted as,

Bhadramase diva dui prahar samay /
Avijit muhurta take jyotisheke kay//
Tahate janmile raja Kalyan Manik/
Lagne o shuthir Debaguru Brihaspati//'

In this very manuscript the benevolent practice of grant of land to the Brahmins is mentioned. It appears that in 1380 S.E. Maharaja Dharma Manikya donated—

namna Sri Dharma Manikya bhupo datavyeyah kriyanidhi
....
Unatrisha-dronamitam bhumi vipravaswesah //'

Practice of traditional medicine can be traced from the ms titled Bhasaktousadhapustika wherein the copyist took pains to mention the remedy for several common ailments as per Ayurveda. Another ms on traditional medical practice reveals the treatment of Diabetes (*'Helanchigacha sameta prate kichu siddha kari marich diya khaile bahumutra khande*).

It was a practice to warn the thieves with a view to protect the mss. from robbery. In the post-colophon of the ms of Mahabharata, the copyist Gangagobinda Das remarked in corrupt Sanskrit:

" *Jatnena likhitam shastra ja*
    Choreyati pustika /
Sakati tasya mata
    Pita tasya garthava //"

The same type of warning was included in the mss

Samudrikastrilakshanam (1681 AD) and Katantravritti-Panjika copied by Ramakhya Dulalaka.

Dr. Panchanan Bhattacharya wrote in the third vol. of his famous book '*Bangla Prachin Puthir Vivaran*' the similar type of warning:

"Chaurat raksha
Jalat raksa
Raksa mum slathabandhanat."

The Nepali language ms of 1105 AD mentions to fondle the mss like one's own son and to bind like the *enemy (Swaputrabat adar o satrubat bandhbe)*.

The warning voice is raised in the Sannyasakarana Vidhi ms of Tripura indicates fear from fools:

"murkhahaste na datavyam
Evam badati putakam"

The same theme is incorporated in a ms of other states *(parahastat gatam raksa evam badati pustakam)*-referred in the book of Dr. Priyabala Saha, *A Descriptive Catalogue of Sanskrit Manuscripts,* p. 11, Ahmedabad, 1964.

Materials and Paintings

The materials used for preparing the manuscripts of the state were locally made from bark of trees (*Balkal*), pulp of cotton (*tulat*) covering of beetal nut tree (*khal*), palm-leaf, bark of birch (*bhurjyapatra*) all being the eco-friendly alternative for paper. These materials were pressed into sheets by conch—shell and stone. Wood, leathers, cloths, cotton wrapper (kantha) were used to make the covers of the mss on which also letters were written.

Paint brush(tuli) shalaka, peacock feather were used as pen Ink of different hues-red, black, brown was made of natural ingredients—juices of plants, Haritaki (myrobalan) and animal bone. In the Sanskrit drama Malatimadhav, shalaka is mentioned as writing material. M.M. Gourishankar Ojha also reported the use of such materials in his book in 1918.

While one of the Ph.D students was undergoing her research work under my guidance, we have come across one fascinating ms preserved in the Sri Sri Nilkantamani Jiur Mandir of Sri Sri Prabhu Bari, Sri Pat, Agartala. The ms of Srimad Bhagavata prepared during the reign of Maharaj Birchandra (1862–96) was found to be wrapped up in cotton wrapper (*kantha*). It was far more fascinating to note that the Kantha has a whole long poem copied on it with needle and red thread by the Muktamala Roy. The poem was lucidly composed by the Maharaja Birchandra:

> *"Ahe Radheshyam aji ki sukher din*
> *Jhulan mangal he bhava makha saraca/*
> *hani jugal adhare hasi sri ange pulak*
> *natha mana saha jhulana dolani Radha//*
> ....
> ....
> *puna Vrindavane jabo jugal rup heriba sukhe*
> *Birchandra Manomohini puro bancha Sri Radharani//"*

The ms on the *kantha* is unique and far surpasses the social importance of kantha gleaned in the famous 'Nakshi Kanthar Matha'—a Bengali lyrical poetical work by Jasim Uddin of East (presently Bangladesh).

Last but not the least, I would like to highlight the paintings on the manuscripts of Tripura which bears testimony to the social appeal of the people towards such activites. Maharajkumar Nabadwip Chandra Debbarman, the son of Maharaj Birchadra Manikya in his book 'Abarjanar Muni' mentions that during the period of his father and grandfather, there was one designated painter Alam Karigar, muslim by religion in the king's realm whose works correspond to Mughal art, the school of art that was widespread in the provinces of India.

Vipra Shiveswara copied Padakalpataru in 1892 AD which bears 13 nos. of paintings by Alam Karigar relating, to *Radha-Krishna lila.* These paintings depict and uphold the devotion of the people of the then period towards Sri Radha-Krishna.

In this context, let us cite the remark of Prof. Kalyan Kumar Ganguly in the Journal of Indian Museum, Pubished 1949:

> "The painting of Manuscripts have preserved the evidence of the continuity of the tradition of Indian painting for long years of which no activity of the painter has survived in any other medium."

In the ms of a fragment of *Ramayana* copied by Gangagobinda Das (1207 B.S.), a painting exhibits Rama seated on the throne encircled by Bharata, Lakshmana, Sugriva, Bibhisana and Hanuman. The painting bears the continuity of Indian tradition of rejoicing the victorious Rama against the evil forces of the society.

To conclude here, it is beyond our admittance and expectation that the manuscripts of Tripura are sufficiently equipped to be the source materials of the history of the state. Not only the manuscripts like Champak-vijaya by Saikh Mahaddi, the Gaji Nama by Manohar Saikh, Krishnamala by Ramganga Sharma and Jayanta Chantai, the Srenimala by Durgamani Ujir, each and everyone of them can unfurl the social enigma of the Princely State of Tripura, if indepth studies are undertaken. However, let us first of all save, protect, preserve these endangered species of source materials then only our young generation of researchers can reckon with.

Prototype of painting by Alam Karigar on the ms 'Padakalpataru'

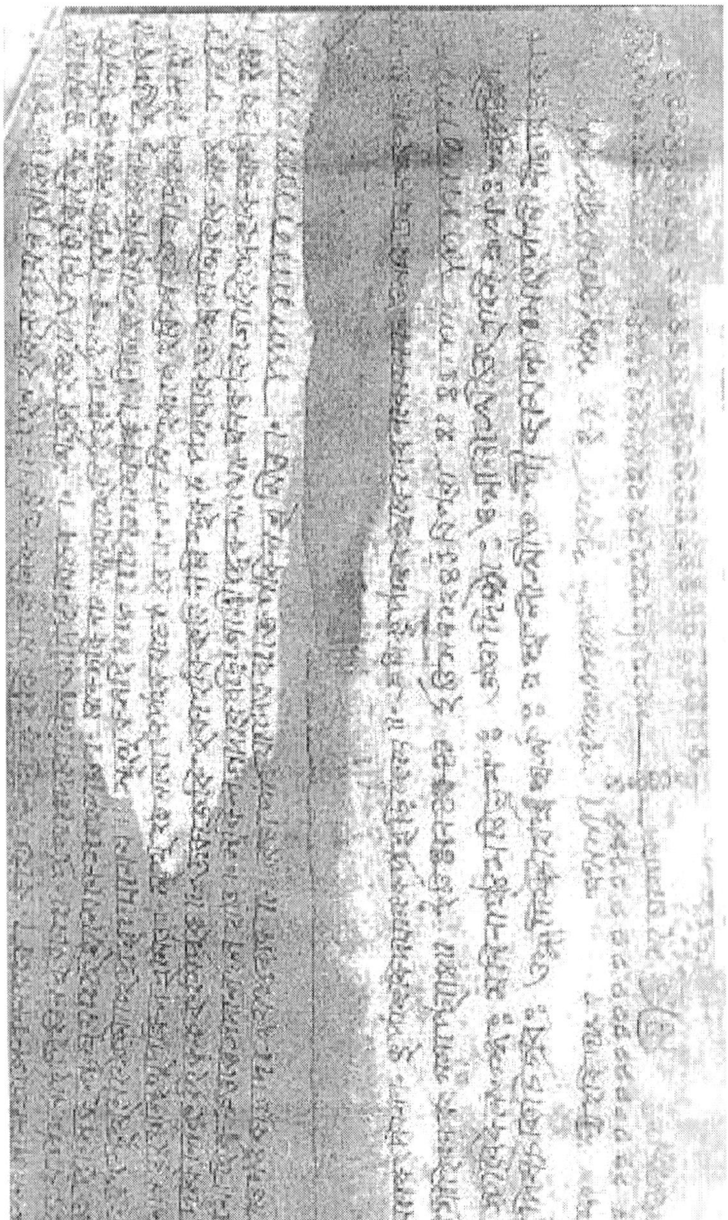

Pushpika of ms Hiranyavadha by Ramanath Kapali., 1931 AD

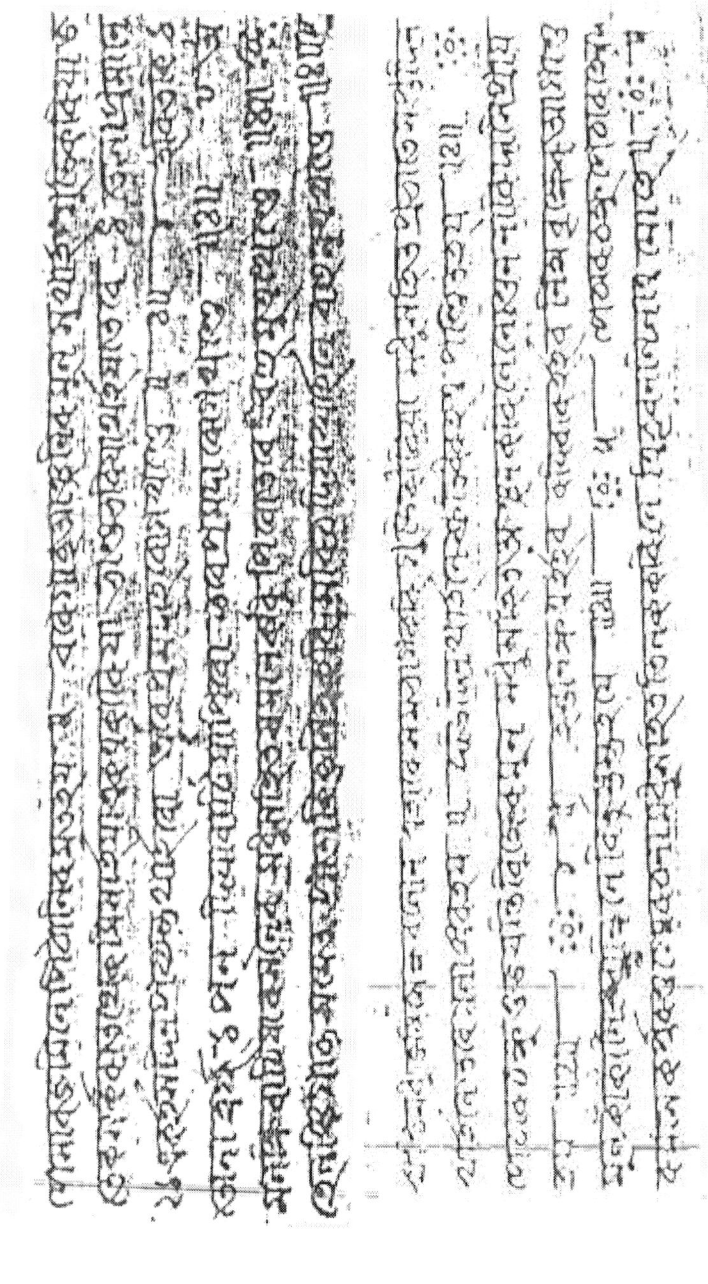

glimpse of ms on traditional medical practice.

6

DIGITAL PRESERVATION OF MANUSCRIPTS, COUNTERFEITING OF INTELLECTUAL PROPERTY AND ITS DIGIT-MICROPHOTO REMEDIES

Ashok Kumar Nath

Prologue

India is one of the most ancient civilizations in the world and one of the largest treasure houses in different fields of ancient knowledge—which are recorded in the manuscripts. In essence these invaluable treasures of creative thoughts or realization and deeds which our great ancestors have bequeathed us must be preserved for posterity. Preservation of past intellectual and cultural documented heritage ensures that these remain intact for our future generation. History, culture and tradition move side by side and every creative literary work of the age reflects its inner urges, its vitality and special characteristics. There is worry that all these vast array of information in philosophical, cultural and religious thoughts available in manuscripts will be too fragile to handle fairly soon. We are often guilty of almost criminal neglect of preserving the accumulated wisdom of the past; hardly anybody is thinking about preserving them in right form, in the right format, in the right time and in the right way. If such repositories of manuscripts and accomplishments are lost, it will leave an incomplete cultural legacy for our children and grandchildren. Librarian as a priest in the temple of scholarship may have charged himself with the reverent custody of our national heritage and their studious preservation in the library.

National Conservation Policy

Government of India is in the process to formulate and standardize National Conservation Policy for preservation of national printed heritage for posterity yet there is a national strategy that concerns the development of the digital infrastructure. The foundation of a scientific policy of protecting and preserving the intellectual, rare and cultural printed heritage of the country seems to be laid and the government is trying to get this conservation policy in operation. The program sought to restore, conserve and upgrade of all valuable manuscripts available in India in any form which will not be affected by adverse environmental factors. The entire archival project of presentation could have generated enormous potential to grasp the significance of our cultural legacy. Center has taken interest and providing necessary funds for restoration and preventing further damage to our national printed heritage, it is essential that the library professionals remain wedded to uncompromising professionalism in matters of security and preservation. Critical problems call for extraordinary, solutions. In accordance with the convention "Protection of the world cultural and natural heritage" adopted by UNESCO India should have succeeded in securing inclusion of a large number of priceless national heritage in the World Heritage List.

Retrospection and present problem

Library authorities today are paying attention to the vital problem of preserving the rich collection of our national heritage particularly when some precious and valuable collection of manuscripts touched advanced stages of decay. The library protagonist know, in the present age of a revolution in library systems even sacrifice and dedication have its limitations because modernization is no longer an option but imperative in modern library services subject to rapid technological changes. Very few libraries in the country meet international standards in terms of infrastructure and facilities. Modernization projects require formidable capital investment and equally large recurring expenditure.

There is adequate evidence that India has the human and capital resources to modernize the preservation sectors at par with other library's of excellence in the world. What is needed is a vision to develop a coherent national action plan to achieve this objective within a specified time frame. Such a mission needs to be backed up a corporate management model endowed with necessary authority.

Digital Imaging of manuscripts in the context of library modernization

Digital Imaging has become an important component for the library's current strategic plan. Digital imaging has dramatically increased access for readers, scientists, researchers, general public and significant information is available through Internet. Every digitization project is different depending on the library's infrastructure, technological developments and parameters, staff expertise, fund for the project and material selected for digitization. Several libraries have adopted digital imaging. Library Congress in USA with its American Memory Project has practical information directed towards librarians and archivists. They have digitized more than fifteen million documentary records of Americana.

Digital Preservation of Manuscripts

Digital technology makes valuable material available to

the library users in such a way earlier generations could only have dreamed about. Major libraries are ready to employ the amazing potential of digital technology and investing large amount of money on ambitious digital conversion project to make their collection more accessible and, too often, believing that they are accomplishing preservation goals at the same time. The persistence of long-term digital information preservation remains an essential challenge. While many countries have put in place notable initiatives or strategies regarding digital preservation of cultural heritage, specific attention to long term preservation of printed heritage needs to be further developed since digitization has unlimited possibilities but loosely referred to as preservation. The strength of digital realm is in the matter of delivery, distribution and access rather than conservation whereas good microfilm could last more than five hundred years. Both microfilm and digitization are equally important and complimentary to each other. Together they can provide viable and more accessible long-term preservation of cultural heritage for the benefit of future generations.

Technological and other limitations of Digital Preservation:

1. Technological obsolescence
2. Legal acceptance of digital image
3. Digital migration of stored information
4. Technical Upgradation
5. Financial Implication
6. Loss of detail in digital images
7. Cyber Security for digital images
8. Technical expertise of digital image conversion
9. Expensive in digital image transfer
10. Temperature and Humidity fluctuation.
11. Computer viruses.
12. Stray magnetic fields

13. Material decay
14. Risk in digital preservation
15. E-Surveillance
16. Plagiarism
17. Light effect
18. Many other known and unknown factors

Digital migration of stored information

Digital migration of documents is a serious and complex issue. If digitized informations are not migrated to new hardware and software before the present ones become obsolete or corrupted, these files are lost. Gazette of India from 1950 to 2002 were digitized in the Central Secretariat Library and made available for search and retrieval. The images were stored in TIFF format and converted into PDF format. OCR was done on the images. The text thus created was stored in the XML format. For search and retrieval. ISYS search software was used. On search the PDF images of the relevant gazette is retrieved. Two Hard Disks of the server went out of order and along with that the 1SYS search software has become obsolete. Now the information could not be retrieved.

Many libraries archive documents to CDs. Eventually, these files will need to be copied to a new medium, DVD. DCVD or some more advanced technology that has not yet materialized. Financial support of the migration plan is an absolute necessity if funding and support are not available, all digitization efforts can be lost within ten years. There is research in the area of emulation. This means that if the proper metadata is recorded at the time of capture (equipment used. settings, color profiles etc.) the original environment can be recreated in order to rescue the lost files. Emulation is not merely a matter of using old software on old equipment. It involves using new technologies to recreate past technologies. The research is ongoing and is not yet a viable option.

Digital piracy of intellectual property

In this era of globalization. digital piracy on intellectual property is a menace that may kill the publication industry both commercially as well as creatively. This is a global phenomena and the Indian market is no exception. Many opine that there is a need to create more awareness in the judicial system against Internet text piracy and about the seriousness of crime. But piracy is treated as a minor offence while judicial leniency is seen as major reason for the rise of this crime.

Counterfeiting and Electronic piracy of Tangible Intellectual Property has spread rapidly in recent years throughout the globe. Executives in Government departments and transanimation companies, from time to time, enunciate, gave warnings as to the effects of piracy, theft. and infringement of the ownership of intellectual property—a hyperbolic term, since it includes text, images. logos, acronyms etc.

Digit-Micro Photo Remedies for preserving printed heritage

For archiving library materials subjected to long-term retention periods, microfilm is the only sensible medium to be chosen—despite the tremendous development of digital storage media. Currently there is no digital storage medium available that could reach the durability of microfilm.

Microfilm technology combining with the electronics of computers is providing major new tools for information science and proper conservation treatment of library documents for posterity. Computer output microfilming plays the most important role in the preservation of library materials in this digital age of modern library activities and of transmitting them to future generations.

Archivist, conservators, computer experts. and the librarians realized that stray magnetic fields, humidity, oxidation. material decay, computer viruses and many other known and unknown factors can quickly erase information stored on the digital media where as the world wide demand for sober security is one of most important module for the prevention of unauthorized access to the digital world.

Hybrid Technology

Most versatile Hybrid Microfilm Camera performs both digital and analog capture in one process—storing of printed heritages (information) as digital data for instant access and microfilmed images for conservation of library materials.

Digitization of microfilms (analog to digital)

Microfilm as an analog and proven age-resistant storage medium could be scanned and digitized to produce necessary back up files for dissemination of information. High *Speed Microfilm Scanner* is effective to disseminate and modernize the Microfilm Preservation.

Computer Output Micro film (COM) process

COM (digital to analogue) for preservation of scanned information on a special type of microfilm converts scanned and stored data directly into microfilm as images for preservation. *Document* Reactive Writer replaces all aberrations in the dissemination of information and conservation of library documents through microforms.

Microfilming of printed heritage

Microfilming is a well established technology with rigorous international standards ensures the longevity of imperiled knowledge. For rectifying library materials subjected to long-term retention periods, microfilm is the only sensible medium to be chosen - despite the tremendous development of digital storage media.

Protection of Intellectual Property

For the protection of Intellectual Property Rights there is a need for reorientation. all nations should work together to fend off cyber attacks in the stored information. Governments throughout the globe are being compelled to amend laws for the protection of Intellectual Property. Symposiums and workshops may be organized to make them understand the gravity of the crime.

Conclusion

It would be a tough superficial to conclude that proper short and effective long term policies should be evolved and care should be taken in order to execute the said policies to be handled by proper persons because misconception, ill-planning, lack of technical knowledge, conflicting priorities, inter-service rivalry and years of neglect still pose formidable obstacles for proper conservation planning of manuscripts in microform.

Every digitization of manuscripts project for national interest should be accompanied by a microfilm copy of the documents to prevent digital destruction and to ensure archival conservation of intellectual property for posterity. It may be a historic blunder if we do not microfilm our printed heritage for preservation along with digitization.

7

BORDER MANAGEMENT AND BORDER FENCING IN TRIPURA

BIHARI JHA

One of the Seven Sisters, the Indian State of Tripura is so located that it borders Bangladesh from three sides i.e. East, West and South. This former princely state was ruled by Maharaja of Manikya dynasty. It was an independent administrative unit under the Maharaja during the British Rule in India, though this independence was qualified, being subject to the recognition of the British, as the paramount power. After Independence of India, as agreement for merger with Indian Union was signed on September 9, 1947 and the administration of the state was actually taken over by Government. of India on October 15, 1949. Geographically, Tripura is the third smallest state of India with an area of 0.32 percent of the total geographical area. Its max stretch measures about 184 km. from North to South and about 113 km from East to West. It has an international land frontier of about 856 km with Bangladesh. Demographically Tripura is home to 0.33 percent of India's scheduled castes and scheduled tribes. During fifties, the growth of the population was recorded at 76 percent approx which was mainly due to influx of refugees from erstwhile East Pakistan (now Bangladesh). The sudden influx which was mainly of Bengali population and finally resulted in armed struggle. The first insurgent outfit was floated in 1960 with support of Debbarma, Chakma and Reang tribal groups. Presently, the main agenda of various considerably from 51 per cent during partition to 31 per cent by 2001. The distribution of population is also highly favorable to the economically and politically dominating Bengali population. The inhabits of most of the economically profitable plain areas and the tribals have been pushed further in the hinterland which is mainly hilly with hardly any development. The religious majority on Indian side is Hindu, while the same across the border is that of Muslims. The people on the either side have commonality in language and culture.

Topographically, Tripura is part of the Provincial, representing a low lying plainpierced by a series of low drawn spurs projecting from the Mizo hills and is part of the Surma valley. There are six prominent hill ranges running parallel from North to South-Jampui, Sakhantang, Longthorai, Atharamura, Sardang and Baramura. The height ranges from 300 meter to 1000 meter and the heights descending from North to South. A large number of short and swift flowing rain fed rivers cris cross Tripura which generally flow in North South direction. The terrain on the Indian side is a mix of hilly, semi-hilly and plains. The hills being low in the South get gradually higher as the boundary line ascends from South to North to enter Mizoram where the heights are more. Over 60 percent of the area of Tripura state is under forest cover and almost same percent of area is hilly. Tripura's eastern borders with Bangladesh falling in Dhalai district. And Tripura South Dist are least developed and almost entire area is hilly covered by thick forest, mainly evergreen wet deciduous forest. The BSF is deployed on the border with Bangladesh district of Khagracheri, Feni and Comilla which are part of Chittagong Hill tracts. Nalkata and Ambasa are the least developed areas of Tripura with almost entire population being tribal. There are only a few means of communication and most of the BOP's in these areas are air maintained. It takes any thing from 3 hours to two days to reach the BOP on foot. The area is free from any smuggling on Bangladesh side and also there is no presence of BDR in these areas. The Western border of Tripura i.e. the districts of Tripura South and Tripura North are quite different from the eastern borders as most of the area bordering Bangladesh is plain with cultivation right up to zero line. Demographically also the population is mostly Bengali and with large towns located in these areas it is quite different from the eastern borders as most of the area bordering Bangladesh is plain with cultivation right up to zero line. Demographically also the population is mostly Bengali and with large towns located in these areas it is quite lucrative to be involved in smuggling. The area being plain is also a heaven for the militants to have their operation and administrative camps in Bangladesh in front of these areas. The militants operate in India and then cross over to Bangladesh. With the fencing coming up in the area these crossings will cease considerably.

The general development varies from well-developed urban areas to under-developed rural areas and underdeveloped interior areas. The economy is primarily agrarian "Jhoom cultivation" is still quite common and largely practiced by the tribal. There is one main highway which connects Tripura to Assam i.e. National highway 44 starting from Churaibari to Agartala. Due to the prevalent situation of insurgency from Manu to Teliamura, a stretch of about 90 kms. is declared sensitive and all the civilian movement of vehicles is escorted by armed escorts of CRPF and TSR. The road communication is fairly developed in the border area but less developed in the interior areas. However, the poverty and unemployment are profoundly manifested equally on both sides of the border.

Border Management

Border management proposes such mechanisms which are necessary to adopt for the country in the era of global terrorism and global connectedness. Border management is a very new concept and it is evolving every day. Border management is the package of various sorts of mechanisms; generally it depends which sorts of needs of the nation which could be fulfilled through regulated and well-managed borders. Sometimes it seems that it is confined merely to secure the borders but gradually newer dimensions are added to explore further advantages.

Gerald H. Blake states that, 'the objectives of border management strategy will be determined initially by national foreign policy objectives. The boundary may even be used as an instrument of foreign policy, particularly if relations between neighbors are poor. The fundamental aims of good boundary management are designed to achieve (a) International Peace, (b) Local and National security, (c) Borderland Prosperity and (d) Effective Local government'.

'Border Management' indicates that it has three major facets. These are (a) Ensuring the security of border areas by preventing trans-border crimes; this would generally lie in the domain of border-guarding forces, (b) Ensuring the welfare of the border population and integrating them in the national mainstream; this would generally lie in the domain of civil administration and other government departments, and (c) Ensuring prompt resolution of all border related problems and maintain cordial relations with the counterpart, especially between counterpart border guarding forces; this would require a certain amount of diplomatic insights on the part of border guarding force commanders and a clear-cut mutually acceptable framework for solving problems.

India's international borders are a unique intermix of mountains, plains, deserts, riverine and jungle terrain with varying degree of habitation and ethnic mix residing. India has been a poor manager of its borders. Border-disputes are evident on almost all its borders. The process of border-demarcation is yet to complete at many borders and a better mechanism of border negotiation is due for a long time. There is no denying of the fact that solving of various border issues with neighboring countries is very complex and full of malpractices of politics due to internal security complex of South Asia. There are various historical, political and economical factors which are responsible to make the matter more vulnerable and tough to cope with.

Border Fencing

The border fencing on the near hand is helpful towards achieving the security concern of the people of the bordering areas and beyond on the other hand has affected the people adversely due to displacement. The present study is focusing upon the West Tripura district having its unique geopolitical position. It is also because the district constitutes the areas of rural as well as urban areas and it seems the displacement has affected all the sections of society. The places such as Agartala check-post, Kamalasagar, Lankamura, Narayanpur, Nirbhayapur, Putia, Bhagalpur, Durgabari, Ashabari, Devipur are Important in this regard. The people of the area have been suffering due to the border fencing and the displacement of the people. In recent years the policy and programs of the Central and State governments have changed from simple fencing and guarding the same to overall management of the same.

Bangladesh was earlier the East Pakistan and before the same the region was the part and parcel of India. Heap of literature has come up on economic cooperation between India and Bangladesh (erstwhile East Pakistan), since the process started long back, attracting the leaders of the two areas. Attempts were made to restore the economy of the border; an agreement was signed between the government of India and Pakistan in 1953 to allow the people from both sides of the border to carry trade and commercial transactions on some specified commodities under some selected heads. However, the arrangement proved to be temporary as trade embargo was imposed by Pakistan in 1965 at the outbreak of Indo-Pak war. The government of Pakistan tried to control the commercial transaction in East

Pakistan (present Bangladesh) by imposing restrictions between the erstwhile East Bengal (present Bangladesh) and adjoining Indian states. This completely stopped commercial ties between the two areas. The relations between India and Pakistan touched the lowest position as India decided to extend full support to the people of East Bengal in their liberation war against Pakistan. Both the Houses of Parliament of India passed a resolution to that effect on March 13, 1971. A war broke out between India and Pakistan, and constant vigil along the border became essential including the border fencing. And the sufferings of the people due to fencing (sociocultural, economic etc.) never caught the attention of the scholars for the study.

With the birth of Bangladesh as a sovereign country in December 1971, it ushered new hopes among the people across the border regarding the normalization of relations especially on the border including the economic cooperation along the border at local level. In a public meeting held in New Delhi in February 1972 the then Prime Minister of India (Indra Gandhi) and the then Prime Minister of Bangladesh (Sheikh Mujibur Rahman) pledged for 'Eternal Friendship and talked of their common goals. This was followed by high powered Bangladesh delegation's visit to India accompanied by Sheikh Mujibur Rahman in 1974. It was further strengthened by the visit of Prime Minister Indira Gandhi to Bangladesh. The delegates discussed various issues related to sharing of Ganga waters, territorial questions and economic cooperation. Both the nations have agreed to solve the border issues and resume trade relations through diplomatic means.

However, establishment of friendly ties and trade and commercial links between the two countries unfortunately could not materialize as Sheikh Mujibur Rahman was assassinated in 1975. After 1975, there were many ups and downs in the relations of the two countries. The successive coups in Bangladesh and drastic changes in the political and constitutional set up from democratic to Islamic nation added new dimension to the politics of Bangladesh with a strong bearing on her relations with India. The security of Indo-Bangladesh border became very important in this regard. However, the aspects of border management (from fencing to economic cooperation between the two sides) and the displacement due to fencing and consequent sufferings of the people did not get adequate attention of the scholars.

Gurudas Das in his article, "Economic relations: Issues in Trade Transit and security" in Gurudas Das and C.J. Thomas (ed.), Indo-Bangladesh Border Trade, provides an analysis of the nature of economic relations that exist between India and Bangladesh since 1970's. The author explores into the structure and trends of the bilateral trade relations between the two countries and the various options available with Bangladesh to reduce her trade deficit vis-ë-vis India. The "Look East Policy" of Government of India also encouraged large number of study related to the trade potentials in the region.

J.N. Dixit in his book Indian Foreign Policy provides useful insight to Indo-Bangladesh relations during the nineties of the last century. He has discussed about the prospect of close contact between the two nations in the context of new government coming to power in both countries. He has highlighted the issues (military confrontations between the Border Security Forces and the Bangladesh Rifles, smuggling, illegal immigration, and anti-Indian propaganda in Bangladesh), which constitute the bone of contention between the two nations. Kuldip Singh in his book India and Bangladesh discusses the development that took place in northeastern neighbor of India from 1970–81. He has covered the wider aspects of relations, including the relations between the East and the West Pakistan, and twist and turn in the relationship between India and Bangladesh after its birth. Virendra Narain in his book Foreign Policy of Bangladesh discusses the problem over a period of ten years i.e. from 1971 to 1981. the author provides a detailed account with regard to the National Liberation Movement in Bangladesh, the cordial relationship that existed between India and Bangladesh under the stewardship of Sheikh Mujibur Rahaman, followed by heavy strain in relation after his assassination in 1975 and the changes in the foreign policy perspective thereafter. The above survey of literature shows that a number of scholarly works on border trade as well as Indo-Bangladesh relations have been undertaken. These studies also help us to understand and the nature of relationship between India and Bangladesh but the issue of border management and displacement of people do not find prominence in any of the works.

Abbreviations

BDR	Bangladesh Rifle
BOP	Border out Post
BSF	Border Security Force
CRPF	Central Reserve Police Force
TSR	Tripura State Rifle

References

1. Jamwal, N.S. "Management of Land Borders" Strategic Analysis, IDSA, New Delhi.
2. Mishra, Ashutosh, "Sir Creek Boundary Dispute": A victim of India-Pakistan Lingake Politics" IBRU Boundary and Security Bulletin, winter 2000–2001.
3. Narain, Virendra, *Foreign Policy of Bangladesh, 1971–81,* Jaipur, 1987.
4. Narhari, N.S., *Security Threats to North-East India: the Socio-Economic Tensions,* New Delhi, 2002.
5. Pemberton, R.B. *Report on the Eastern Frontier of British India,* Guwahati, 1966.
6. Singh, Kuldeep, *India and Bangladesh,* New Delhi 1987.
7. Thomas, C.J. ed,, *Engagement and Development, India,* Northeast India and Neighborliness countries, New Delhi, 2006.

8

COLLECTION AND PRESERVATION OF MANUSCRIPTS IN BANGLADESH: A STUDY

KALPANA HALDER BHOWMIK

Since the early ages of civilization, human beings have attempted to convey their achievements to their future generations. Since ancient age, humans have been trying to collect and preserve valuable articles and documents out of their own needs. And the collection of such important artifacts is the National treasure of a country.

Bangladesh has been playing an advance role of preserving such significant assets. Before August of 1947, the only archive of ancient information was the Imperial Record Department in Delhi. During 1972, after independence, Bangladesh established the national archive to collect and preserve such records. In this archieve, all records found in Bangladesh since 1800, especially those that belonged to Nawab Estate in Dhaka, Royal Estate in Bhawal, and many other important records are preserved. A Bengali manuscript from Lisbon, Portugal has also been added to the collection.

In other way, library is called the backbone of a country. There are many libraries in Bangladesh; among these Dhaka University Library is known as the biggest library. Its importance is uncountable to many countries of the East. It has got the reputation of a vast preservatory of rare books, periodicals and old manuscripts.

Some document in the 'rare branch' on this library are, The Calcutta Gazette (1901–44), The Gazette India (1906–35), Eastern Bengal District Gazetteers (Tippera, 1901), Eastern Bengal and Assam Gazette (1908), Asiatic Quarterly Review (1894–1907), Journal of the Asiatic Society of Bengal (1835), Rajamala (1st Lahar, 1311 Yripurabda.) General History of Tripura can be found in Rajamala. In short, to find the historical elements of Tripura, Rajamala is a priceless asset.

Every nation or race can find or know about their past traditions from their ancient literatures. We find such antique texts from the ancient manuscripts. Thus, collecting and preserving such manuscripts are an important task for a nation or country.

Collection

A lot of manuscripts are collected in different places of Bangladesh. Notable places are, Dhaka University Library, Bangla Academy, Central Public Library, Dhaka Museum, Rammala Library of Comilla, Public Library of Kishoreganj, Sylhet Central Muslim Literature Collection Centre, Bangladesh Asiatic Society, Nazimuddin Muslim Hall Library, Barendra Museum, Rajshahi Library, etc. Dhaka University Library Archives is important among these because it is significant in size and rarity of collection not only in Bangladesh, but also among all Archives in South Asia. Over 30,000 rare and valuable documents are preserved here.

The Barendra Research Museum has 3,000 manuscripts. Among these, on 2,600 Sanskrit Manuscripts have been catalogued jointly by Professor Kanailal Roy and Professor Chittaranjan Mishra. Out of 3,000 manuscripts in Bangla Academy, 526 Bengali manuscripts have been published as a list and edited by Sri Sukumar Choudhury. Currently the present writer is working on to identify 1500 Sanskrit Manuscripts and publish a catalogue titled, "*Sanskrit*

Barnanamulak Puthi Parichiti (Introduction to Sanskrit Descriptive Manuscripts)" from Bangla Academy.

Method of Collection

The first initiative to collect manuscripts began after establishment of the University of Dhaka. On this purpose, a seven member-committee was formed in 1925 whose President and Secretary were Professor S.K. Dey and Nalinikanta Vattacharya. The committee operated during the first two years from Dhaka Museum and later was transferred to the central building of the university in 1927. The committee was satisfied for being able to collect 3,000 manuscripts in their initial year. In the following year, the committee appointed a few agents to collect manuscripts from other districts, such as Faridpur, Sylhet and Mymensing. One of those agents was Bireswar Roy, who collected manuscripts from Faridpur region. The committee also employed a person to classify and to catalogue the collections on April 6, 1926. On 1926–27, 3 more persons named, Mathuranath Majumdar, Abinash Chandra Basu and Subodh Chandra Banerjee also began working on the same task as cataloguer, accessioner and assistant. In 1933–34 session, an agent called Mukunda Behari Das was employed who was a roaming agent and collected many manuscripts from various parts of Dhaka, Pubna, 24 Parganas, Bardhaman, Nadia, Assam, Medinipur, Hugli, Barisal, Faridpur (Kotalipara), Bakherganj and Noyakhali. He asked the magistrate of Dhaka to issue orders to Panchayet Chiefs of Manikganj and Dhamrai, instructing to help Mr. Mukunda Behari Das on manuscript collection.

Besides, efforts of the committee, many people donated manuscripts personally. During 1925–26 session, the landlord of Muktagacha, Mr Krishnadas Acharchya donated 573 manuscripts. Next year, Pandit Joshadhakanta Chakrabartee of Faridpur district donated 109 manuscripts. Next year, Pundit Kalikrishna Smrititirtha donated 41 bundle, Abhaypada Bhattacharya of Bardhaman donated 9, Pundit Rakhalananda Tagore Shastree donated 15, and Banagopal Goswami and Bijan Goswami of Katoya donated 43 manuscripts. Also some manuscripts were donated by a pundit named Chaitanya Charanya Vattachargya. In this manner up to 1940–41 session, thirty thousand manuscripts were collected at the library archives.

For collection of Urdu and Farsi manuscripts, a committee was formed in 1928 by the academic council. Members of this committee were, Head of the Farsi and Urdu Department, Fida Khan, Magruf Ahmed, Jafar Hussain Azad, a professor of Farsi department and Dr. Sunil Kumar De of Sanskrit and Bengali department. The committee published a large advertisement on the newspaper asking for donation of manuscripts and received great response. Within 1929–30 academic year, almost 300 manuscripts were collected. A member of a respected family of landlords, Khan Bahadur Choudhury Kazimuddin Ahmed Siddique and a notable person of contemporary India, Hekim Habibur Rahaman donated large collcctions of rare manuscripts to the university. Most of the collection came from the donations of various landlords and liberal persons. Some of the manuscripts were also purchased from various sources.

After 1940–41 sessions, not many collections were made. This field was totally neglected in the Pakistan Era. Later in 1951–52 sessions, the university again took initiative to collect manuscripts. In 1952, Abdur Rahim Sahittyabisharad donated 585 manuscripts to Dhaka University.

No significant additions were made to the archives since 1954 and before the independence. But after independence of Bangladesh, new initiatives were taken to collect and preserve historical artifacts. A subcommittee was formed on that purpose and as per as the decision of the committee, Mr. Ali Ahmad began working on the collection of microfilms of manuscripts stored at various archives in Bangladesh. During 1975–76 sessions, microfilms were taken of 666 manuscripts of Bangla Academy (Dhaka), Barendra

Research Museum (Rajshahi) and Rammala Library (Comilla.) During 1980–81 sessions, the collection of microfilm was further increased to 1053.

With financial assistance from Ford Foundation, a new project was taken for manuscript collection. The former director of Indian National Archives, Dr. Katpalia was an advisor of this project who took up this job after being advised by Dr. V.C. Joshi, a consultant to Ford Foundation. This project continued till June of 1988. This project was able to collect almost 3,000 manuscripts from Rammala Library of Comilla, Bangla Academy, Central Public Library and Kishoreganj Public Library. After cataloguing and microfilming, the manuscripts were returned to the archives. In 1998, 50 manuscripts from Srihutta Sanskrit Collage and in 2002 some manuscripts from Buddhist Monestrary in Comilla and Ramu (Coxs Bazar) were received. Finally during 2007, the family of notable educationist, Professor Ahmad Sharif donated 406 manuscripts. These manuscripts were mainly collected by Abdur Karim Sahittyabisharad and preserved by Professor Ahmad Sharif. Until 2011, the number of microfilms and manuscripts in the archive is 31000.

Identity of the collection

Here, among the collected 31,000 manuscripts, twenty thousands are Sanskrit. Most, among the rest, are Bangla and only a few are in Arabic, Farsi and Urdu. These manuscripts have been provided with short summery of identifications and serial of collection numbers. 17699 out of 20000 Sanskrit Manuscripts have been completely identified and have been listed on a literature of 8 volume titled as "*An Alphabetical Index of Sanskrit Manuscripts in the Dhaka University Library.*" Scholars who have contributed to the identification of these manuscripts are, Pundit Manindranath Samajdar, Dr. Kalpana Halder (Vhoumik), Professor Narayan Chandra Biswan, Professor Dilip Kumar

Vattacharya, Professor Dulal Kanti Bhoumik and Barendra Richa (Rajshahi).

Method of Preservation

An air-conditioned room is there to preserve the collected manuscripts. Both traditional and modern methods of preservation are used there. According to the traditional method, the pages are tied within two wooden plates and then the plated are bound by red/blue cloth. In the conditioned room, the manuscripts are kept in netted cabinets so that they are stored cold and in the presence of sufficient light and air. To control temperature, air cooler is used and to control humidity, dehumidifier machine is used. Fragile and difficult to preserve manuscripts are laminated with hand and modern hydraulic machine to make them durable and preserve their original appearances. Also, microfilming of the manuscripts began a few years ago and those can be easily read with the help of a microfilm reader. Pest infested manuscripts are disinfected with the help of fumigation treatment at the laboratory. For prevention of infestation of bug on the uninfected items, chemicals such as naphthalene and anti-infestation spray are used.

Compact disks of digitalized manuscripts are also collected in the archive. On this purpose, the required supply of digital cameras, computers, and printers have been purchased. Currently, images of the manuscripts are stored in the CD with the help of scanners and digital camera. These help the readers and researchers to read and make copies of the valuable manuscripts very easily while the original manuscripts remain protected from damages.

Specialties of the Archive

The manuscripts in the archive are written and copied within fifteenth to ninteenth century. They had been written on interesting materials, such as, Bark, thatch, tereta page, banana pages, tulata paper, press made papers etc. Among the subjects, there are the *Veda, Upanishada, Ramayana, Mahabharata, Purana, Smriti* and *Dharmasastra, Tantra, Literature, Drama, Vyakarana , Astrology, Alankara shastra, Chanda, Vedic Sastra* and *Kosha Grantha*. Some of the notable manuscripts are, *Vajasaneya Mantrabhasya* (Vaidic), eight Upanishads along with *Isha-Upanishad, Adhyatmya Ramayana, Adbhuta Ramayana*, A few chapters of *Mahabharata, Kurma Purana, Brahma Baibartya Purana, Dayabhag, Manusamhita, Sarada Tilak, Nirvana Tantra, Raghuvangsha, Kumarasambhaba, Gitagovinda, Bhatti Kavya, Meghadutam, Abhijyanasakuntalam, Maha Nataka, Kautuk Ratnakar, Bidagdhamadhaba, Katantra, Mugdhabodha, Adbhuta Sagar, Jyotishtattva, Kavyaprakash, Kavyachandrika, Pingala Chanda, Chandomanjari, Srutabodha, Chikitshatattva, Roganishchayanidana, Amarkosha, Shabdaratnabali, Laili-Majnu, Shatya-kalivivadsambad or Jugasambad, Madhumalati, Chandravali, Nabibangsha or Rasulcharit, Sikandarnama, Sayful Muluk Badiuzzamal, Chandrabati, Kavindra Mahabharata* etc. Also some genealogies of Mughal, Pre-Mughal periods, Hindi *dohas* written in Devanagari Script, land trading documents from Nasiruddin Shah era, slave trading documents from the time of Sultan Mahmud Shah and Emperor Shah Jahan.

The manuscripts are written in languages like, Sanskrit, Bengali, Asamese, Maithili, Persian, Urdu and Arabic. Scripts are mainly of Bengali, but some also written in Devanagari, Urdu, Persian, Arabic, Burmese scripts.

Antiquity of the Collection

It is difficult to say when manuscripts were first used in Indian subcontinent. The oldest text, *Rig Veda*, is assumed to be written in 2500 BC and is said to be in oral form initially. It is likely because the Vedas were written in verses. But what about the Brahmin Literature which was written on extensive texts? Aranyak Literature? The Upanishads written in later ages both in verses and prose? And the *Ramayana* and *Mahabharata* from fourth century BC? These texts were surely in black and white. But manuscripts from such old ages are not supposed to last till today. We have them on our hand now because they have been copied over and over through ages. The oldest manuscript ever discovered in India is a part from a Sanskrit Drama written on Palm Pages which is deduced to be from second century AD. Dr. Ludas was the publisher of the manuscript. The oldest manuscript preserved in Dhaka University library is "*Sarada Tilaka*", a book of Tantra Sastra, from 1439 AD which was written on bark.

Significance of the Archive in Bangladesh

The significance of the archive in Bangladesh is immense. These priceless gems from the archives are the greatest means of portraying Bangladeshi heritage to the world. Enter to the world of those dusty pages of the manuscripts and one would wonder at the treasures of our past. So many works on literature, theology, economics, sociology, medicine, ethics, magic and many other known and unknown topics are kept in all these archives throughout Bangladesh. But I worry whether we would be able to present their existence to the world before their demise.

A handful few of illuminated personalities of this country have accumulated treasures from these troves and glorified the nation. Most of the riches of the glorious Bengali Literature have been amassed from these archives. These archives are treasure troves for not only Bengali literature, but also for Sanskrit Literature too.

Historical Importance of the Manuscripts

Many manuscripts collected in Bangladesh provide valuable historical information. For example, in ancient Bhulua (Modern Noyakhali), the all four dynastic kings were poets. They are, Lakxman Manikya, his son Chandramanikya and Amar Manikya and the grandson Rudra Manikya. The dramatic verses written by them are preserved at Dhaka University Library. The court poet of Lakxman Manikya, was

Kabitarkik. *Kautukratnakar* is one of his notable creations. From these books, the original genealogy of Manikya Dynasty has been correctly identified than other erroneous historical information. In some other sources, Gandharbamanikya and his son Lakxmanmanikya are said to be two brothers and without the scripts written by the Manikya the misinformation would have prevailed. Also, I used to consider Manikya Dynasty to be same with Tripura Dynasty and I looked into the history of Tripura. There I did not find the name of Chandramanikya and felt frustrated. Finally when I researched the books of Bhulua, I discovered the true history. Manikya kings of Tripura and Bhulua are really similar.

We all know about the language movement of 1952, but many of us do not know that many years before the language movement, the Sultanat Rulers contributed to establishment of Bangla Language. In reality, while discussing about the contribution to the Bengali Language, sixteenth century Sultan Alauddin Hussain Shah and Paragal Shah should be appreciated first for their bold role to promote and establish the Bengali Language. The *Kavindra Mahabharat* bears the witness to their contribution. Even though Muslim Rulers were in power in Bengal, Bengali Language was oppressed and neglected by the Brahmin Society which was established during Sen and Pala dynasty. Brahmins had shunned away Bengali language. During that time the medium of education had been Sanskrit. Any considered educated scholar was judged whether he was conversant in Sanskrit. Along with such situation, Bengali Language had also been in the primitive state. Kavindra Parameswar Das was a Sanskrit scholar by family tradition whose father had the title of 'Gunaraja' and fame of being a great leader. Alauddin Hussain Shah titled Parameswar Das "Kavindra" (Best among poets) and assigned him as the court poet of his subordinate ruler of Chittagong, Laskar paragal Khan. This Paragal Khan heard about the glory, art of war and politics from The *Mahabharat* and became greatly interested. But he did not have the time or patience to learn the whole of Sanskrit *Mahabharat* because of its enormous size. That was probably why he instructed Kavindra Parameswar to write a *Mahabharat* worthy of listening within a day in Bengali Language. Following that instruction, Kavindra wrote a shorter version of *Mahabharat* in his own language in Bengali, which is called the *Kavindra Mahabharat*. Because, that *Mahabharat* had been written by demand of Laskar Paragal Khan, it is also called *Paragali Mahabharat*. Because, Kavindra was foremost a Sanskrit scholar, his *Mahabharat* is a great asset of Bengali Language. The writing style, scripts, language, rhythm, garnish, poetic quality of *Kavindra Mahabharat* makes it a distinct place in literature. This *Mahabharat* was read in the court of Sultan and the audiences were the Sultan, Courtiers, Citizens and Common people. Through this, we can detect a purpose of advertising and promoting Bengali Language. Even within the dominance of Sanskrit and Brahmins, one can earn greatness through Bengali Literature and Alauddin Hussain Shah had proved that by awarding Kavindra title to Parameswar Das. The power and glory of the independent Tripura Kingdom has a presence in the background of writing of this literature. Alauddin Hussain Shah had suffered many defeats to conquer Chittagong from the Kingdom of Tripura. Even though he had conquer Chittagong,he could not sustain his hold over the city for long. His contemporary king of Tripura, Dhanyamanikya, was a very powerful ruler. We hear about many defeats of Alauddin Hussain Shah in the hand of Dhanyamanikya from the Dhanyamanikya chapter of Rajamala—

> *'Bhay Paiya Gaur Sainnya rane bhanga dilo*
> *Tripurar Sainnya shabe prolay karilo.'*

Hussain Shah and Paragal Khan were worried about the influence and power of the King of Tripura. That is probably why they commissioned the Bengali *Mahabharat* to learn about the politics described in Sanskrit *Mahabharat*.

The manuscripts of *Kavindra Mahabharat* are preserved in the Dhaka University Library. After studying this *Mahabharat*, we learnt that it is the first ever translation of *Mahabharat* in Bengali and even 200 years older than Kashiram Das. From general consideration, the *Kavindra Mahabharat* bears immense importance for the history of Bengali text, language and literature.

Similarly, many other manuscripts bearing historical information are preserved in this archive which may be realized by more research.

Research on the collection

In order to research, which is to say editing and publishing, a committee called 'Oriental Text Publishing Committee' was established in November 8, 1927 by the vice chancellor. The president of the 6 member committee was the professor of Sanskrit, Radhagovinda Basak. This committee was assigned to select Manuscripts, Editor and Reviewer and publish if the manuscript was declared worthy of publishing by the reviewer. First publishing of the committee was *Kichakabadha* by Nitivarma. It was edited by S.K. Dey and was published in 1929. The reviewer was Professor Thomas of Oxford University. S.K. Dey edited a second publication, *Padyavali* of Rupgoswami, in 1934. Third and fourth publications were *Ghatakarporkabya* by Radhagovinda Basak and *Krishnakarnamrita* by S.K. Dey in 1938.

The divide of India in 1947 became a great barrier against the work on Sanskrit Manuscripts, because most of the Sanskrit scholars living in Dhaka left for India. As a result, works on both editing and collection stopped. Many years later in 1991, the writer of article, received PhD. degree from University of Dhaka for her work on *Apadesh Shatak* by Bhuluaraj Chandramanikya. This thesis was printed and published by the Bangla Academy, Dhaka in 1993. Afterwards, Dr. Dulal Kanti Bhowmik wrote on a prahashan called "*kautukratnakar*" by Raghunath Kavitarkik, the court poet of King of Bhulua Lakxmanmanikya and earned his PhD degree from Ravindravarati University in Kolkata. The book was published by the University of Dhaka in 1997. He also worked on the *Apadeshiyashataslokamalika* by Rudramanikya, son of Vijaymanikya. It was published in 1999. Manaranjan Ghosh, a student from Sanskrit Department of the University of Dhaka, also worked on another manuscript, Shantishataka by Sihlan and earned PhD degree from Jadavpur University.

Editing of Bengali Manuscripts

After the partition of India, the editorial work of Bengali manuscripts continued on personal capacity. From 1957, Professor Ahamad Sarif edited a few manuscripts from the collection of the Dhaka University Library. He edited the following texts: *Laily Majnu* by Daulat Uzir Bahram Khan(1957, Bangla Academy, Dhaka), *Vidyasundar* by Sridhar Kabiraj (1957, Sahityapatrika, Department of Bangla, University of Dhaka), *Tohfa* by Alaul(1958, University of Dhaka) , *Satya-Kali Vivad Sam*bad (1959, University of Dhaka), *Jaynaber Chautisha* by Seikh Fayjullah, Arbi tirish akkhare munajat by Muhammad Fasih, *Madhumalati* by Muhammad Kabir, Musanama by Muhammad Akil (1960, Bangla Academy), *Padasahitya and Mushanama* by Muslim Kabi (1961, Bangla Academy), Madhayuger Bangla Giti Kabita (with Muhammad Abdul Hi, Dhaka University), *Rasul Bijoy* By Jayenuddin (1964, University of Dhaka), *Nitisastrabarta* by Mujammil (1965, Bangla Academy), *Shabarid Khan Granthabali* (1966, Bangla Academy), Syed Sultan Granthabali (1967, Dhaka University), *Chandrabali* by Kureishi Magan Thakur(1967, Bangla Academy), *Byaribhaktitarangini* by Bidyapati (1968, Itihash Parishad Patrika), *Nashihatnama* By Afzal Ali (1969, Bangla Academy), *Sayful Muluk Badiuzzaman* by Donagazi (1975, Bangla Academy), *Sikhdar Nama* by Alauddin (1977, Bangla Academy), *Nobibangsha and Rasulcharit* by Syed Sultan (1978, Bangla Academy), Kifayetul Mushallin and Kaydani Kitab by Seikh Mutalib (1978, Bangla Academy), *Chaitanya-tatvapradip* by Brajamohan Das (1978, Bangla Academy), *Hajar Mashayel and Nurnama* by Roshang Poet Abdul Karim and Sariyatnama by Nasharullah Khondakar (1997, Bangla Academy). The manuscript titled *Usuf Julekha* by Shah Muhammad Sagir and edited by Dr. Muhammad Enamul Huq was published from the University of Dhaka. The writer of this article has earned her D.Lit degree from Jadavpur University for editing and researching on *Kavindra Mahavarat* by Kavindra Parameswar Das and her work was published in 1999 by Bangla Academy. Another manuscript by the same researcher, a romantic tale called *Chandrabati* by Dvija Pasupati, is to be published by Bangla Academy soon.

An American researcher, Tony Stuart, have edited the work of a manuscript called, *Satyanarayan Pachali* or *Satyapir Pachali* from the Dhaka University Library. This is to be published soon as well. This manuscript describes the good relation between Hindu and Muslim societies and explains philosophically that Allah and Bhagavan are just two faces of the same God.

Conclusion

The western researchers were the first one to show the great importance of the manuscripts. Researchers from USA, UK, France, Italy, Russia, Australia, China, Japan and other countries have researched on our manuscripts and are currently doing so too. Realizing the importance of the manuscripts, the British Rulers took many of them away when leaving the subcontinent during the partition. Now, when we need them, we have to incur high expenses to loan or to copy those manuscripts from them. Even though what we have are like priceless treasures, but are mostly unknown to us. How many of us have realized their importance? Those who realize are unable to do anything for lack of scopes even though they are capable of doing the job. Only their silent pains remain as the witness to the demise of our national heritage. The great task of discovering treasure from those dusty and forgotten manuscripts is as tough as harvesting pearls from the bottom of the sea. And if we give up, our heritage will be lost forever behind the black veil of time a bit by bit. A type of ink used by the ancients is made of iron particles to give it a bright black texture. But unknown to them was that this ink was the source of destruction for their manuscripts. Even though the pages remain intact, the scripts written by those ink dust away. We have many such manuscripts in our collections, which are just stored under conditioned rooms. But the only way that is worthy of their preservation is to research and work on them. Only if we can utilize our talent after such task, then we would be able to save our knowledge of the past and our treasures.

Sri Dinesh Chandra Vattacharya said about storage and preservation of Manuscripts in his book "Bangalir Sharswatta Abadan" that, Through the pages of the manuscripts we find the remains of old lifestyles; as the general rule, in the city archives, the manuscripts only sleeps well dressed in beautiful rooms; if we could check their pulses before their final journey to mortuary, our archeological asset would have been richer.

Most of the manuscripts in Bangladesh have reached the last stages of their life. Probably most archives in India are also in the same state. That is why, we should not allow them to rest in their sleep, we have to wake them up. And then our language and history will find their glory.

9

THE KOKBOROK MANUSCRIPT

NARESH CH. DEV VARMA

The Kokborok, language of the major tribes of Tripura, has rich hidden treasure of folk-literature. There were numerous folk-tales and folk-songs which have been in vogue orally amongst the Kokborok speaking tribes hereditarily from the remote past. Besides, the Kokborok folk-songs had been composed orally by the Kokborok singers till the recent past. But the folk-tales and folk-songs were not in writen form or published in the past. Some of the folk-tales and folk-songs have however been collected and are getting published by some researchers now-a-days.

The oral literature of folk-tales and folk-songs were not written in the past because of absence of education of the tribal communities in those days. The educational schemes of the tribals under the Royal patronage of the State seem to have been taken up during the last part of the nineteenth century. It is found that even in 1892, the Royal administration expressed its views in a proceedings that the number of schools was very inadequate and the enrolment of students was also very poor in comparison of the population of the State. Except the capital, all other areas were inhabited by the weaker sections of the people. The prevailing conditions did not lead them to feel the necessity for higher education.

There should have been good number of Pathasalas to improve the condition and to meet the demand. Therefore, it was suggested to establish requisite number of Pathasalas in a planned way.

However, there are some hints and references of old literature written in the Kokborok language under the Royal patronage. First, there is a mention that the "Rajmala" "the chronicle of the Tripura dynasty, was written in the Kokborok by Durlabendra Chantai. King Dharma Manikya during his reign (1431–62 AD) engaged two brahmin-brothers Sukreswar and Baneswar for translation of the "Rajmala" from Kokborok Language to Bengali. But, the manuscript of the Kokborok "Rajmala" is still missing.

The second reference of the Kokborok manuscript is "Surchya Pujar Khonaimani" (worship of the Sun-God) as published by Santimoy Chakraborty in his book "Kok-boroker Utsa Sandane" in 2000. The manuscript is being preserved in the Agartala Museum. The manuscript contains the Mantras (incantations) for the Sun-God and other Gods and Goddesses as were worshiped by the tribal people of the State. There are forty slokas (verses) each containing eight lines .

According to the views of Santimoy Chakraborty this Kokborok manuscript is the oldest one and was probably composed in 590 AD. It is comprehended that the manuscript was transcribed many a time during the successive reigns of the kings of Tripura. It is mentioned in the verse no. 5 of some Mantra (incantation) that manuscript was last transcribed by some Krishna Ballav Deb Sarmano during the reign of king Mahendra Manikya in 1699 AD. It was further stated in the verse that Shri Durgaprasad Narayan Tripur was the custodian of the manuscript. The original composer of the Mantras (verses) was not indicated anywhere. Thorough research is also required regarding the antiquity of the manuscript.

Mention of the Kokborok cultivation by Prince Radhakishore Manikya in the Official Reports is quite significant. T.E. Coxhead, Esq. C.S. Officiating Political Agent, Hill Tipperah in his Annual Report of 1876 stated, "The Joobraj has, moreover, at my suggestion, set about the compilation of a Tipperah vocabulary. He is perfectly acquainted with the vernacular of the hill people, and I am in hopes that the result of his undertaking will have some scientific interest." (No. 134, date Agurtollah, the 26th June, 1876).

In the next year, C.W. Bolton, Esq. Officiating Political Agent, Hill Tipperah, in his Annual Report of 1877 stated.—"The Jubraj is still engaged in the compilation of Tipperah, Bengal Dictionary." (No. 196, dated. Agartala, the 17th July, 1877).

But the aforesaid work of the Jubraj was not published and the manuscript thereof was not found elsewhere.

Doulat Ahammad was the pioneer with regard to the venture of composing the Kokborok Grammar. He wrote a book of Kokborok Grammar "Kokborma aung Tripura-Byakaran" published in 1897/1899 AD. (Poush 1307 Tring). After publication of this book he wrote another Kokborok Grammar "Kokma Kalai" (Easy Grammar), but it was not published. At the instance of Nehar Uddin Ahmmad, the youngest son of Doulat Ahammad, the manuscript was found in thier homestead Kulubari, Sonamura, in 1970.

The cover and the first four pages of the manuscript were missing and the pp. 5–10 were torn. The manuscript contains seven chaptes (sanket). The seventh chapter indicates poem-prose. But only three kokborok poems are found in this partly damaged and illegible. So, it is presumed that there might have been some kokborok stories, folk-tales etc which are lost in the torn part.

The "Kokma Kalai" manuscript was published by Hachukni Khorang Publishers, Agartala, in 2007 as edited by myself.

10

TRIPURA ON THE PATH OF PROGRESS: A STUDY ON SOCIAL AND RELIGIOUS REFORMS

NEERU WAHAL

From the early decades of the nineteenth century there was a growing awareness in all parts of the country of the backwardness of Indian society and of the need for its betterment. Some of the social evils and superstitions had become associated with religious beliefs. The Practice of killing infant girls, child marriages, Sati or the burning of widow on the funeral pyre, regular trade of slaves are inhuman, customs and practices prevailed in the Indian society over the years.

The rising tide of nationalism and democracy after the revolt of 1857, not only led to the struggle for freedom but also found expression in movement to reform and democratize the social institutions and religious outlook of the Indian people. Thoughtful Indians began to look for the strengths and weaknesses of their society and for ways and means of removing the weaknesses. They realized that social and religious reformation was essential condition for thedevelopment of the country in modern lines and for the national unity and solidarity. Rammohan Roy pioneer among the reformers; worked hard all his life for the social religious intellectual and political regeneration. Debendranath Tagore (father of Rabindra Nath Tagore), Ishwar-chandra Vidyasagar in Bengal, are other leading personalities who dedicated their lives to the cause of social reform. Deeply influenced by the ideas of rationalism and humanism and of human equality socio-religious reform movement spread in western and southern India also.

Tripura, the small state of southwest corner of the north eastern region, also .received the spurt of these reform movements. The enlightened monarchs of Tripura influenced by humanist and radical ideas made efforts to eradicate social evils from the state. They also realized that education could only help the society to get rid of abuses. An attempt has been made to trace these 'royal' and 'public' efforts of social and religious reforms that paved the path of progress for tribal state.

Tripura—A background

With an area 10,477 Sq Km. Tripura is the smallest of the seven Sister states of North-East India. It is the second most populous state in North-East India after Assam. According to the census of 2011, Tripura has a total population of 36,71,032 with 18,71,867 males and 17,99,165 females. There are nineteen tribal communities of which Tripuris are distributed all over the state. The others are, Noatia, Jamatia, Reang, Chakma, Halam, Garo, Kuki, Lushai, Mog, Oraon, Santhal, Uchai, Khasi, Bhil, Lepcha, Bhutia, and Chaimal[i]. The Tribal population formed majority before independence. The Tripuris, had there tribal religion modified by Hinduism. At the same time, under the patronage of the Tripura. Rajas, a good deal of their pre-Hindu religion and its rituals are preserved as a part of their religion.

An overwhelming majority among the important tribes in Tripura—the Tripuris, Reanges, Jamatias, Noatians, and Halams are to all intents and purposes, Hindus and practices all the Hindu religious rites like any other Hindu. Like other Hindu sobrieties of India the rigid social conventions and customs prevailed among these tribes: They believe in the existence of spirit possessing supernatural power of doing harm. Child marriage among the chakmas, the custom of Jamaikhata among the Reangs, Halams and Tripuris, dowry system in Jamatias, Polygamy among the Bhil tribe and such other social customs were prevalent among most of the tribes of the state.

Some of the rigid social conventions and customs of the tribal society of Tripura

In the Tripuri, Reang and Halam tribal family youngman who wished to marry a girl had to serve for some years in the prospective bride's house. This practice was known as Jamalkhata. During this period of stay the youngman had to undergo certain rigorous practices. He had to get out from bed early at dawn, fetch water for the family, sweep the house, prepare breakfast for the members of the family. When it was still dawn, he had to process bamboo and wood for use as fuel. Before sunrise he had to serve breakfast to all the members of the family.

Before Marriage and during the period of Jamaikhata, it was prohibited for the would-be couple to talk to each other. The would-be wife however, would serve dish to her would-be husband during dinner and prepare for him a hookah. (an instrument of smoking with tobacco) at night. But while doing so she could not talk with him. If he was up to her choice, she would keep secretly a boiled egg covered with rice on his dish beyond the knowledge of anybody. The would-be husband, then could understand that she likes him. Contrarily, she would keep ashes on her dish, covered with rice, thus indicating that she did not like him. In such case the would-be bridegroom would leave the house in no time.[3]

Thus his manners, likes, dislikes, behaviour pattern all are deeply and closely watched. The groom is sent to cultivation, husbandry of cattle, fencing of the garden, making of household articles. If the groom runs away before the period of jamaikhata he forfeits all claim to the bride who can now be married to anybody else even if the boy and girl fall in love for each other[4]. The period of such probation varies from tribe to tribe.

This practice was inhuman and undignified. It was a cruel exposure of selfishness on the part of would be farther in law. It was a custom based on exploitation.

Another evil practice prevalent mostly among the Jamatias and Kukis was the custom of paying bride's price. In many cases even after observing the custom of Jamaikhata a bride's price was to be paid. Besides, the groom's party had to spend a lot of money in the actual wedding cermoney while taking the bride to their own house.

The Sati system or the burning of the wife with the dead body of her husband which had been prevalent in India was practiced from a very early period in Tripura. The term 'Sati' literally means 'a pure and virtuous woman'. It is used in the case of devoted wife who contemplates perpetual conjugal union with the husband life after life, and as a proof she burns herself with the dead body at the pyre of her husband.

Francois Bernier, a traveller from France visited the subcontinent in the seventeenth century. In his account 'Travels in the Mughal Empire' he has given a detailed description to this practice of Sati. He noted that while some women seemed to embrace death cheerfully, others were forced to die. This is perhaps one of the most poignant descriptions by Bernier:

> "... I saw a most beautiful young widow sacrificed, who could not, I think, have been more than twelve years

of age. The poor creature appeared deader than alive when she approached the dreadful pit the agony of her mind cannot be described. She trembled and wept bitterly; but three or four of the Brahamanas, assisted by an old woman who held her under the arm, forced the unwilling victim towards the fatal spot, seated her on the wood, tied her hands and feet, lest she should run away, and in that situation the innocent creature was burnt alive, I found it difficult to repress my feelings and to prevent their busting forth into clamorous and unavailing rage. . . ."[6]

Polygamy was in vogue in the Tripuri society. The practice of marrying for the second time while the first wife was alive appeared to be a fashion at one stage, while a woman has no right to live with two husbands at a time. It is disgraceful and persecuting for a woman.

Untouchables of Tripura—there is a good number of tea garden labourers in Tripura. Among them there are Santhal, Sabar, Munda, Oriya, Tanti and the like. They were called coolies (agricultural labourers) in Tripura. It was a common believe that one would loose their caste if one drank water or ate cooked food from their hands.

Like many other human societies some women were taken for witches in Tripuri Society also. It was a common belief that illness or death of children or boys or girls was due to the women who were witches. In Tripuri society there was fear among many about this type of woman and they tried to avoid them. The villagers sometimes offered pujas by sacrificing tortoises or cocks in order to appease the witch. There was not a single village where someone or the other was not suspected—to be a witch. The common people are used to utilize the services of ojjah (sorcerer) to identify which woman was a witch and there after she was killed. This inhuman treatment was purely based on superstition.

The practice of slavery like other Indian societies, also common in the society of the nobility of Tripura. It appears from Ibn Battuta's[7] account that slaves were openly sold in the markets like any other commodity and were regularly exchanged as gifts. All the 'Thakurs' irrespective of their status however enjoyed certain economic privileges. One such privilege was the traditional right to maintain domestic slaves. This system of domestic slavery provided the Thakurs with domestic servants at no cost. The political agent in his report of 1857–76 writes:

> "It is not an uncommon thing for a Hillman when in difficulties to sell him for a period in consideration of the debt incurred being liquidated. Sometime he sells himself without any restrictions as to the term of his slavery, sometimes he sells himself with his wife and children. Women also dispose of themselves for the same reason but it is not so much on account of those who have more or less voluntarily incurred bondage that the custom is so hateful, but on account of the effects to their posterity. Their children are slaves, and remain so if their parent's have died when in slavery or have run away leaving them. If they are girls, the position they sometimes come to occupy in their masters household may be understood.[10]

Lack of education was the root of all these evils and superstitions. The hill people were innately conservative in their mode of life. They were all much given to drink, having the sanction of their religion for doing so, spirits were indispensably necessary for more of their ceremonies.

Transformation and Modernization of the society under the enlightened Monarch of Tripura

Every human society has been undergoing a process of social reformation. In some society it started earlier while in others later on. Generally the tribal societies have come late into process. Modern era in Tripura maybe said to have begun from the reign of Birchandra Manikya (1862–96).

Till 1813 British authorities followed the policy of no-interference in the religious, social and cultural life of the country but after 1813 they took active steps to transform Indian society and culture. The rising industrial interest after the industrial revolution which had begun in the middle of the eighteenth century tempted them to make India a big market for their goods. This required the partial transformation and modernization of Indian society.

The eighteenth and nineteen centuries witnessed a great ferrent of new ideas in Britain and Europe. All over Europe new attitudes of mind, manners and morals were appearing. The great French revolution of 1789 with its message of liberty, equality and fraternity generated powerful democratic sentiments and unleashed the force of modern nationalism. In the realm of thought, the new trend was represented by Bacon, Locke, Voltaire, Rousseau, Adam Smith and Bentham, in the realm of literature by Wordsworth, Byron, Shelly and Charles Dickens. The impact of new thought, the product of the intellectual revolution of the eighteenth century, the French revolution, and the industrial revolution were naturally felt in India and to some extent affected the official notions of the government.

The three outstanding characteristics of the new thoughts were rationalism or faith in reason, humanism or love of man and confidence in the capacity of man to progress. Humanism was based on the belief that every human being has an end in him and should be respected and prized as such. No man had the right to look upon another human being as a mere agent for his own happiness. According to the doctrine of progress all societies must change with time: nothing was or could be static. Moreover man had the capacity to remodel name and society, on rational and just lines. Thus modernization of India was accepted by English officials, businessman and statesman because it was expected to make Indians better customers for British goods and reconcile them to the alien rule, To this elaboration of the theory of modernization was added the concept of "good government." It included useful public works, promotion of 'public education, provision for suitable medical agencies, abolition of' undignified social customs and maintenance of public order. Lord Mayol had clearly formulated one cardinal principle that the rights and privileges of the prince would be respected only if they provided "good government" to their people and on this background reforms were introduced in Tripura under Birchandra Manikya (1862–96) and his successors. Radhakishore Manikya (1896, 1909), Birendra Kishore Manikya etc. future dealings in slavery are stopped. The Maharaja's action in this matter deserves praise.

By the famous regulation, XVII, 4 Dec. 1829 AD. William Bentpick declared Sati system illegal in India. But in Tripura this system was still continued for a long time. Personally Maharaja. Birchandra was not in favour of the abolition of the Sati. as it was a very old practice in Tripura and people considered it as sacred one. The commissioner of Chittagong Mr. D.R. Lyall wrote to the political Agent on 2nd Oct 1888:

> "I request that you will place—the matter again before- the Maharaja strongly. advising him to pass a law to the same effect as regulation XVII of 1829 and to see that it is "enforced".[12]

After receiving this letter, the political agent for Tripura. again requested Maharaja to abolish Sati within three months. It was due to the initiative of Umakant Das, the assistant political agent for Tripura that Bir Chandra Manikya prohibited the practice of Sati in Tripura by a duly promulgated order in 1889 AD.[13]

He also recognized judiciary in 1873–74 and the first written laws were introduced in the state. The imperial post office began to function at Agartala from October 1875[14] vaccination operations against cholera and small pox started in the state in 1875–76[15], female education began in 1876–77 with the establishment of a pathshala or elementary school at the Christian village of Mariam-nagar. A charitable hospital was opened at Agartalla in May 1873[17].

In recognition of Birchandra's loyality and his earnest endeavour to improve the administration of his state the title of 'Maharaja' was bestowed upon him in 1877 as a personal distinction.

Birchandra Mariikya patronized a good number of scholars, musicians and artists and accorded libral grants to the Pundits for publication of literary works. Himself, a lyrical poet he earned the most covetous but appropriate title of Vikramaditya from the people of Bengal.[18]

It was Birchandra Manikya who first recognized the genius in the poet Rabindra Nath Tagore after reading his book of Poems "Bhaganahridya." At a time when the poet was quite young and his writings were known to few besides his own intimate friends and relations, Birchandra sent an emissary to congratulate him as a great poet. The poet was thrilled at this. This simple yet, momentous event proved as a stepping stone not only for a close link that followed since then between the royal family, and the poet but through this followed a close cultural tie between two states, Tripura and Bengal.

After Birchandra's death in 1896 his son Radhakishore Manikya (1896–1909) took over, the administration of the state. Like his illustrious father he was also a great reformer. His administration was oriented towards the welfare of the people. He set up model farm to educate and encourage the cultivators to cultivate on modern lines. He built few departments like education, health, agriculture, public works and police. He promoted the cause of learning in the state and cultivated friendship with many eminent personalities of Bengal. In 1904 he gave away all the valuable laboratory equipment of the defunct government college at Agartalla to the then newly founded Brahma Vidyalaya at Shantiniketan, which became the nucleus of Vishvabharti University later on. For the foundation of this Vidyalay itself, he donated Rs 5,000.[19] The Bengal technical institute of Calcutta which formed the nucleus to the present Jadhavpur University received handsome donation from him.[20]

Radhakishor Manikya gave financial help to the great scientist Jagdish Chandra Bose for his researches in science. He also gave financial help to the blind poet Hem Chandra Banerjee. A contemporary newspaper records, "The Maharaja of Tripura has offered to fix a pension on baboo Hem Chandra Banerjee, the distinguished Bengali Poet, who owing to blindness has been incapacitated from carrying his profession as a pleader and is with his family at Benaras."[21]

After the death of Radhakishore Manikya in March 1909, the crown Prince Birendra Kishore Manikya (1909–23) succeeded him. He also worked for the spread of education among his people. He founded English high schools in different places. A circular was issued in 1920 from the department of education urging upon the Darogas, Nayebs and Tehsildars to take special interest in the matter of increasing staff in meeting the requirement of the schools. He opened a Model school for agriculture education and training.

The most important achievement of his reign was the

establishment of tea industry. This industry increased the revenue of the state and gave employment opportunities to the people.

Himself being an artist and painter, he was a patron of drama, music and literature. He died in 1923 at the age of forty only.

Bir Bikram (1923–47) was the last ruling prince of Tripura. Like, his illustrious predecessors he did his best for all round development of Tripura: it was due to his initiative that an aerodrome for Agartala was constructed at Singarbil. 'Bir Bikram passed away a few months before independence on 17 May 1947. But before his death he could foresee that Tripura's fate must be tagged to the rest of India. He therefore settled the question of Tripura's merger with Indian Union. Tripura's merger agreement was signed on 9th September 1949 in New Delhi. Maharani Kanchanprava Devi as Regent and on behalf of her minor son, signed the agreement. Formal integration took place on 15 October 1949.

Efforts of Tribal Youth of Tripura to reform and modernize their society

Education is the rearing ground of culture, and an integral part of the regions' development process. Spread of education among the Tribals and development of their consciousness was the prime necessity of the time. The kings of Tripura took some steps for the education of their subjects but these were not adequate.

A group of educated Tribal students and youth being actuated by a desire to awaken their tribal commoners embarked on a mission to spread education among them, for education only helps the society to get rid of abuses which disfigured the social life. With the object of spreading mass education in the hills of Tripura and to eradicate poverty of the tribal masses, to carry out social reforms, to motivate the people, to abandon superstitions, to develop cottage industries and to take up settled cultivation Vanasiksha movement was started in 1945. Janasiksha or the movement for enlightenment was organised by Tripura Janasiksha Samiti. It was the first Tripuri (tribal) protonationalist organization formed on 27 Dec. 1945. Samiti got support from Mr. Brown, then Education minister of Tripura. The President of the Advisory Committee of the Samiti was Hriday Ranjan Deb Barma, retired judge and Dhiren Krishna Deb Barma was its Vice President. Biren Datta, Aghore Deb Barma, Dasarath Deb Barma; Nilmoni Deb Barma, Sudhannya Deb Barma and many others were the members of' the Samiti. 'It is impossible to organise the tribals in the rural area, wrote Biren Datta, merely on the slogans for personal liberty, democracy and socialism without unleashing a struggle for their development.'[23] Not only in the hill areas inhabited by the tribes but also in the plains inhabited by the Bengalees, schools came up at the initiative of Janasiksha Samiti. Besides removing illiteracy, the Janasiksha Samiti also embarked a mission to remove poverty. It steered a movement against squeezing of the tribals by the mahajans (businessmen/ moneylenders). The organizers of the Janasiksha are Birchandra Maniknya (1862–96), Radhakishore Manikya (1896–1909). Birendra Kishore Manikya (1909–23), Bir Bikramkishore Manikya. 1923 movement made extensive use of songs and rhymes in Kok-Borak (Tripuri dialect) and thus pioneered a movement for the development of this language and literature.

The Janasiksha or people's education movement drew wide support from the people. It ceased to exist in 1948. Though short in time span it had an impact of long term value.

The mass-awakening aroused by the Janasiksha movement and the sense of pride and national feeling gave courage to the people of Tripura to raise their voice, unitedly against the conspiracy to annex Tripura State to Pakistan. The conspiracy was plotted specially after Chittagong Hill Tract, Chakla Roshnabad, Sylhet district had gone to Pakistan leaving Tripura isolated and cut off from the mainland. We are proud to say that when communal frenzy overtook different parts of the undivided India, Tripura cautiously guarded herself from falling a victim to it. No communal riots was ever held in the state. Carrying the legacy of the Janasiksha Samiti the Tripura Rajya Mokti Parishad, embarked on a mission of socio-cultural reforms of the Tripuri Tribal Society. This organisation came into existence in May 1948. It was due to its efforts that some social abuses and practices like the child marriage, jamaikhata, bride's price, polygamy, marriage between uneven ages, untouchability, witch hunting etc. were restricted and some of these were even stamped out. Parishad championed the cause of women, especially their right to paternal property.

Thus these two organisations Tripura Janasiksha Samiti (1945–48) and Tripura Rajya Mukti Parishad (1945–51) aroused a strong interest among the tribal people who were inspired to look forward. These two, in fact, paved the way for social tranition of the Tripuri Society.

Conclusion

Inspired by the humanitarian impulses of the 19[lh] century socio-religious movements, the enlightened and benevolent rulers of Tripura Birchandra Manikya (1862–96), Radhakishore Manikya (1896–1909). Birendra Kishore Manikya (1909–23), Bir Bikramkishore Manikya (1923–47) made their best efforts to modernise their society. Their efforts further strengthened by the enthusiastic, energetic, newly educated youth of Tripura. They strongly stood against the rigid social conventions and outdated customs of the society, laid stress in mass education, Tripura today has a higher literacy percentage 87.75%

compared to the national average of literacy rate 74.04%. Far from the capital city of country, with its isolated situation and vulnerable geographical location, bottleneck communication, this tiny state of Tripura is on the path of progress and occupied a position of importance on the eastern border of India.

References

1. Census of India, 1961, XXVI, Tripura, part V-A.
2. S.N.GuhaThakurta: Tripura, Publish by the Director, National Book Trust, India, New Delhi, 1986, p. 54.
3. Bijan Mohanta : Tripura in the light of Socio-Political movements since / 945, Progressive Publishers, Kolkata, 2004, p. 48.
4. Ray. S.KÑ., India's North-East and the Travails of Tripura, Minerva Associates Pvt. Ltd, 2003, p. 51.
5. Mohanta: Tripura, op. cit., p. 51.
6. Bernier, Francois: Travels in the Mughal Empire.
7. Ibn Battuta a traveler from Morocco, in the North-Western Africa visited the subcontinent in fourteenth century.
According to K.C. Singha, it was Kalyan Manikya, 625–1659, who first introduced the title of Thakur to distinguish the, Raj Kumar (princes) from others of nobility In the course of time however the title Thakur become synonymous with the nobility of Tripura as such.
9. Annual Administration: Reports of the Political Agency of Hill Tipperah for the year 1875–76, p. 6, para 13.
10. Viceroy of India, 1869–72.
11. Reporf for the year, 1877–78, p. 7.
12. Bengal Administrative Report I, 888–89.
13. Ibid.
14. Report for the year 1875–76, p. 10, para 26.
15. lbid., p. 10, para 24.
16. Report for the year, 1876–77, p. 3, para.
17. Report for the year 1873–74, p. 14, para 55.
18. Ñ Chaudhari .D,K: *The Political Agents and the Native Raj,* New Delhi 1999, p. 74.
19. S:N.G., Thakurta: Tripura, p. 21.
20. Ibid., p. 56.
21. Ibid., p. 51.
22. The Indian Nations, 31 july 1899, Quoted from Thakurta, p. 57.

23. Tripura State Gazette, vol. XIX, no. N, 12.
24. Dana, Biran, 1982: 25, Amar Smritite Tripurar Communist 0 ganatantrik andolaner patabhumi 1900–925. Calcutta,
25. Roy Choudhury,N.R, *Tripura through the Ages,* New Delhi, p. 77.

11

TAKHEN (TRIPURA) AS REFLECTED IN THE MANUSCRIPTS OF MANIPUR (FORMER KANGLEIPAK)

NG. KANGIIA MANGANG

The former name of the present state Manipur was Kangleipak according to a number of manuscripts like *"Wakoklon Thine! Salai Amailon Pukok"*, *"Cheitharol Kumpaba"*, *"Kangleipak Meetei lmpham"*, *"Panthoipi Khongkhul"* etc. According to the Manuscript *"Sanamahi Laikal"*, the Sanskrit word "Manipur" came into existence, for the first time in Kangleipak, during the reign of King Pamheiba (1709-1748 A.D.) who was the first king of Kangleipak to take Hindu Ramayet Cult. Before King Pamheiba, all the kings of Kangleipak professed Sanamahism (Sanamahi Laining) as State religion. The national Script of Kangleipak was Kanglei Script popularly known as Meetei Mayek (Meetei script) and its national game was Sagol Kangjei (Modern Polo).

Tripura State was mentioned by the name "Takhen" in a number of manuscripts written in Meetei Script like *"Takhen Ngamba"*, *"Cheitharol Kumpaba"*, *"Sanggai Phammang"*, *"Langthaballon"*, *"Pamol Khunthoklon"*, *"Nongchup Haram"* and others. The manuscripts called Assam by the name "Tekhao", Cachar by the name "Thongnang" and Burma (modern Myanmar) by the name "Awa". The ancient kingdom Kangleipak (Modern Manipur) had bilateral relations with the neighbouring kingdoms since ancient times.

Kangleipak itself was a united kingdom of seven principalities—(1) Mangang Kingdom ruled by Mangang dynasty king; (2) Luwang Kingdom ruled by Luwang Dynasty king; (3) Khuman ruled by Khuman dynasty king; (4) Angom ruled by Angom dynasty king; (5) Moirang ruled by Moirang dynasty king; (6) Khanganba by Khanganba dynasty king; and (7) Leisangthem principality ruled by Leisangthem dynasty. It is clearly written in the manuscript *"Wakoklon Thallel Salai Amailon Pukok"*. These seven kingdoms had a common language "Meeteilol", a common religion "Sanamahi Laining" and common traditional and cultural practices. These small states had jointly enjoyed the sovereignty of the United Kingdom of Kangleipak and maintained its territorial integrity. Travellers from the mainland of India and western countries had passed the United kingdom of Kangleipak for China, Burma and other South-east Asian countries. Due to geographical and historical reasons people from east and west had settled in Kangleipak and its original people had also settled in the far and near neighboring states.

Inter-state migration between Takhen (Tripura) and Kangleipak (Modern manipur) : It is written in the old manuscript *"Khamlangba Khunkumion"* that Khamlangba, a well known adventurer, in the first quarter of the first century AD, left Kangleipak for Takhen (modern Tripura). It is mentioned in the manuscript that the Takhens (people of Takhen, Tripura) had known him as "Kalika". In Khamlangba's return journey to Kangleipak, he was accompanied by a group of emigrants and they had settled at Uripok near Imphal City and Kakching in the south-east region of Kangleipak. It is the first recorded inter-state or inter-community migration episode between Takhen (Tripura) and Kangleipak (modern Manipur). Khamlangba had a wife during his journey. Eminent scholars are of the opinion that his wife was a Takhen woman. It is also opined that some of the Meeteis (major community of Kangleipak) who were associated with the adventure journey of Khamlangba had setteled in Takhen having Takhen wives.

It is written in the manuscript "Cheitharol kumpaba (Royal Chronicles) meaning *"Queen of Takhen Akoijam Chanu Yangnu had returned to Takhen."* It was in 1609 during the regime of king Khagenba (1597-1652 AD)

The manuscript *"Pamol Khunthoklon"* had recorded a series of emigrants from Takhen (Tripura). During the regime of Lamkyamba (1512–23 AD) emigrants from Takhen (Tripura) to Kangleipak (Manipur) were Narayon, Bitambora, Mishripanda, Brahmachari, Dibadi, Sarangki, Natwa, Langkachoron, Tanta Dhara, Nakhak, Nandirai, Bakindra, Raghunath, Thradas, Sanesegiri, Kriparam, Bichitra Punt and his son Cheiteino Dasho and other 63 Takhens. They had settled at different places of the seven principalities of the united kingdom of Kangleipak. King Lamkyamba and his royal court had given Meetei surnames *"Nakakmayum", "Samurailatpam", "Aribam", "sija Kurumayum" and "Kuru Aribamayum"* to the Takhen emigrants. Takhen emigrants were many and in series during the regimes of Kanglei Kings.

The chain-episodes of Takhen emigrants may be shortened by observing some interesting facts. (1) All the Takhen emigrants are no more emigrants in the present state Manipur. They are all Meetei indigenous people; (2) There is a vast scenic region in the eastern part of Manipur inhabitated by thousands of native people of Manipur the name of which is "Takhen" (Tripura of Kangleipak;. (3) A number of Meetei clan names are coiled adjusting the very word "Takhen". Some vivid examples are Takhenmayum, Takhenchangbam and Takhenlambam. The name of a big locality near Imphal city is "Takhen Leikai".

Meetei (in larger connotation, Manipuri) settlement in Tripura was mostly the outcome of the matrimonial relations between the royal families of the two kingdoms. Another one is historical reason.

The manuscript "Sanggai Phammang" had recorded that Meeteis had settled in Tripura (Takhen) in groups. Many family groups including Meetei clan chiefs (Sagei Pibas) had settled in Takhen following Burmese invasion in Manipur causing "Chahi taret khuntakpa", a version often quoted in the historical manuscripts of Manipur meaning "Seven Years Devastation". Hundreds of Meeteis had migrated and settled in Takhen during this seven years devastation of Manipur.

On the other hand, matrimonial relations are the important causes of Meetei settlement in Tripura. Some selected examples may support the fact. During the regime of Meetei King Khagemba (1597–1652 AD), Akoijam Chanu Yangnu was married to Takhen king and she became "Takhen Leima", Takhen queen as recorded in manuscript "Cheitharol Kumpaba". Meetei attendants of Takhen Leima and retinues had permanently settled in Tripura.

Harisheshori, a daughter of King Chingthangkhomba (1759-1798 AD) was married to King Rajadhan of Tripura (1785–1804 AD). Meetei Princess Kutilakshi had been married to Tripura King Kashichandra Manikya (1826–1829 AD) and Krishna Kishore Manikya and Birchandra Manikya the following kings of Tripura had Meetei ranis. All the attendants and retinues of the Meetei ranis had settled in Tripura. Here, the reigned periods and some names of Tripura Kings are not mentioned in the Meetei manuscripts. These are added from other sources for convenience.

Inter-State Military Conflict: The manuscripts "Ningthourol Lampuba", "Cheitharol Kumpaba" and "Kangleirol" had mentioned a number of battles fought between Tripura and Manipur. Mention may be made of a few of them. In Maliya Kum 2926 (Kangleipak era used since the regime of King Maliya Phambalch coronoted in 1397 B.C.), that is, 1529 AD, Langai (an area of Langai river, a tributory of barak river) was a region of Tripura. Kangleipak King Kabomba (1524–42 AD, that is, Maliya Kum 2921–2939) had sent a military force to invade Langai region of Tripura. Langai region was attacked and occupied by the Meetei troop in 1929 AD. To take a revenge, Tripura force attacked kangleipak (Manipur) in 1533 under the command of Pancham. The Tripuri troop advanced upto Leimatak area of Kangleipak. The Meetei troop had defeated the invaders and some important persons were captured. To commemorate the victory, Takhen Khong (Tripura Canal) was dug jointly with Takhen personalities and they became bonafide citizens of Kangleipak. There were also military conflicts between the two kingdoms during the regimes of King Chalamba (1545–62), Mungyamba (1562–97), Charairongba (1698–1709), Pamheiba (1709–48) and others.

But the conflicts could not affect the closeness of Tripura and Manipur. In 1663 AD, Tripura King had offered a Tripuri girl with an elephant as a present to the king of Manipur. King Khuniaoba (1652–66 AD) in return offered a princess along with an elephant to the king of Takhen. A friendship door was; thus, opened in the political and social history of both the Kingdoms.

During the reign of Charairongba (1698–1709) also a post-conflict alliance was made between the two kingdoms. After King Chingthangkhomba (1759–98 AD) there was no more military conflicts between Tripura and Manipur. Helping hands had been extended to each other.

Religious Aspects: Since the second quarter of the eighteenth century AD, the Meeteis (Manipuris in larger connotation) had professed two religions viz., Sanamahi Religion (Sanamahism) and Hinduism. In Tripura also, the Manipuri emigrants had brought Sanamahism with them along with recently adopted Hinduism. But before the second quarter of the eighteenth century AD, they had settled in Tripura professing only Sanamahi religion. Under the Patronage of Tripuri Kings, four dieties of Sanamahi religion were formally worshipped in Takhen. A temple of goddess "Panthoibi" was constructed at Likman Khuman in Taltola and another temple of goddess "Lamden Lairembi" at Bajal Ghat. A temple of the same goddess "Lamden Lairembi" had also been constructed at Bamutia in Tripura. Two temples of the two male gods "Pakhangba" and "Puthiba" were constructed at Banamalipur and Abhoynagar in Tripura.

The Tripuri emigrants had also professed two religions Sanamahism and Hinduism as they had been native Meeteis.

Both Tripuri and Meetei Manipuris are mongololids. Their appearance, facial cuts and skull forms are the same. Therefore, assimilation and adaptation process is quick and speedy and that is why indigenous Tripuris are all bonafide Meeteis in Manipur. They are never mentioned as Tripuris in the manuscripts of Manipur which are written in Meetei script.

12

INCANTATION, SUPERSTITION AND MEDICAL TREATMENT—A CASE STUDY OF TRIPURA ON THE LIGHT OF MANUSCRIPT

NIRMAL BHADRA

This paper highlights the role of incantation and superstition in connection with the medical treatment in Tripura during the second half of the twentieth century. It also attempts to make a focus of study on the social-religious condition of the then Tripura.

In this work, my effort has been given on a manuscript, which is collected from the custody of Mr. D.C. Bhadra, living at Kamalghat under Sadar Sub-Division. Mr. Bhadra is now near about 70 years old. He got this manuscript as gift from a Fakir or Mohammedan mendicant age. It had written by water-ink with bamboo pen on ordinary paper. Linguistically the manuscript was written in simple Bengali language, which is very common among the people living under Sadar Sub-Division of Tripura and the people living under Brhmanbariya Sub-Division of today's Bangladesh. The entire manuscript is full of incantation for various diseases like differing pains, fever, infection, eruption/smallpox, air of evil sprit etc. However, not all the incantations are very clear for reading out.

It is really a difficult job to discuss the social history of Tripura because of the great scarcity of data in this regard. Besides, some accounts given by few colonial writers on North East India and some administrative reports of the British Political Agents stationed in Tripura almost no reliable informations are found. It has already been stated that, *Rajmala'* is confined to the life of the kings of the state and the different political events during their reign.

However the scarcity of historical sources during this period till the beginning of the twentieth century continues. Some elite scholars like Mr. Brajendra Chandra Dutta, Kali Prasanna Sen, Thakur Somendra Chandra Debbarman had produced some written documents during the period under discussion. Nevertheless, those documents are not sufficient for unraveling the social history of Tripura. Even Rabindranath Tagore, who visited the state seven times during this period and composed novel, drama, poem, song etc, has also centered among the Royal house. Under such circumstances, the present manuscript will be a valuable one. As because

i. The manuscript was obtained for the first time at Rasulpur of the then Tipperah district of British Bengal, which was 15 to 20 km far from Agartala.
ii. Some weekly markets like Newhabeli, Bamutia, Mohanpur, Sidhai, Laxmilunga, Debendranagar, Fatikchara, Kalachara, Mantala, Narasinggarh etc was very near to Rasulpur. Not only that, those markets were the epicenter for the people of this region as well as hill tribes of Tripura'.
iii. The language, which was used in the manuscript, is a common language practiced by the people of this region.

Infrastructure of the Medical Department of Tripura from 1890 to 1940

Table

Year	Dispensaries	Patients treated	total population
1890–91	04	5079	137442
1899–00	09	25366	173325
1910–11	15	73880	229613
1920–21	16	81816	304437
1930–31	20	107317	382450
1940–41	21	163893	513010

Source:

1. Chakraborty, M., ed., *Administration Report of Tripura State,* pp. 363, 862, 1456.
2. Govt. of Tripura, *Tribal Research and Cultural Institute,* Report on The Administration of the State of Tipperah 1890-91, Agartala, 2004, p. 36.
3. Dey, R.K., ed., *Report on The Administration Of Tripura State,* 1898–99, 1899–1900, 1943–46), *Varanasi,* 1997, p. 56 .

We can clearly observe from the above table that, by 1940-41 there was a development of medical facilities in Tripura. Whereas the number of dispensaries in Tripura was 04 in 1890–91 in 1940–41 it rose to 21. The number of patients in each decade was more and patient's service improved substantially. However, in comparison with the total population it has seen that, there were a- few people who used to go to the government hospitals for medical treatment. We have also seen from the reports of the political agents in the nineteenth century that the subjects of the state, especially the tribal people suffered a lot due to attacks of cholera, kalajar, smallpox etc. It means, in hill Tripura modern medical facilities were not available. As a result, when a person had illness like fever, leprosy etc he took the help of the Ojhas. The Ojhas treated the patient with spells.[2]

In the meantime it is also observed that, during the financial year of 1903–4, the head dispensary of Agartala was renamed after Queen Victoria in memory of the queen and was upgraded into modern medical centre[3]. Later on, a Medical school, named Edward Memorial School was opened to prepare doctors for the state with Dr. S.C. Das as Superintendent. This school was started in 1910 AD[4]. It is found in the administrative report of 1916–17 that with three Aurvedic practitioners and two Homeo-pathic physicians, facilities for Ayurvedic and Homoeopathic treatment were opened[5]. By appointing Dr. A. Sengupta Bacteriologist in 1928–29, pathology department was improved[6]. An anti Rabic treatment centre was opened in V.M. Hospital with Dr. N. Debbarma as H.O.D. in 1933–34[7]. Two leprosy clinics were opened—one at Agartala and one at Khowai under the supervision of Dr. Parbati Charm Sen, MB. In this connection Dr. P.N. Ghosh, leprosy propaganda officer of Bengal spent about a year in the state to provide special training in this connection[8]. Later on, an X-ray unit was added to V.M. Hospital on 16 March, 1937[9]. However, it was not sufficient for attracting the general people to the government hospitals for treatment.

In this context it is necessary to mention some incantations of the manuscript as follows—

1. Incantation for headache
   "Ek hanuman lankai bosea nacharea matha—Kar montrea agga hoi? Hanur mantrea agga hoi. Duhai ustad mahadever dohai"
   The incantation means that- A Honuman hold his head sitting in Lanka,— Whose incantation permit it? Hanur mantra permits it. Sake of boss God Mahadeva.
2. Incantation for air of evil sprit
   "Ek namjoshi are bataser kana—allahar kadut

dinemar gazi. Nai kichu nai are Fatemer dohai, Fatemer dohai."

The last line of the incantation means that, nothing else sake of Fatema.

3. Incantation for recovery from confined or tying position—

   "Halt bandi gait bandi maharogir jirba bandi—Aarnar gyan larbasarba trish koti debater math katba." The last line of the incantation means-

   "If my knowledge moves then heads of thirty crore Good will cut down."

4. More incantation for recovery from confined or tying state—

   No—"Purba bandi paschim bandi, uttar bandi dakhshin bandi—Aamar jadi gyan lorea iswar mahadever jata china bhumite pare,"

   The last line of the incantation means- "If my knowledge moves then Mahadeva's matted hair will fall on earth.

Besides them, there are so many incantations for various diseases like gynecological problems of the women, conjunctivitis, snakebite, fish bite etc. There are some mantras to extinguish a fire, to seize a thief, to run away of ghost etc.

If we carefully annotate the incantations then we can observe deferent socio-religious historical information from them. From the number 1 incantation, we find the name of Hanuman. It is surprising to note that worship of Hanuman was popular in the northern India. Most probably, it had an effect of the popularity of Bengali Ramayana in this region. Side by side Hindu god Mahadeva, Kali, Manasa, Ambassadors from heaven etc was very popular as expressed in these mantras. We also observe the existence of Allaha, the mighty God of the Mohammedans and Fatema mother of Hassan from the second mantra mention above. So it suggests that there was a strong co-habitation among the Hindus and Muslims in this region.

Interestingly it is observed from the incantations that the composer of the mantras or the folk Ojha swear the name of Hindu God or Allah in the end of every incantation. The person use to blame to the mighty God of Hindu or Muslims in every failure. That clearly indicates the unconsciousness, foolishness and weakness of the people with religious philosophy. Side by side, it also reveals that some cheaters dominated the field of medical treatment. In this context, we have so many memorandums from the Royal court of Tripura.

The incantations in second and third mentioned above clearly indicate the beliefs of evil sprit, like Daini system and other superstitions among the people leaving in this region. However, in hill Tripura in the nineteenth century, modern medical facilities were not available. As a result, when a person died from fever, leprosy etc. as there were no means to test them, or suffered from T.B or any other disease, the tribes believed that it happened due to the influence of the Dainis. Hence, they took the help of the Ojhas. The Ojhas treated the patient with different spells and mantras. In case they failed, they gave the excuse that the Dainis were more powerful. Therefore, the tribals were always in fear and in doubt of these Dainis. In some cases, they suspected some one in their Para. If all of them suspected the same then that man or woman was murdered. As a result, in both the cases, the tribals led a life under the terror of Daini system, which was superstition and as a result the innocent people were killed. K.P. Sen the writer of Rajmala gave an illustrated description of such an instance, where he said that in 1881, in the Sonamura division of Tripura, one person was murdered in front of his wife. Although there was severe Punishment for those who suspected people as Daini and killed them, this superstition system has been liberally practiced in Tripura.

In conclusion, it may be argued that the expansion of modern medical facilities did not benefit the people living in this region, until the first half of the twentieth century. There was a strong role of the folk incantations and Ojha or exorcist on the ground of Medical treatment. Side by side, the society had a strong faith on such exorcist. It also concludes that the people of this region were blind by several superstitions. Finally, it is noteworthy that there was a well co-habitation among the Hindus, Muslims and the tribes of Tripura so far as folk treatment and blind superstions are concerned.

13

THE HISTORICAL PERSPECTIVE OF TRIPURA SUNDARI TEMPLE

PRADEEP KUMAR DEEPAK

This article attempts to explore the historical background of Tripura Sundari Temple in the light of several literary sources, manuscript, inscription, oral records and traditional findings. Actually, the universal energy personified in the mother Goddess delivers the concept of Sakti. The beliefs and ideals of the Nomadic people like Proto-Austroloid, Mediterranean, Mongloid and Alpine mingled with those of the heterogeneous people helped to develop a new civilization.[1] Added to such waves of racial elements Aryanisation of the socio-religious practices formulated a cultural complementary to the religious set up of Tripura, Incidental evidences relating to the position of the supreme Goddess can be gleaned from the earlier literature where mere appearance of some designations of the mother can hardly be recognised as having the role of Shakti worshipped by the shaktas of the later age.[2] Sri and Bhadrakali in the Sankhyana-grihya-sutra of Rigveda,[3] Bhavani as the wife of Bhava in the Hiranyakesi Grihya Sutra,[4] Kali and karali mentioned in the Mundakopanishad,[5] Haimvati and Uma as personified Brahmavidya in kenopanished,[6] Ambika, the sister of Rudra in the Vajasaneyi-Samhita are all designations of the mother, but bearing no concrete evidence of the development of her cult. It is the Taittariya Araanyaka of the Black Yajurveda,[7] where Ambika is described not only as the spouse of Pashupati Rudra, but is identified with Devi.[8] Two more designations viz Katyayanki and Kanyakumari in the Durga Gayetri of the same text[9] furnish a point of significance in the later history of Shaktism.

If we look at Kubjika Tantra (Patala VII) manuscript No-3174 (RASB),[10] we find the reference of Tripura as a great shakta centre.

> " Sruyatam Savadhanena Siddha Pitham Pativrate
> Yasmin Sadhanamatrena Sarvasiddhisvaro bhavet
> Mayavati Madhupuri Kasi Goraksakarini
> Hingula ca Mahapitham tatha jalandharampunah
> Jvalamukhi Mahapitham Pitham Nagarasambhavam
> Ramgirirmahapitham tatha Godavaripriye
> Nepalam Karnasturanca Mahakarnam tatha priye
> Ayodhya ca kurukshetram Simhanadam manoramam
> Manipuram Hrsikesam Pragyanca tapovanam
> Badari ca Mahapitham Ambika ardhanalakam
> Triveni ca mahapitham Gangasagarasangamam
> Narikelanca viraja uddiyanam Mahesvari
> Kamala Vimala Caiva tatha Mahismati Puri
> Varahi Tripura Caiva Vagmati Nilavahini
> Govardhanam Vindhyagirih Kamrupam Kalauyuga
> Ghantakarno hayagrivo madhavasca sureswari
> Ksiragramam Vaidyanatham Janiyadyamalocane."

The wide development of Shakti Worship in Tripura caused the production of a large variety of such Devi images. The worship of the female deities is even today a common feature in Tripura. Shakti worship prevailed originally among the Indo-Mongloid[11] race of Tripura as Matai Katarma. Shaktism is the blend of Aryan and Non-Aryan streams of thought. It is a federation of the cults where the main principle is to reach the goal 'Tantric way'. Tantricism was practiced in Tripura and this tantric worship gradually developed in Iconography. Tantricism was the predominant religion of Tripura from eighth centuries AD.[12] The God and Goddess of the Shaiva form of Hinduism became the deities of the Sakta-tantra.

As a matter of fact, Tripura Sundari Temple is one of the 51 holiest Shaktipeetha (shrines of the Goddess of power) in India as per Hindu mythology. A verse of the 'Pithamala Tantra' to this effect is,

"Tripurayam daksa-padadevi Tripura-Sundari
Bhairavas Tripuresasca Sarvabhista-pradayakah."[13]

(In Tripura, the right leg of sati fell, and so, the Goddess is called 'Tripura Sundari' There The Bhairava is called Tripuresa (Lord of Tripura), who is the bestower of all things desired.)

We can get the authencity of this fact from the famous holy book of Hindus named, 'Brihaddharma Purana' in which it is mentioned,

"Yatra-yatra Satidehbhagah Petu Sudarshanah
Te te desha dhara bhaga Mahabhagah kilabhavan
Tetu Punyatma Desha Nityam Devyadhishisthitah
Siddhapithah Samakhyeto Devanamapi Durlabhah
Mahatirthani Tanyasan Muktikshetrani Bhutali."[14]

"Wherever the limbs of Sati fell, the places became religious place and were known as Siddhapith and these places were considered as the Muktikshetra for all the creatures."

One of the greatest historians Dr. Dinesh Chandra Sarkar has searched a manuscript based on 'Pitha Nirupana Tantra' and found out the word 'Tripuraneel in place of 'Tripuranal'. The meaning of the word 'Neel' is Sundari. So, Dr. Dinesh Chandra Sarkar's view is based on this fact that the 'Mahapeeth' was established in Tripura and it was established on the right leg of Sati.

The Tripura Sundari Temple inscription of Dhanya Manikya bearing the data Saka 1423 (1501 AD) is an important source of information regarding the Shakti religion in Tripura. This inscription is of two parts, first one is engraved on the east side of the temple and second on the south side of the temple. It is recorded that in ancient times there lived an accomplished king named Dhanya Manikya. It is said that his charity was comparable with that of Karna of the Mahabharata. Being pleased by his worship Indra descended to the Earth from the Heaven. In 1423 Saka (1501 AD) he constructed a Skyscraper temple in the name of the Goddess 'Ambika'.[15] After him Maharaja Kalyandeva, ruler of Tripura brought the Earth oppressed by enemies under his control. His son Govindadeva, a warrior was prominent among the kings. The dedicatory inscription gives the name of the founder of temple, 'Dhanya Manikya,' the foundation year of temple in 1423 Saka or 1501 AD and other two devotee kings Kalyan Manikya (1626 AD to 1656 AD) and his son Govinda Manikya.

Another inscription tells us that the Rama Manikya, (1673–85 AD) son of king Govinda Manikya, renovated and repaired this temple. A devoted worshipper of Ambika, the king Rama Manikya took up this project of beautification of the temple in 1603 Saka era (1681 AD). Tripura Sundari Temple is the presiding deity of this revered temple.[16]

> As per Sri Rajmala, the historical chronicle of Manikya rulers, we can say with surety that Maharaja Dhanya Manikya installed the idol of Tripura Sundari in 1501 CE. It is believed that in a revelation dream he was ordered to bring the idol of Mata Tripura Sundari from Chattagram.

"Bhagwati Rajate Swapna dekhay ratrite
Ai kaha ama sthapya raja Mahasakte
Chattagrame chateswari tahar nikat
Prastarte ami achhi hoiya prakat
Tatha hote ani ama aie matha pujo
Paiba behul bar sei mato bhajo.[17] (*Sri Rajmala,* pt. ii)

According to A.C. Bhattacharya, "Dhanya Manikya signalized the victory over the Nawab of Bengal by building in 1501 AD the famous temple of Tripura Sundari at Udaipur and immortalized himself by various works of public utility."[18]

Biman Dhar is also of the opinion that the Tripura Sundari Temple is situated in south-west direction of Udaipur at Matabari and was built by Dhanya Manikya in 1501 A.D. After 175 years of its construction, it was renovated by Ram Manikya.[19] As per his view this temple is Paschim Mukhi (opened to west side)[20]

Historian Kailash Chandra Singha also writes, "It was constructed by Dhanya Manikya and the installation of statue was historically approved." This is also accepted by Priyabrata Bhattacharya in his book 'Tripurar Debadevi O Mandir'.[21] Dr. Harekrishna Acharya also accepts this view in his book 'Tathyasutra Tripurar Itihas.'[22]

The author Sudhir Krishna Devvarma in his book 'Tantrasar' has expressed his views in 'Pithadevi Shri Shri Tripura Sundari Prasang,' "The area of Tripura Sundari is a Siddha Pitha. Its reason of being 'Sidhapitha' is also mentioned in this book and the place where animal sacrifice is offered, that place is called as Siddha Pitha."[23]

Subroto Roy in his book 'Encyclopedia of Tripura', mentions, "The Shakti image of Matabari, the Tripura Sundari Devi of Udaipur, South Tripura was the collection of a Maharaja after his Chittagong conquest.[24]

Regarding the statue of Tripura Sundari Temple, mention can be made that there are two statue in the Garbhagriha of this temple. The bigger one is the statue of

Tripura Sundari, whereas there is one little statue called 'Chota Ma' means 'Kali' or 'Chandi' statue, which is the carbon copy of big statue. Probably the 'Chota Ma' statue was accompanied by Manikya rulers during war time to worship the deity before starting of any war for victory purpose.[25] The statue of Tripura Sundari mata is made of Kashtipathar (black stone) and the height of the statue is 1 metre 57 cm and its width is 64 cn.[26] From the inscription, it is clear that in 1681 AD it was renovated by Ram Manikya Dev.[27]

Date of the temple of Tripura Sundari

According to Sri Rajmala, the temple of Tripura Sundari was erected by Dhanya Manikya in the saka year 1423.[28] Numismatic evidence determines the period of Dhanya Manikya from saka year 1412–42 AD.[29] Ramdev Manikya (1676–58 AD) repaired this edifice and put an epigraphic note on the black wall which narrates the date of erection of the temple as 1423 saka year.[30] Thus, we can say that this temple was built by Dhanya Manikya in 1501 AD.

Architecture of the temple

If we examine the architectural style of the temple of Tripura Sundari, we can gather a fair idea about the Manikya ruler's architecture from sixteenth century to eighteenth century. Generally, like other temples of Tripura, Tripura Sundari Temple is built with thin bricks, sand, mortar or lime. This temple stands on tortoise-shell shaped high hillock, it is also known as 'Kurma-Pith'. Ratna Das is of the opinion, "Only two cult-icons with black slab, have so far come to our notice. Both of them are worshipped now. The image of Tripura Sundari (5 feet 2 inch high) carved on coarse-grained sandstone is installed in the Tripura Sundari Temple, Udaipur dated—1501 AD.[31] The edifice was dedicated to Goddess Ambika. Later, it underwent repairs many times. This is a living temple and the Tripura Sundari is the presiding deity. The temple has apparently lost its original character due to periodical maintenance. The floor of the sanctum and the cirucumbulatory passage are now paved with mosaic tiles. Several coats of plastering have hindered to find out architectural modes and features such as the technique of vaulting and the method of construction of doorways. The walls take semicircular shape with four moulded lines towards the top which merge with the hut-shaped roof; above the roof rises the stupa-crowning with a row of small niches of the shape of lotus petals at its base.[32]

Generally, the walls of the temples are very thick. For that reason the space of Garbhagriha is quite small. The outer measurement of the Tripura Sundari Temple is 24 feet and the walls are of 8 feet thick, so only 156 sq.feet is used as sanctum.[33] All other temples have only one door, but Tripura Sundari has two gates, the main gate facing the deities in the west and another on the north side. The height of Tripura Sundari Temple is about 75 feet. The crown of the temple is visible from quite a distance from the plain land around it. It is considered to be one of the oldest Pitha-Sthan. Tripura Sundari temple at Udaipur "consists of a square type sanctum of the typical Bengali-hut type above which rises a conical dome with a continuous series of low niches at the base simulating lotus leaves. On this rises the amalaka, which has been made elongated in order to confirm to the shape of a cone."[34]

Conclusion

Thus, on the basis of above facts we can say with surely that Tripura Sundari Temple occupies a very pivotal place in Tripura. The reference of Tripura as a great Sakta centre is found in the Kubjika Tantra (Patala VII) manuscript. We also get the historical authencity of this fact from the holy book 'Brihaddharma Purana' and the 'Tripura Sundari Temple Inscription' of Dhanya Manikya. Sri Rajmala, the historical Chronicle of Manikya rulers also narrates that king Dhanya Manikya installed the idol of Tripura Sundari in 1501 C.E. Many renowned historians and legends also confirm the authenticity of this temple. This is why, Tripura Sundari Temple is considered as one of the main sacred pilgrimage centre of Indian Sub-continent.

References

* Inspection note of Directore-General of Archaeology Govt. of Tripura, 1952, p -3. Quoted in Tripura District Gazetteers, p- 397

1. Chatterjee, Rama, 'Religion in Bengal', Calcutta, 1985, page – 173
2. Palit, Projit kumar, 'History of Religion in Tripura', Kaveri books, New Delhi, 2004, pp. 109–10.
3. *Rigveda,* II, 14, 15.
4. Ibid., II, 7, 8.
5. Mundakopanished, 1, 2, 4.
6. Kenopnishad, III, 55
7. Mitra, R.L, 'Taittriya-Aranyaka, Calcutta, Asiatic society of Bengal 1872, Namo hiranyavahave hiranyavarnaya hiranyarupaya hiranyapatiye, mbikapataye umapataye Pashupataye namo namah.
8. Ibid., X, 1.
9. Ibid., X, 1–7.
10. The same is quoted in the Pranatosani Tantra Vasumati, p. 234 and Palit Projit kumar, 'History of Religion in Tripura,' Kaveri books, 2004, pp. 111–12.
11. Sarkar, J.N., 'India Through the Ages; Calcutta, 1951, p. 35.
12. Palit, Proji Kumar, 'History of Religion in Tripura, Kaveri books, New Delhi, 2004, p, 112.
13. Dr Narendra Chandra Nath, 'Sri Rajmala' (Eng. Version), Tribal Research Institute, Agartala, 1999, p. 16.
14. Priyabrata Bhattacharya, 'Tripura Debadebi O' Mandir, Agartala, 1989, p. 2.
15. Brahmavaivartta Purana, Vang edn, L VII, 17.
    ' Sarvan mokshan prapayati janmamrityujaradikam
    Characharamischa Vishvathen sharvanitoana kirttita.'
16. Palit, Projit kumar, 'History of Religion in Tripura', Kaveri books New Delhi, 2004, p. 113.
17. Sri Rajmala, part II, Dhanya Manikya yantra, p. 30.
18. Bhattacharya A.C. 'Progressive Tripura, Inter-India publication New Delhi, 1985, p. 21.

19. Biman Dhar, 'Rangamatir Itikatha Udaipur,' Bina Prakashan, 2011, p. 134.
20. Ibid., p. 135.
21. Priyabrata Bhattacharya, 'Tripurar Debadebi O' Mandir' Agartala, 1989, p. 6.
22. Dr Harekrishna Acharya, 'Tathyasutre Tripurar Itihas, Agartala, 2011, p. 41.
23. Ibid., p. 3.
24. Subroto Roy, 'Encyclopedia of Tripura', Agartala, p. 180.
25. Priyabrata Bhattacharya, 'Tripurar Debadebi O' Mandir, Agartala, 1989, pp. 1–10.
26. Ibid., p. 6.
27. Ibid., p. 7.
28. Sep,, K.P., 'Sri Rajmala', vol. II, p. 97.
29. Majumder R.C., 'Bangladesher Itihas, op. cit., pp. 488–90.
30. Vidya Benode Chandrodaya, op. cit., p. 6.
31. Ibid., p. 6.
32. Ratna Das, 'Art and Architecture of Tripura, Agartala, 1997, p. 68.
33. Dr. D.N. Goswami, 'Temple of Tripura', Agartala, 2003, pp. 17–18.
34. S.N. Guha Thakurta, 'Tripura', National Book Trust, New Delhi, p. 131.

14

WEDGED BETWEEN TUI-VAI AND KHOLONGMA—RECONSTRUCTING TIPPERA MIGRATION TO TRIPURA

RUPAK DEBNATH

The importance of manuscripts, especially chronicles in the reconstruction of early history cannot be denied; however, manuscripts also tend to reflect opinionated versions of actual facts. Where parallel accounts lack, the process of event reconstruction becomes particularly problematic. In case of Tripura. the recorded history prior to the fifteenth–sixteenth centuries contains vast super-impositions, which steadily dwindle backwards into domains of brazen fabrication. Oral traditions too are scanty, and a few stories that still exist are either neglected or remain unexplored. What the *Rajmala* reflects for those centuries is de-historicising the actual past in face of an eastward expanding Aryandom. However, there are times when the unwritten converges on the written. The present paper focuses on one important event of the southward migration of Tipperas in the fourteenth-fifteenth century AD, as it reflects within a comparative frame, in the state chronicle as also in one neglected oral tradition of a subjected tribe, and attempts to discover that event, may reconstruct a significant episode in the early history of a Tibeto-Burman tribe that eventually saw the establishment of a Tippera kingdom in Tripura.

The Argument

Usually written materials warrant better documentation of human cultures than unwritten sources. Yet, if written records contain opinionated versions of events, especially in the absence of parallel accounts with counter-representations, the problems of reconstructing the actual past can become really arduous. This is precisely the situation one faces in cementing a coherent history of the Bodo-Garo tribes in general and the Tipperas in particular. These tribes lived in long oblivion previous to their notice in the *Ahom Burzmji*. Scriptural accounts from mainland India flocked diverse races (Mongloids, Austrics, and the Malay tribes) of the eastern country into the *kirata* fold in violation of their ethno-linguistic diversities and racial-cultural differences. At a later time, in the fifteenth-sixteenth century AD, Hinduised tribal-rajas sought to legitimatise their temporal status within an expanded Aryandom by commissioning Bengali scribes to compose state chronicles, which did document contemporary events but, on the other hand, also de-historicised the oral past with superimposed Hindu myths and exotic-ancestries.

This paper analyses, within a comparative frame, the southward migration of the Tipperas as recorded in the *Rajmala* and in one oral tradition and shows how vital it is sometimes to sleve out fabrications that have penetrated deep into the commissioned documents of culturally assimilated peoples of the Northeast.

Centralised polity among Tipperas

The Tippera's name for himself is *Borok* or *Borok-sa*, and the language he uses is Kokborok. He is called *Takhen* by the Meithei, *Vai* by a section of the Halams and *Mroung* by the Rakhines. Linguistically, Tipperas along with Boro, Rabha, Garo, Tiwa, Dimasa, Koch. Deori and Moran belong to the Bodo-Garo group of the greater Bodo-Konyak-Kachin sub-branch of the Tibeto-Burman subfamily of Sino-Tibetan. The time around which the Bodo-Garo tribes separated from their Kachin relatives of upper Myanmar and came to settle in the Brahmaputra valley is an issue that deserves separate space and treatment; for the present, it would suffice to say that for several centuries before the advent of the Ahoms in 1228 AD, these tribes occupied the extensive tract along the Brahmaputra River. In fact, an old name of the Brahmaputra, 'Ti-lao,' which occurs in the *Ahom Buranji,* is of Bodo-Garo

A majority of the Tipperas are Hindus, having adopted the religion around the 15th century AD. Asked about his descent, the average native refers the matter to the *Rajmala,* which recounts a legendary descent of the Manikya royalty from the Kuru dynasty of pre-Mahabharata times. This genealogy was constructed in the fifteenth century by two scribes from Bengal, Sukresvvar and Banesawar, under the royal patronage of Maharaja Dharma Manikya. In later centuries, it was revised a couple of times. With the Tippera's closest ethnic relative, the Dimasa, we have an analogous case of the ancestry of temporal rajas pushed back to fabricated antiquity. A family-tree prepared as late as in the mid-18th century linked the Dimasa rajas of Maibong and Dimapur to Ghototkotch, a giant born of the demon Hidimba and Bhirna, one of the five Pandavas. Historically, the Tipperas split from the Dimasas more than hundred years before the *Rajmala* was first composed. Their southward migration led to the emergence of a centralised state, sandwiched between Bengal in the west and the Kuki country in the east. If the popular 15th century tradition of a Tippera king, Dangur-pha (alias Ratna-Manikya), subduing his seventeen brothers, each a 'king' of his own small 'kingdom,' to become the undisputed ruler of the hill state is viewed in proper light, one discovers the shift from older ways of tribal chieftainship to a centralised polity under a territorial authority. A Meithei account, the *Cheitharon Kumpapa* (or the Court Chronicle of the Kings of Manipur) contains the earliest reference to Tripura against the year 1467 AD.

Migration Tipperas to Tripura

Withdrawal of the Bodo-C;aro tribes (especially the section known in late 19th and early twentieth century ethnographic literature as 'Kachharr) from the Brahmaputra valley occurred in the wake of Sukhapa's invasion of Assam (referred to as 'Mungdun-chunr̃kham' in the *Burunji)* in 1228. The ethnic name Dimasa' means 'children ("sa") of the big ("-ma") river ("di").' The 'big river' is probably Ti-lao whose valley the Dimasa occupied before they retreated to the Dhansiri valley. Gait (1963: 300–301) accounts for Dimasa withdrawal in the following terms: 'In the thirteenth century, it would seem that the Kachari kingdom extended along the south bank of the Brahmaputra, from the Dikhu to the Kallang, or beyond and included also the valley of the Dhansiri and the tract which now forms the North Cachar sub-division. . . . Towards the end of this century, it is narrated that the outlying Kachari settlements east of Dikhu river withdrew before the advance of the Ahoms.' The *Ahom Buranji* (Barua 1985: 52) records the first war between the Ahoms and the Dimasas (spelt 'Ti-,o-cha' in the *Buranji*) in lakni Kapshan, corresponding to the year 1490 AD.

In the 'Dakshin' and the Kholongma' episodes of the *Rajmala,* it is narrated that after a war with the Kachari raja (name is not mentioned), the Tippera prince, Dakshin withdrew to the upper region of the Barabakra (Barak) river, settling at Kholongma among the Ľangrong' (a corruption of the ethnonym 'Ranglong') and other Kuki tribes that eventually accepted him as their king. In the early part of the narrative, the boundary of the Tippera kingdom is thus demarcated: Tuiruong in the north, Roshang (Arakan) in the south, Koch-banga (Koch-Bihar?) in the west and Mekhli (Manipur) in the east. Incidentally, Tui-rong is the local name of the Barak river, which forms a confluence with the Tui-vai at Tipaimukh, a place identified by the Ranglongs as early settlement.

A parallel version of the migration occurs in an oral tradition prevalent among Ranglongs who came under Tippera domination during the latter's southward migration, The Ranglongs are a section of the Hallam group of tribes; linguistically Old-Kukis, the Hallam tribes usually refer to themselves as *Mi-hriam* or *Hriain-mi.* In the Ranglong oral- tradition, it is stated that in former times, when the *Hriams* lived in the region of the Tuiŕvai, they had one *Hriam-reng* (literally, 'king of the Hriams') who became enamoured of the physical beauty of his own daughter. Soon people came to know of it, and, in humiliation, the king jumped into the river. As he fell, he was miraculously transformed to a rock. From that day, the place acquired the name Tamlung (literally 'the Jumping Rock'); it lies south of Senbaum, close to the Manipur border. His crown fell into the Tuivai. As it was being carried downstream, a Tippera chief *(Vai-reng-te,* 'the small king of the Val') picked it up and placed it on his head. The Hriams, then having no king of their own, made the Vai (Tippera) their ruler and followed him to *Reng-pui-ram* ('land of the great king'), the Halam name of Tripura.

Cause of migration

Intense ethnic rivalry for territorial domination seems to be a major cause of the Dimasa-Tippera split. The Dimasa version is given below:

> Trilochan, the king of Hidimba, had several sons. Two of them, Drikadhvaja and Dakshin, were ambitious and aspired equally to succeed their father to the throne.

Trilochan was aware of the intense rivalry between the two brothers. One day, he summoned them and said that he had a dream in which the goddess Chandi told him that she would disguise herself as a serpent and lie near the river bank. The one who dared to catch the serpent would be considered the rightful heir to the Hidirnba throne. On the following morning. Drikadhvaja woke up very early and hastened to the river bank where he found the serpent; no sooner did he hold it by the tail than it transformed into a glittering sword. When Dakshin arrived at the spot, he saw the sword and knew what had come to pass. Promptly, he tried to snatch away the sword from his elder brother; in the tussle that followed, the sword broke and Dakshin was left holding the hilt. Disappointed by the failure, he assembled a train of followers, which included his younger brothers, and, migrated southwards along the course of Kholongma to reach the Kuki country, where he established a new kingdom.

In the *Rajmala,* it is narrated Dakshin ascended the Hidimba throne after his father's death but could not retain possession of it for long. His elder brother, who was already king of Hidimba, wished to be king of the Tipperas too. On hearing that his younger brother has succeeded to the Tippera, he was overpowered with rage, and collecting a huge army, marched against Dakshin. An intense battle broke out between the armies of the two brothers and it continued for seven days. At last, Dakshin was defeated and forced to retire southwards. Ten younger brothers accompanied him in the journey that ended in establishing a new kingdom at Kholongma.

Time of migration

As far as the dating of Tippera migration toward Tripura

is concerned, neither the *Rajmala* nor the oral repertoire of the Dimasas is of much help. Even at this stage, the native rajas continue to bear Aryan names. At the same time, internecine tribal feuds are magnified by scribes into formally pitched battles. However, a fairly accurate stock of the situation can be made from oral references to Old Kuki settlements in Tipaimukh region. A major dispersion of the Kuki-Chin tribes occurred in the 13th-14th century AD, when the Shans made inroads into the Chindwin valley (Debnath 2010: 44-45). By the time, the city of Kalemyo was built (in 1395) to mark Shan domination in Chindwin, the Hriams had left the Chin Hills and entered Northeast India through the Champhai route, settling in the northern parts of Mizoram along the Cachar border, even penetrating into southern parts of present Manipur (called *Moitai-ram'* in Ranglong). The first place they settled was *Ruong-le-vai-suo* (Tipaimukh), from where they attempted to push northwards through Manipur Hills but were prevented by the 'Rongmai' Nagas, whence, they retreated to the Tuivai region, where they came under Tippera domination. This occurred at the close of 14th or in the early fifteenth century. Around that time, the Dimasas inhabited the region east of the Dikhu, chiefly in areas around present-day Dimapur.

Acknowledgements for oral sources

For oral traditions sourced in this paper, I remain indebted to three individuals in particular, Rev. Tara, alias Tamborlian Halam of Bagbasa, North Tripura, and Gopal Thaosen and Keneng Daulaguphu of Diphu, Karbi Anglong, Assam. Acknowledge is also due to Nirphunjoy Halam of Zoitang, North Tripura and to my friend, Robert Lumphuid of Jagirod, Assam.

References

Barman, Nalindra Kumar, *The Queens of Cachar or Herambo and the History of the Kachchari,* Silchar: Lakshmi Prasad Barman, 2007.

Barua, Golan Chandra, *Ahom Buranji: From the Earliest Time to the End of the Ahom Rule,* Guahati: Spectrum Publications, 1985, reprint.

Chatterji, Suniti Kumar, *Kirata-Jana-Krti,* Calcutta: Asiatic Society, 1974, second edn.).

Debnath, Rupak, *Exploring Highlanders of Tripura and Chittagong Hill Tracts,* New Delhi: Akansha Publishers, 2010.

Endle, Sidney, *The Kacharis,* London: Macmillan and Co., Limited, 1911.

Gait, Edward, *A History of Assam,* Calcutta: Thacker Spink & Co. 1933, P. Ltd, 1963, Revised third edn.

Guha, Upendrachandra, *Kacharer Itibritta,* Guahati: Asom Prakashan Parishad, 1971.

Parratt, Saroj Nalini Arambam, *The Court Chronicle of the Kings of Manipur: the Cheitharon Kumpapa,* London & New York: Routledge, 2006.

Sen, Kaliprasanna, Sri Rajmala, Agartala: Tribal Cultural Research Institute, 2003, Reprint, Sinha, Kailas Chandra, *Rajmala or Annals and Chronicles of Tripura,* Comilla, 1896.

Rupak, Debnath is presently assistant Director in the Directorate of Distance Education, Tripura University.

15

HISTORY OF TRIPURA: ITS ROLE IN LITERARY LIFE OF RABINDRANATH TAGORE

Sanjukta Mandal

The State of Tripura has a long history. The Kingdom of Tripura in its peak included the whole eastern region of Bengal from the Brahmaputra river in the north and west, the Bay of Bengal in the south and Burma to the east during the fourteenth and fifteenth centuries AD. This (Sanskrit: *Tripura,* Anglicized: *Tippera)* was one of the largest ancient kingdom of the Tipra people of the Bodo-Kachari ethnicity in the Northeastern region of the Indian Subcontinent having a chronicle of 186 Kings till the present times (Maharaja Pradyot Kishore Manikya, better known as Kirit Pradyot Deb Burman).

The history of Tripura was very long, impressive, interesting and thought provoking; most of the kings were very powerful, strategic and skillful in battle and very cultural minded, progressive and above all the great patronizers of art and literature and many of them greatly loved Bengali culture. They engaged Bengali intellectuals at the *Royal Court.*

It was told nobody returned empty handed from the *Royal Court of Tripura.* Rabindranath Tagore, the great poet of Bengali literature and many of Bengali intellectuals knew this truth and took advantage of it and thus earned name and fame not only in India also recognition world wide. But it was so elaborated and large and time consuming; that's why I will try to confine my topics in those parts of literary history which was related to Rabindranath Tagore.

I would like to quote some comments by Rabindranath Tagore in

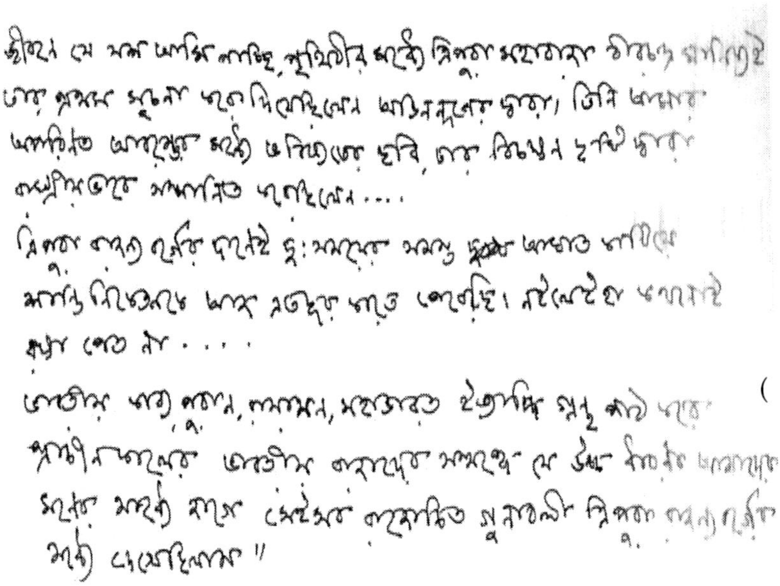

(The name and fame which have been bestowed on me from the nation, world, the honourable king of Tripura, Birchandra Manikya at first started it by greeting me. It is he who with his far-sightedness, discovered in my present immature writing, the future picture of a poet.

It is only for financial help from Kings of Tripura I have overcome all crises and placed Santiniketan at its present form; otherwise it was quite impossible.

The kingly qualities I am familiar with after reading Hindu epics, Mythology, the Ramayana, Mahabharat, etc. I have seen them in all kings of Tripura.)

Our great poet Rabindranath Tagore lived 80 years; out of this more than 60 years were involved with people of Tripura and *Tripura Royal Court (Raj darbur)*. At that time he was so entangled with soil, people and nature of Tripura that their music of flute, arts, dance delighted him, the flowers and its scent maddened him, its structure of buildings impressed him and above all botanical gardens of Tripura overwhelmed him so much that he spurred to bring different kinds of plants from there to Visva-Bharati university campus at Shantiniketan, Bolpore in West Bengal, India. Not only that he brought from Tripura different kinds of Bamboo, espetially Muli Bamboo, plant of trees and hemp (a kind of plant) and at present those trees become very big and spread shade on the campus and thus delight viewers with their beauty. (Source: Tripura of Rabindranath by Haroon Habib)

The relationship between the kings of Tripura and Rabindranath Tagore was reciprocal. The kingdom of Tripura and its people felt honoured for being in touch with the great poet, Rabindranath Tagore and at the same time the poet also felt venerable with their everlasting love, respect and indebted to them for donations, grants which he expended for the development of Bishwabharati. Rabindranath Tagore also introduced many prominent contemporary Bengali intellectuals to Tripura Royal Court and received unending financial help from Kings of Tripura and thus made places not only in India also in the world, some of them are:

- Scientist Jagadish Chandra Bose;
- Dr. Dinesh Chandra Sen;
- Pundit Ramnaran Bidayratna;
- Famous poet Hem Chandra Banerjee;
- Painter Shashi Kumar;
- Ashutosh Choudhury;
- King of nature, Jagadindra Nath;

- Rajendra Nath Mitra;
- Taraka Nath Palith;
- Rasbihari Ghosh;
- Darakanath Chakrabarti;
- Great Artist Allaudin Khan;
- Ranganath Jadubhatta.

Beside these, along with Rabindranath Tagore, many other persons of Tagore family also received presents, financial helps from the Royal Court of Tripura whenever they were in need.

Rabindranath Tagore was well known to four prominent kings of Tripura and had had their blessings, they are:

- Great King Bir Chandra Manikya (1862–96)
- Radha Kishore Manikya (1896–9)
- Birendra Kishore Manikya (1909–23)
- Bir Bikrom Kishore Manikya.(1923–47)

These four kings deeply admired him and helped him financially.

By age Great King Bir Chandra Manikya was like RabindranathTagore's grand father, Radha Kishore Manikya was like his father, Birendra Kishore Manikya was like his brother and Bir Bikrom Kishore Manikya was like his son. This relationship was one of great episodes of history of Tripura, it proves how magnanimous, philanthropic, patronizer of literature and cultural minded were the kings of Tripura, they were sponsors of education also, it is only for active participation, cooperation of these kings Rabindranath Tagore's hurdles to bring his many dreams into reality might have been overcome. All the time royal court of Tripura encouraged art, literature, culture of Bengal.

Rabindranath Tagore received noble prize on 13 November, 1913 and after 18 years of this great event Bir Bikrom Kishore Manikya inaugurated Rabindra fair and art exhibition at

Kolkata town hall in 25 December, 1931. In his speeches addressed there, he admitted how his great grand father Great King Bir Chandra Manikya was impressed by the amazing beauty of the rising sun, Rabindranath Tagore, since then they also maintained this relationship unabated. The King also recalled how Rabindranath Tagore also greatly influenced people belonging to Royal Court of Tripura. For the first time at one occasion the king addressed him as *poet of Tripura,* before that he was only the poet of Bengal, India and world. We come to learn from his speech that world of Rabindranath Tagore was not only limited to literature only; he hoped and expected that humanity of the world would be enriched and ventured great efforts to implement it. His essay on *'Deshia Rajja'* was first read in the literature convocation in Tripura.

In 7th January, 1939, Rabindranat Tagore on behalf of Visva Bharati, paid a respect of tribute to Bir Bikrom Kishore Manikya with great enthusiasm; the poet was then 77 years old. That day from his speech we learn how deep rooted was the relationship between the poet and Royal Court of Tripura. He recalled then Bir Bikram Kishore Manikya was not born when his great grand father the Great King Bir Chandra Manikya sent Sri Radha Raman Ghosh, one of his ministers to the Tagore family at Jorashako in Kolkata to inform the poet that he wanted to confer on him the title of the best poet (*sresta kobi*) as he envisioned a great literary future in him by reading his collection of poems *Bhagna Rhiday*. Till then he only received criticism from his contemporary Bengalese which was known to Great King Bir Chandra Manikya. For the first time the poet was honoured from the people of his nation, though it was outside the Bengal. At one occasion he acknowledged, 'the recognition which I have been paid from the nation, the world, it started from Great King Bir Chandra Manikya, the king of Tripura. He also took Rabindranath Tagore along with him when he went to Karsiang for a change of weather for the sake of his health, though he was older than the poet but openly discussed different sides of literature with him. He had deep knowledge of songs and loved to listen to songs of the poets. He shared with the poet his plan for the development of the Bengali literature, asked his advice and wanted to have the poet as co-partner to execute this plan, he also wanted to establish an individual printing press with one lakh taka from where only the poet's publications would be printed. But soon after he died, the poet then apprehended his relationship with the royal family of Tripura might be jeopardized. But as this relationship was perennial, his son Radha Kishore Manikya made him free of his apprehension and embraced him with fatherly affection, though at that time the king himself was immersed in great financial crisis . But he ignored his personal crisis and patronized the works of the poets with hospitality and grants. Tagore established a school (1901) at Santiniketan, in Bengal, to teach a blend of Eastern and Western philosophies with financial help from Tripura. Dizendra Chandra Dutta in his book, Rabindranath and Tripura' quoted that Radha Kishore Manikya, the king of Tripura gave at a time 5000 taka for establishment of a school at Santiniketan and sanctioned yearly 1000 taka for its development. He also sent many scientific apparatus and furniture to Santiniketan from Tripura. His contributions in education and culture was tremendous, he financially helped to found Victoria College in Comilla, Bangladesh and Jadavpur University in Kolkata. At his time the king invited the poet at a grand cultural program in Aagartala, the people of Tripura received him with so enthusiasm he was overwhelmed with joy and wrote a collection of poems '*Kahini*' and dedicated this book in the name of Radha Kishore Manikya . In another occasion the king was invited to Kolkata, there at Park Street in the house of Sateyndra nath, where his drama *Bisarjan* was acted, Ranindranath Tagore himself played the role of Raghupati. After his death his son Birendra Kishore Manikya sanctioned 10,000 taka for establishment of a hospital at Santiniketan. Rabindranath Tagore published a collection of essays, *'Bichitra Prabandha'*. At that time Vishva-Bharti was in a great financial crisis and to overcome it, he wrote to Jatindra Nath Bose, then the Bengali minister in Tripura to request the king of Tripura to buy some volumes of these collections. At his request the king bought not only some of volumes, but started random distribution of collection bought by him and as a result after fifty years there are more than fifty copies in the library of Tripura Kingdom. Thus the Vishva-Bharti was offered direct or indirect help from the kings of Tripura all the time.

The richest, the best asset of all humanity lies in its culture, in the supremacy of minds of its people. Most of the kings of Tripura knew it and always tried to enrich their culture, their intellect by blending them with other culture. And this cultural blending made bondage between them and Rabindranath Tagore. Bir Bikram Kishore Manikya ascended the throne in 1923. He was the last independent king of Tripura. The poet had been offered helps in cash and kinds from the king. The Second World War began in 1939. Bir Bikrom Kishore Manikya sheltered many devastated Bengalee in his kingdom with great care and generosity. At that year the poet invited the king along with his ministerial *(Raj parishad)* for the anniversary of Santiniketan. Tripura joined the war and helped the Allied Force. WhenTagore approached him with the ambition of establishing a department for songs (Sangit Bhaban), the king without hesitation agreed to finance it and donated an additional 20,000 taka and for constructing a great Theater Hall P.P. Chakrabarti referred it in *Rajmala.*

In 25 Baishakh of 1348, Bengali year Bir Bikrom Kishore Manikya arranged Rabindra Jayanti at the Darbur Hall of 'Ujjanta Rajprasad'and at that grand occasion conferred on him the title of *Bhārat Bhāsvar.* The poet through his literature; novels, drama, poems prayed for the best wishes of Tripura.

Rabindranath was very impressed by the Manipuri dance. He visited Tripura probably eight times. Once in 12 Falgun, 1332 Bangla year Tripura arranged a grand cultural program in his honour. Brajendra Kishore Debsharma, the then Prime Minister of Tripura supervised the overall program himself. The Manipuri artists performed *Rash Dance* before Rabindranath Tagore, the poet was overwhelmed and wanted to introduce it in Vishva-Bharti and asked the Prime Minister to send an expert in this regard. He conveyed the message to the king, Bir Bikrom Kishore Manikya and he sent Mr. Buddimotta Singh, a dance expert of Agartala to Vishva-Bharti. But he was send for a temporary period and the poet wanted to have someone permanently. When the king learnt it he sent the wife of Mr. Buddimotta Singh who started teaching Manipuri dance to the girl students of Vishva-Bharti. Since then it has been taught there. In Bangladesh, it is very popular and our artists also practice it with great care and earn and great accolade.

The Kings of Tripura made him the poet of Tripura. The poet realized how he was indebted to Royal Court of Tripura and he expressed his endebtness to them on many occasions. He wrote the famous novel *Rajarshi* on Gobinda Manikya after collecting sufficient information from Bir Bikrom Kishore Manikya. He sent Tagore the history of Gobinda Manikya. Being impressed by his generosity Tagore spurred to write a novel, *Rajarshi*. His drama *Bisarjan* was also based on some parts of the novel of *Rajarshi*, related to Gobinda Manikya. Gobinda Manikya (1660–76), the son of Kalyan Manikya (1626–60) ascended the throne in 1660. He was religious, righteous and affectionate; that's why Rabindranath Tagore, addressed him as *Rajarshi* in his novel. He left the throne in 1661 for his brother Nakhatra Roy, who conspired with the *Raj purohit*, to have the *Rajmikut*.

He was the most righteous and tolerant king. When he realized Nakhatra Roy, connived with Raghupati to dethrone him, he got alarmed and to avoid bloodshed left the kingdom willingly and lived a life of hermit in the jungle. This concept inspired Rabindranath Tagore to write the novel *Rajarshi* and in another drama *Bisarjan* he engraved the character of Gobinda Manikya. In this drama he narrated how the king got emotional when he witnessed the scene where the armed guard started to take his brother Nakhatra Roy from the court. He got down from the throne and uttered:

Again we see how righteous he was in his judgment when he told:

Thus we see the Royal Court of Tripura played a very vital role in the literary life of Rabindranath Tagore.

REFERNECES

1. Tripura Jatir Itihas o Songskriti (History and Culture of the Tripura)' Provangshu Tripura.
2. Tripura Jati, Shova Tripura
3. Rabindranather Triparoon Habib

16

MANUSCRIPTS AS HISTORICAL SOURCES: TRACES OF TRIPURA IN TAGORE'S WRITINGS

SOMA BASU

This particular seminar which has history of Tripura as its objective but at the onset I want to discuss the multifaceted importance of studing the manuscripts. I will then try to cast a brief glance on the princely state that is Tripura with relation to Tagore's writings, i.e., how Tripura has come in his writing or how it has cast its spell on Tagore's mind so much so that he was inspired to take up his pen.

The first part, therefore, is about manuscripts, from genesis to modern age—

> A manuscript is the handwritten information that has been manually created by someone or some people, such as a hand-written letter, as opposed to being printed or reproduced some other way. The term may also be used for information that is hand-recorded in other ways than writing, for example inscriptions that are chiselled upon a hard material or scratched (the original meaning of graffiti) with a knife point in plaster or with a stylus on a waxed tablet (the way Romans used to make notes), or are in cuneiform writing, impressed with a pointed stylus in a flat tablet of unbaked clay. The word 'manuscript'

derives from the Medieval Latin *manuscriptum*, a word first recorded in 1594 as a Latinization of earlier Germanic words used in the Middle Ages: compare Middle High German hantschrift (*c.* 1450), Old Norse handrit (*c.*1300), Old English handgewrit (*c.* 1150), all meaning 'manuscript', literally, 'handwritten'. Handscriften kunde means 'Manu-scriptology' which has been recently replaced with 'Codicology'

Manuscripts inform us about social conditions, relations and expectations—

Information preserved in manuscript form is the primary source databank of written material from the earliest period. Manuscripts provide not only the most authentic witnesses to life, but also a record of what aspects of life were considered to be of sufficient importance to immortalize in the medium. Every manuscript written in the medieval era is an authentic artifact of that era. However, every manuscript was not penned by its author, and every author was not a living witness to the events he or she penned. Scribes existed in every era, chronicling events of many generations of past. After all, they were writing for their times, not for curious readers of hundreds of years in the future. Written records can be used to make inferences of historical questions which could not have been in the minds of the scribes who penned the words. The granting of privileges or the dispensing of justice reveals much about social conditions, relations and expectations.

Manuscripts are invaluable sources of cultural history—

Manuscripts are primary sources of heritage knowledge. Various fields of human achievements were brought forth on variety of medias viz. clay tablets, stones, metals, tree barks, palm leaves, animal skins, cloths, papers, etc. Manuscripts are available throughout India in several languages and scripts, which cover art, philosophical, historical, literary and scientific subjects.

Manuscripts may be in book form, scrolls or in codex format. Illuminated manuscripts are enriched with pictures, border decorations, elaborately engrossed initial letters or full-page illustrations.

The traditional abbreviations are ms for manuscript and mss for manuscripts. The second 's' is not simply the plural; by an old convention, it doubles the last letter of the abbreviation to express the plural, just as pp. means 'pages'.

Before the invention of printing in China all written documents had to be both produced and reproduced by hand. Historically, manuscripts were produced in form of scrolls (*volumen* in Latin) or books (codex or codices in plural). Manuscripts were produced on vellum and other parchments, on papyrus, and on paper. In Russia birch bark documents as old as from the 11th century have survived. In India the Palm leaf manuscript, with a distinctive long rectangular shape, was used from ancient times until the nineteenth century.

When Greek or Latin works were published, numerous professional copies were made simultaneously by scribes in a scriptorium, each making a single copy from an original.

The oldest written manuscripts have been preserved either placed in Egyptian tombs, or reused as mummy-wrappings or stored in dry caves (Dead Sea scrolls i.e., the Hebrew manuscripts). Manuscripts in Tocharian languages, written on palm leaves, survived in desert burials in the Basins of Central Asia. Volcanic ash preserved some of the Roman library of the Villa of the Papyri in Herculaneum.

The oldest known dated Arabic manuscript on paper in Turkey libraries dates back to 931 AD but ironically, the manuscripts that were being most carefully preserved in the libraries of Antiquity are virtually all lost. Papyrus has a life of at the most a century or two in relatively moist Italian or Greek conditions; only some of those works copied onto parchment have survived.

Originally, all texts were in manuscript form. In China, and later in other parts of East Asia, Woodblock printing was used for books seventh century onward. The earliest dated example is the Diamond Sutra of 868. In the Islamic world and the West, all books were in manuscript form until the introduction of movable type printing in about 1450. Copying of manuscript continued for at least a century, as printing remained expensive. Private or government documents remained hand-written until the invention of the typewriter in the late nineteenth century. Because of the likelihood of errors each time a manuscript was copied and different versions of the same text became a fundamental part of the study.

In case of Asia—

In Southeast Asia, in the first millennium, documents of sufficiently great importance were inscribed on soft metallic sheets such as copperplate, softened by refiner's fire and inscribed with a metal stylus. In the Philippines, specimen documents were not inscribed by stylus, but were punched much like the style of today's dot-matrix printers. This type of document is rare compared to the usual leaves and bamboo staves that were inscribed. However, neither the leaves nor the paper were as durable as the metal document in the hot, humid climate. In Burma, Buddhist manuscripts were inscribed on brass, copper or ivory sheets, and even on discarded monk robes folded and lacquered. In Italy some important texts were similarly inscribed on thin gold plates: similar sheets have been discovered in Bulgaria. Technically, these are all inscriptions rather than manuscripts.

The case in Europe—

The study of the writing of in surviving manuscripts is termed paleography. In the Western world, from the classical period through the early centuries of the Christian era, manuscripts were written without spaces between the words (*scriptio continua*), which makes them especially hard for the untrained to read. Extant copies of these early manuscripts written in Greek or Latin and usually dating from the fourth century to the eighth century, are classified according to their use of either all upper case or all lower case letters. Hebrew manuscripts, such as the Dead Sea scrolls make no such difference. Manuscripts using all upper case letters are called majuscule; those using all lower case are called minuscule. Usually, the majuscule scripts are written with much more care. The scribe lifted his pen between each stroke, producing an unmistakable effect of regularity and formality. On the other hand, while minuscule scripts can be written with pen-lift, they may also be cursive with little or no pen-lift.

Modern variations

In modern times in the context of library science, a manuscript is defined as any hand-written item in the collections of a library or an archive; for example, a library's collection of the letters or a diary that some historical personage wrote.

In book, magazine, and music publishing, a manuscript is an original copy of a work written by an author or composer, which generally follows standardized typographic and formatting rules. In film and theatre, a manuscript, or script for short, is an author's or dramatist's text, used by a theatre company or film crew during the production of the work's performance or filming. More specifically, a motion picture manuscript is called a screenplay; a television manuscript, a teleplay; a manuscript for the theater, a stage play; and a manuscript for audio-only performance is often called a radio play.

Preparation of the pages for writing : Pricking and ruling the leaves—

> The first step is to set up the quires. The quires are a group of several sheets put together. Raymond Clemens and Timothy Graham point out, in *Introduction to Manuscript Studies*, that "the quire was the scribe's basic writing unit throughout the Middle Ages".
>
> Clemens and Graham define pricking and ruling perfectly. "Pricking is the process of making holes in a sheet of parchment (or membrane) in preparation of it ruling. The lines were then made by ruling between the prick marks" and on ruling "The process of entering ruled lines on the page to serve as a guide for entering text. Most manuscripts were ruled with horizontal lines that served as the baselines on which the text was entered and with vertical bounding lines that marked the boundaries of the columns."

After this stage, the scribe would get to work copying from the original work to his collection of sheets of parchment.

- Now for text-editing a few words on textual criticism, the scribe, the editor and editing principles of a text on the basis of manuscripts-

The literary heritage of India dates back to nearly 4000 years. Sanskrit literature, available today, encapsulates all branches of human knowledge but the major part of this literature, unfortunately, has not yet been published in text-critical editions due to lack of proper training in methodology.

Moreover, literature of olden days is written in variety of scripts in the form of manuscripts. Today, many scripts have become obsolete and script experts are also becoming rare, which hinders the process of preparing text critical editions by collecting, comparing and collating different manuscripts procured from different regions. Every manuscript is a unique artifact and for the last 200 years the ancient manuscripts remained a subject of study and research by the Indians and western scholars.

But despite the best efforts made by the experts only 25% of ancient Indian i.e., Vedic and classical literature could be published. It is, therefore, a desideratum that more and more texts on various branches of Indian literature, particularly those bearing on sciences and arts should be brought out in good text critical editions.

A text-critical edition aims at the reconstruction of a text which will be nearest to the work of the original author. However, preparation of text critical edition of old texts is a difficult work. An editor of such text must be conversant with the methodology of textual criticism.

The collection of manuscripts, cataloguing and classification, microfilming or photocopying are most important procedures for the purpose of editing a particular text. They involve highlighting of methodology of critical editing: genealogy of manuscripts and preparation of *stemma*, technical terms in the science of editing, selection of correct readings and also fixation dates of manuscripts, decoding the dates from colophons, origin and development of large variety of Indian scripts.

Thus manuscriptology plays a significant role and becomes inevitably necessary for any kind of meritorious work on manuscripts, i.e., deciphering a manuscript and taking it up for research and publication. It is not an easy task to bring out critical edition of a text without good knowledge of manuscriptology.

Textual criticism does not itself include the 'higher'

criticism (i.e. the enquiry into the sources and methods of an author), but only the transmission of the completed work, either directly or in translation or by quotations by other writers. We have to distinguish between the 'authentic' or 'transmitted' reading of the archetype and the 'true' reading of the original.

The mere collection of the transmitted evidence and the choice between extant readings is the work of *recensio.* But as what has been transmitted to us even in its earliest form (i.e. the archetype) may not be what the author wrote, dictated or intended to say, it is sometimes necessary to go behind the archetype by the work of *emendatio.* This distinction is particularly useful in application to the peculiar conditions under which classical texts have come down to us. In practice the two operations cannot be kept distinct, as the choice of any reading in preference to another implies that we know what ought to have been written.

The object, then, of textual criticism is to discover the 'right', not merely the 'transmitted' reading. The theoretical approach may be analyzed in a number of ways into many processes which in practice overlap and are never truly scientific. The results of collecting all the evidence, after testing by transcriptional probability, are further shifted by transmission probability and finally scrutinized by intrinsic probability. This should logically result in the reconstruction of the earliest transmitted text or archetype, which can only be improved by emendation—the most interesting, difficult, deceptive and elusive aspect of textual criticism.

If the manuscripts are unequal in matter and volume, then how is it possible to go back to the original text while editing? It is to be remembered that only number of verses or passages cannot be the decisive factor. It is very difficult to decide who has copied from whom. Transcription and collation have to be done faithfully. While transcribing we should not change or correct and while collating we should note down only the variants. Collation sheets are like mirrors so much so that internal features of manuscripts are recorded in collation sheets. After collation, we get a complete tabular record of the manuscripts; if the collation is very faithful then it might be possible to go back to the original text. If the critical apparatus is recorded very exhaustively and critically it might be possible to trace the lost original text. In case of citations we have to consult critical editions or the testimony. Testimony has to be consulted or compared when the citations are unknown to the editor.

While editing a very old text it may be useful to compare as many numbers of manuscripts as possible. But that is not possible for an individual researcher. One has to be selective. Most of the available manuscripts were compared in BORI, Pune, while editing the *Mahabharata.* The more manuscripts we consult the more the possibility of coming across the variants. The ultimate goal is to find out the readings most akin to the author of the text. If the manuscripts belonging to a single region are collated, there may be the chance of their being copied from one and similar source and hence may contain similar scribal errors or variants, which obviously will not serve the real purpose. So while collecting manuscripts we should be careful about the fact that manuscripts should be collected from different regions.

There is not a single rule of text-editing. Knowledge of script is the first requisite but that does not make text-editing easy. There is no punctuation in between the *slokas* or lines in manuscripts. While editing the text, this proves to be a great difficulty. To consult catalogues is the primary task of text-editing which means, searching for manuscripts and their subsequent collation. Panditaparampara, Vaidika srotriya-sakha parampara, hastalekha-parampara especially maintained by the pandit*s* all over India, should be consulted. One has to research the king's places, personal collections also. In case of printed catalogues not always available, scholars have to make contacts with the institutions or personal collections directly for procuring photocopies of manuscripts. In case of manuscripts not yet recorded the editor has to depend on hastalekha-parampara.

- The task of the editor is to determine the nature of the subject matter of the manuscripts to give it a name and then proceed. First, we have to detect and identify nature of the text—whether it is srauta or kalpa or a jyotisa text or any other branches of ancient Indian wisdom.
- The duty of the editor is to secure them as soon as they are located. In case of manual transcripts, the editor is to compare it with the original and rectify in it any scribal or other type of errors common to happen due to the personality of the transcriber. Copying of manuscripts was for more reading, broader exposure and popular use of the text.
- The editor has to observe the codices in hand for determining which is the oldest or latest; he has to evaluate, or judge omissions, commissions, colophon and beginning, whether they are giving some reading or not internally. The relation among the manuscripts i.e. the genealogy, stemma codicum of manuscripts are to be determined. From reading is determined stemma. This constitutes a large part of higher criticism. The Introduction or the Higher Criticism begins with a description of the critical apparatus which has been utilized by the editor for his work. The editor clearly gives the abbreviated sign for the manuscript technically known as *siglum* by which the editor denotes its readings in the critical apparatus. Then there is a general account of the manuscripts, the number of manuscripts actually examined and the reasons for selecting the Manuscripts collated. A writer composed a copy – that was the original copy. There were other copies for preservation and propagation – those were manual copy, hand-written. They were distributed and

copying was done by copyists. Scribes or copyists were not always necessarily scholars. That gave rise to different difficulties. Handwriting may not be legible. While copying, scribes may make certain mistakes. To err is human. It is not possible to copy the texts exactly in totality, certain percentage of original texts may get lost, mutilated, scrapped. We should try to go back to the original.

- Only one manuscript is not sufficient because of the fact that when a single manuscript of a text is available then it is very difficult to edit. But in order to make that text available to the people in case of unavailability of other manuscripts that can be published even from a single manuscript which is most important.
- The manuscript in hand may have many errors because the copies are not in most cases faithful, thus we have to select five or six manuscripts though we know that the numbers of manuscripts are very limited.
- A manuscript may travel from one country to another— we have to trace the history of that particular text.
- The manuscript in hand, if it is quoted in some other already critically edited works, also can be compared with the orthodox texts. If any manuscript quotes verses or quotations in correct form then we should accept the manuscript in hand as faithful. For example, the original work composed by Carvaka is not known to us but his views are known, because the verses are quoted in different later works, and from supporting evidence we can come to know about the field of work. The meaning of prastara in Vedic context is prastare havih . . . oblations are not to be placed on stones but on kusa grass known as prastara. Thus there is difference in meaning of technical terms.
- The first two stages of editing are only clerical, but these two steps should be done faithfully. There should be no alteration or change done by the editor in these

initial steps. But the next steps are very responsible for editing. Text-editors are masterminds. Those who have mastery over the field can be expert text- editors. The caliber of the editor can be tested by how successfully he can edit a text. It is very easy to edit a text badly. There are classical scholars who are expert text-editors.

- One should not abandon any variant found in different manuscripts. Those variants which are rejected by one as wrong may be adjudged as correct. So they are given as footnotes. They should be given in the form of critical apparatus. Sometimes there may be very insignificant variants, still according to scholars, critical apparatus should be as exhaustive as possible, i.e. what is appearing as insignificant to me today, may appear as significant to other people in coming days. The editor has to be careful while tackling the errors from the pen of the author. No change should be done with the errors from the pen of the author. If it is decided that errors are scribal errors then the editor should change while reconstructing the original text. This is regarding the critical edition of the text.
- A detailed account of the manuscripts contains generally the *siglum*, followed by the place of deposit, name of the library, the press-mark of the library, the number of folios, the number of lines in each folio and the number of letters in each line, the material on which it is written, the style of the handwriting of the scribe as well as the orthographical peculiarities of the manuscript, its nature and condition, existence of sections, lacunae, if any, the beginning and end of the text and the intermediate colophons (at the end of each chapter) in which some information about the text or its history, or the name or place of the scribe or the patron, place or date of transcription exist. Sometimes two colophons are found in some manuscripts (a) Author's colophon and (b) Scribe's

colophon. Sometimes colophons supply besides concluding note about the title, date and place of his working etc., other information such as whether the copyist has compared the copy with any other important copy to get the best readings, for which he has copied the text and how to protect the text from external damages etc. Sometimes an expression of pious thanks at the end of the book is also found to be recorded.

- If the manuscript bears a title it should be indicated in the detailed account. If the style of handwriting is found to vary in the same manuscript, it should be pointed out whether the manuscript is in one uniform hand writing or whether several scribes were at work on it. Some importance is to be given with regard to the additions or corrections entered in the margin or in-between the lines or with regard to deletions, omissions etc. There should be given clear reason regarding the manuscripts which have been eliminated; in case of the partial collation of any manuscript, places where such collation begins and ends are to be indicated, if possible, in the tabular form for easy access of the critical reader.
- A detailed information of the testimonial such as ancient commentaries, adaptations and *florilegia* etc, the relationship of the manuscripts as expressed in a genealogy in the form of a pedigree or *stemma codcium,* the probable or exact recorded date of the manuscripts utilized must be furnished.
- Exact transcription is known as calligraphy which is done usually by restoration or conservation section. For restoration, calligraphy is mainly done. Now we get codex i.e. copies of manuscripts, e.g., from Ms A, B is copied. From which manuscript is copied is known as archetype. To B, A is archetype i.e. pratnarupa. For copying archetype as well as exemplars are required – antarvarti-pratnarupa-sub archetypes or hyper

archetypes- these copies are called codex (in singular) and codices (in plural).

- Supposing six manuscripts are available, their relation is to be decided. The manuscript must be dated.
- If the manuscript is not dated its script is to be considered to determine the period when it was written.

From *lexilio deficilio* it can be determined i.e. difficult words are to be taken as older. Palaeographically regional type of writing different sects, interpolations comes when transmission of manuscripts starts. In one copy if we get two earlier streams of one tradition, i.e. C_4 – two streams from C_1 and C_2 is found, then C_4 is called conflated copy. C_2 is being carried to C_2 (1), C_2 (2) and C_2 (3) – again if C_5 contains all the three streams then the earlier three mss. C_2 (1), C_2 (2) and C_2 (3) – all should be important than C_5. In case of collation, C_5 is not so important.

- The archaism may be considered/determined according to area, or group or recessions. Manuscript containing same stream but much older has to be credited with more importance. The relation among the manuscripts which are in hand for collation has to be determined. Transcription of manuscripts is to be completed first, then collation with different manuscripts. Manuscripts which are most complete, legible, oldest, more correct, best preserved and in good condition have to be taken up for collation. Limited number of manuscripts is to be taken up for study and collation. Collation should be started taking up manuscripts area wise, taking up texts from different regions. Then the study is more comprehensive and accurate.
- No judgment is expected to be given in this stage. Once final reading and redaction of the text is done,

quotations are to be traced in original texts which are critically edited; variant readings, recensions have to be taken care of.

- For variant reading (1) *lexio vario* - from commentary, older manuscripts also are to be accepted.
- (2) *lexio deficilio*—more difficult readings are to be accepted as they are more akin to the original text.
- (3) *lexio recensio*—the status of manuscripts is to be determined first—whether it is codex etc. Omissions, commissions determine the groupings. History of the text is influenced by the nature of the manuscripts.
- (4) *stemma codicum*—matrkanam vamsa-visesah—the relation among manuscripts in hand has to be evaluated.
- Then there are vulgate editions, students' edition, and popular edition. Critical edition should fulfill maximum conditions. In a critical edition references should be of a standard edition. One text may be critically edited many times. In that case the edition should mention the latest edition. If the text is hitherto unedited and unpublished, it can be edited satisfactorily. If it is satisfactorily edited then one should not go for editing that text for the second time.
- Vulgate edition
- *Popular edition*—They may be taken from a vulgate edition or from a critical edition; they also do not have the critical apparatus; or other information regarding the manuscripts or of the text. For a popular edition, the editor does not necessarily have to consult manuscripts.
- Students' edition—The editor picks up text from the critical edition or vulgate edition and also from popular edition.
- Conflation may give amalgamation of two copies of manuscripts, even of two copies belonging to different recensions. Thus conflated copies are most troublesome and perplexing. While editing we must

know the historical and philological background and development, age, date of the text. If it is decided that errors are scribal errors then we should change them while reconstructing the original text. Best example of conflated copies may be given as a manuscript in which 2/3 or other manuscripts are found combined. Conflation may give amalgamation of two copies of manuscripts belonging to different recensions. Readings (*lexio vario*) or recensions (*lexio recensio*) may vary in conflated copies. Thus conflated copies are most troublesome. While editing the text Maulasarvastivada when discovered in Central Asia Turfan it was found that *lexio vario* and *lexio recensio* are amalgamated there. In such cases the editor must know the history of the texts, philosophical as well as background, development, age, date etc. In case of different recensions keeping note of variants (*pathantarabheda*) is most important. In the critical edition of the *Mahabharata*, we get a long eulogy of Sri Krsna where in the portion of vastraharana of Draupadi, when she says if dharma is there, and then let it prevail, originally two verses were there. As time passed by, copyists keep on adding eulogies, praises towards Lord Sri Krsna. It is now decided that these verses are definitely interpolations but while preparing critical editions of the *Mahabharata*, scholars kept these verses as they are, since culture is involved and Indian sentiment is glorified there.

The final part involves Tripura and Tagore.

To say something about Tripura for the people of Tripura is difficult indeed. The history of Tripura is a long drawn story which dates back to the time of the *Mahabharata*. In the 14th Century the history of Tripura witnessed a change with the sifting of the capital from Kailashahar to Udaipur. It was around the same time that the Tripuri kings adopted the title of Manikya and the Manikya dynasty which had an Indo-Mongolian origin ruled Tripura for around 3000 years.

This was probably the most glorious episode of the history of Tripura and the dominance of the Manikyas was also acknowledged by the Mughals who were the central rulers.

The etymological origin of the word Tripura explains its origin to a large extent. The compound word of Tripura when broken gives two separate words, 'Tui' (water) + 'Pra' (near). The geographical location of the region thoroughly justifies its name.

It is also argued that Tripura is a distortion of the word Twi-bupra which means confluence of waters and many of the Tripuri Villages are named after the confluence of different rivers.

Being dominated by the Bengalis, the state's prevalent culture is Bengali. In fact, Tripura is also home to thousands of migrants from West Bengal and Bangladesh. Bengali is spoken and understood by more than 50% of the state's population. However, Tripuri as well as Bengali are the official languages of Tripura. Hinduism is the most practiced religion in Tripura. Both Bengalis and Tripuris follow Hinduism with ardent fervor. Islam, Buddhism and Christianity are also followed by people in minority.

Another very strong probability of Tripura - origin of name is the Temple of Tripureshwari. This Temple in Udaipur is a major pilgrimage spot in the region and is one of the Shakti peeths.

The main gods worshipped by the people are Lord Shiva and Goddess Tripureshwari. This is a rare specimen of temple architecture which was built by Maharaja Govinda Manikya near the old Royal palace of Maharaja constructed during 1660–75 AD.

The Tripura Bhuvaneswari Temple is immortalized in two of Rabindranath Tagore's plays—namely 'Rajarshi' and 'Bisarjan'.

And Tagore

Rabindranath Tagore (1861–1941) was a Bengali poet, philosopher, artist, playwright, composer and novelist.

Known mostly for his poetry, Tagore wrote novels, essays, short stories, travelogues, dramas, and thousands of songs. India's first Nobel laureate, Tagore won the Nobel Prize for Literature in 1913 for his book 'Song Offering' 'The *Gitanjali'*. Tagore travelled widely and became friends with many notable tweitieth century figures such as William Butler Yeats (who wrote the Introduction to the English translation of 'The *Gitanjali'*), H.G. Wells, Ezra Pound, and Albert Einstein. His body of literature upholds universal humanistic values and was often deeply mystical. He composed national anthems of both India and Bangladesh.

Of Tagore's prose, his short stories are perhaps most highly regarded; he is indeed credited with originating the Bengali-language version of the genre. His works are frequently noted for their rhythmic, optimistic, and lyrical nature. Such stories are mostly borrowed from deceptively simple subject matter: commoners. Tagore's non-fictions are grappled with history, linguistics, and spirituality. He wrote autobiographies. His travelogues, essays, and lectures were compiled into several volumes.

'Rajarshi' is the name of the novel by Rabindranath Tagore based on the life of a king of the state of Tripura, named Govinda Manikya.

Tagore's 'Visarjan' is a drama in verse in elegiac lyrical style. Raghupati, a priest and an earnest and pious devotee of the goddess Kali, wants to offer animal sacrifice to propitiate the goddess. Govinda Manikya, King of Tripura, is sincerely opposed to this and issues a mandate against animal sacrifice.

'Visarjan' explores the meaning of true religious devotion and exposes the heinous, barbaric and brutal acts perpetrated by the fundamental religious orthodoxy, in the name of religion and God.

As many are adherents of animist-Saktism , Govinda Manikya, Tripura's monarch, issues a ban on slaughters at the altar of the Goddess on realizing the futility of blood sacrifices. Raghupati, the high priest who decides to infuriate everyone against the king, encouraged the people to cause a general discontent in the state. Initially he starts playing with the emotions of the childless queen Gunavati subsequently moving on to Nayanray, the crown prince, and then finally to Nakshatraray, the king's brother. However, he failed in all of his efforts until Jaisingha, a Rajput by birth, who has unquestionable faith in the deity and his mentor, came into the picture. As a result of witnessing the clash between Raghupati and Govinda Manikya, Jaisingha, caught between blind faith and a mixed sense of morality, finally decides to sacrifice himself as the only solution to the grave problem.

The dialogue on sacrifice featuring in the drama is said to be a literary masterpiece. Raghupati conspires to dethrone the king. The priest deprives a poor girl of her only and favourite goat to offer it as a sacrifice. Raghupati's disciple Jayasingha who loves the girl is incensed at this. The conflict in his soul between his reverence for his Guru and his love for the girl and for her pet is a fine subject for dramatic handling and is very beautifully described. He offers to give his own heart's blood to propitiate goddess Kali rather than allow the goat to be killed. His other works fuse lyrical flow and emotional rhythm into a tight focus on a core idea, a break from prior Bengali drama. Tagore sought "the play of feeling and not of action". In 1890 he released what is regarded as his finest drama: Visarjan (Sacrifice). It is an adaptation of Rajarshi, one of his earlier novels. "A forthright denunciation of a meaningless [and] cruel superstitious rite[s]", the Bengali originals feature intricate subplots and prolonged monologues that give play to historical events in seventeenth-century Udaipur. The devout Maharaja of Tripura is pitted against the wicked head-priest Raghupati.

17

SANSKRITIC CULTURE IN THE PRINCELY STATE OF TRIPURA

CHANDAN KUMAR CHAKRABORTY

At this high tech age of human civilization when Sanskrit has apparently lost its past glory and modern prudents have shelved it, the Prime Minister of India Dr. Manmohan Singh declares unequivocally in presence of the assembled scholars of more that 33 countries "संस्कृत भारत की आत्मा है"– Sanskrit has been the soul of india. He had been inaugurating the 15th World Sanskrit Conference in the Vijyan Bhawan of New Delhi on the 5th day of this month of January, 2012.[2] He had rightly suggested to the cultural heritage of India which is primarily based on Sanskrit tradition. There is no denying of the fact that the highest knowledge and wisdom as reflected in the Vedas, the sprituality and immortality as in the Upanisads, the ethics and culture as in the great epics and the sublimity and exquisiteness as in the classical literature, are all produce of the eternal tree of Sanskrit language. It is also a fact that Sanskrit, with its unbounded vitality and potentiality has been surviving through the centuries, and exercising power as cementing force of unity in multifarious diversity through the true concept of "वसुधैव कुटुम्बकम्".

The eternal flow of Sanskrit has drenched all the parts of Indian soil. But it is surprising that the deep forests and cluster of hills surrouding the North East, did not stand on the way of Sanskrit, and the Sanskritic culture was eagerly embraced by this princely state of Tripura even in the mysterious past. The cultural history of Tripura would have been written in a different manner had there been no favourable attitude of the tribal kings towards Sanskrit. Tripura was ruled by various kings in different phase of history, and it had produced a distinctive heritage of its own. Tripura has a long historic past. It is stated in the Rajaratnakara about the state's antiquity—

> "अति प्राचीनमेवेदं राज्यं त्रिपुरसंजितम्।
> महादेवविहारार्थं ब्रह्मणा निर्मितं पुरा।।"

With its attractive hills and forests, this small tribal state of North-east India has been able to generate attraction of the galaxy of luminaries from different fields of knowledge and proficiency far and wide. The kings ofTripura possessed a generous heart and cultural mind. They also had great quest for quenchless knowledge. So the state was able to bring to its close contact the greatest souls like Rabindranath Tagore, Acharya Jagadish Chandra Bose and many others. The state is thus rightly praised—

> "नाना गुणज्ञैर्विवुधैश्च धन्या चिरप्रसिद्धैः किल राजवंश्यैः।
> सङ्गीतसिद्धैस्तपसा प्रसिद्धैः सा दीप्यतां भारतभूमिभागे।।"

In such an exquisitely beautiful and sacred land of the North-east, series of 183 kings once ruled. So far the earlier history ofTripura is concerned, it can be learnt from available manuscripts, different inscriptions, coins, deeds, oral traditions and other records. The history of Tripura is primarily recorded in the Rājamālā, the state chronicle and the Rājaratnākara, a Mahākāvya, written in Sanskrit in two parts pūrva vibhāga and dakṣiṇa vibhāga of which the latter part is yet to be recovered. It is stated that the royal lineage of Tripura kings belong to the lunar dynasty. Some authors think that the Puranic myths of lunar origin of the early rulers came into being when the royal dynasties of Tripura came in touch with the aryan culture through some Brāhmaṇa pundits. Kailasha Singha, the author of Rājamālā maintaind this view. Due to the influence of Aryan culture, the names of tribal kings have had their Sanskrit origin.

The Brahmanical culture apparently stepped in the state of Tripura for the first time during the middle of seventh century AD while Ādi Dharmapā was reigning the state. History, however, tells us that the Brahmanical culture and religion had already spreaded in Bengal and Assam in the sixth and seventh century AD . It is therefore, reasonable to believe that Tripura could not steer clear of the influence of that culture.

At the request of Ādi Dharmapā, the then Mithilā king Balabhadra sent five erudite Vedic Brāhmaṇa scholars to the capital of Tripura state. The five brahmins were Sri Nanda, Ānanda, Govinda, Srīpati and Puruṣottama belonging to Vatsa, Vātsya, Bharadwāja, Kṛṣṇātreya and Parāsara gotras respectively. They performed a great Vedic sacrifice at the behest of the king in the district of sylhet. The name Ādi Dharmapā was conferred on the king for his religious bent of mind. A copper plate inscription, written in Sanskrit states that those five Brāhmaṇas were favoured with grant of land for their stay in the kingdom—

त्रिपुरापर्वताधीशः श्रीश्रीयुक्तादिधर्मपा।
समाज्ञं दत्तपत्रञ्च मैथिलेषु तपस्विषु।।
वत्स-वात्स्य-भरद्वाज-कृष्णात्रेय-पराशराः।
श्रीनन्दानन्द गोविन्द श्रीपति पुरुषोत्तमः।।
प्रातीच्यामुत्तरस्याञ्च वक्रमा क्रौशिरा नदी।
दक्षिणस्याञ्च पूर्वस्यां हाङ्काला कोकिकापुरी।।
एतन्मध्यां सशस्याञ्च टेङ्करीककिर्षितां।
प्रलभ्यदत्तां तद्भूमिं तेषु पञ्चतपस्विषु।।

मकरस्थे रवौ शुक्लपक्षे पञ्चदशी दिने।
त्रिपुरा चन्द्रवानाव्दे प्रदत्ता दत्तपत्रिका।।

(Rājamālā sec. Lahar, p. 101)

The date of the inscription appears as 51 Tripurābda. Those Vedic Brāhmaṇas had drawn subsequently five other Brāhmaṇas from Mithilā belonging to the Kātyāyana, Kāśyapa, Moudgalya, Swarṇakauśika and Goutama gotra together with their Brāhmaṇa attendents and barbers. Influx of Brāhmaṇas from other parts of India also continued. One copper plate inscription reveals that during the Gupta period Brāhmaṇa priests, belonging to different Vedic recensions and expert in sacrificial rites, came from North-west India to settle down in the state of Tripura. In this way exuberance of Sanskrit learning came into being by way of establishing many Sanskrit schools in Bengal. Sanskrit learning became firm-footed in the state during the fourteenth century AD due to arrival of many Brāhmaṇa pundits, and also with the composition of many valuable books by them on philosophy literature, smṛti, astrology and āyurveda. Since then the flow of Sanskritisation continued in the royal culture of Tripura. At a much later date, during the regime of King Dharmadhara, the son of King Megha, a great Vedic sacrifice was performed in Kailashahar (in 1195 AD). This is stated by Sri Dinesh Chandra Sen in his book 'Bṛhat Baṅga' (Part II, p. 1086). A copper plate relating to donation of land as an offering, 'dakṣiṇā' to the sacrificial chief reads as follows:

"त्रिपुरा पर्वताधीशः श्रीश्रीयुक्तधर्मपा।
समाज्ञं दत्तपत्रञ्च मैथिलाय तपस्विने।।
श्रीनिधिपति विप्राय वात्स्यगोत्राय धर्मिणे . . ." etc.

It is intersting to note that during the last part of 14th century AD when sylhet came under the Muslim rule, then too Sanskrit tradition in Tripura did not cease to continue.

Some land deeds, written in Sanskrit during that time, as mentioned in the 'Srihatter Itivritta,' bear the truth of this statement. We are aware that Mahārāja Dharma-Māṇikya took resort to the Sanskrit Pundits Bāṇeśvara and Sukreśvara to record the history of his ancestors. Kailash Chandra Singha's Rājamālā records the fact of the arrival of many Brāhmaṇa pundits at the time of King Ratna Māṇikya built the temple and installed the idol of goddess Tripura Sundarī Kāli and orderly placed a stone slab in the temple bearing a śloka inscribed on it. "Sri Chandrodaya Vidyabinode" Bhattacharjee mention it in his book 'Shilālipi Saṁgraha'. The śloka runs thus—

> "माया मुरारेरियमम्बिका या।
> मुञ्चत्यमुष्या निकटं कदाचन।।
> प्रान्ते भवाण्याः ध्रुवमास केशवः।
> श्रीधनमाणिक्य कथं तु विस्मितः।।"

The other inscriptions, written in Sanskrit, also bear the name of Dhanya Māṇikya–

> "आसीत् पूर्वं नरेन्द्रः सकलगुणयुतो धन्यमाणिक्यदेवो।
> यागे यस्याम्बरेशः क्षितितलमगमत् कर्णतुल्यस्य दानैः।।
> शाके वह्नक्षिवेधोमुखधरनियुते लोकमात्रेऽम्बिकायै।
> प्रादात् प्रासादराजं गगनपरिगतं सेवितायै स देवैः।।
> तत्पश्चाद् भूमिपालस्त्रिपुरनरपतिधीरकल्याणदेवः।
> खिन्नां पृथ्वी शशास प्रवलरिपुगणैः केवलं स्वीयशक्त्या।।
> तत्पुत्रो भूपसिंहः समरपतिवरो धीरगोविन्ददेवो।
> दानैर्भूदेवयोषिद् कणकमयकृतः साम्बराज्ये विराजे।।"

After Dhanya Māṇikya, inscriptions inscribed in Sanskrit ślokas, were installed in different temples and buildings at different times by Mahārāja Kalyāṇa Māṇikya, Vijaya Māṇikya, Rāma Māṇikya, Govinda Māṇikya and Rādhā-kishore Māṇikya. In 1901 Mahārājā Rādhākishore Māṇikya installed a stone inscription while laying the foundation stone of the magnificient Uajjayanta Palace at Agartala. The Sanskrit inscription reads as follows:

> ''शीतांशु द्वन्द्वरन्ध्रोदधिजपरिमिते शाकवर्ष सुलग्ने
> वैशाखे सुरजाहे गगन विधुमिते रोपिता यस्य भित्तिः।
> सोऽयं नाम्नोज्जयन्तः सुरगणकृपया पूणर्णतां प्राप्य सौधः
> श्रीश्री राधाकिशोर त्रिपुरनृप पादस्पर्शयोग्यो विभातु।।''

Besides the inscriptions, use of Sanskrit by the kings of Tripura could be found in the coins also. The book 'Coinage of Tripura' records the herd of Tripura coins, royal orders, decoration, medals and seals etc and a good number of them bear Sanskrit writings inscribed on them, some in Devanagari script and some in Bengali. Many of the Māṇikya coins bear the names of the queens along with the rulers, thus reflecting the status of royal women in those days of antiquity. It is very interesting to find that Sanskrit was being learnt in the royal harem of Tripura. Nanua, the wife of Dharma Manikya II, Jahṇabi Devi, wife of Mahārājā Krishna Māṇikya, queen Sumitrā Devī, wife of Durga Māṇikya, their daughter Anandāmoyee Devī and also many other learned ladies of royal harem were versed in Sanskrit. Sanskrit was frequently used in the holy places, worksites of reconstruction, images of animals and at the top of the certificates of recognition on the distinguished personalities as noble titles. Such as—''स्वस्ति। विनय-समर-विजयी-महामहोदय-पञ्चश्रीयुक्त-महाराज (name of the ruler) देववर्मा-माणिक्य-बाहादुर-नरपतेरादेशोऽयं कारकवर्गेषु प्रचरतु, परमस्य विराजते राजधानी हस्तिनापुरी।'' Mahārājā Birendra kishore's wife Prābhāvati Devī reconstructed the temple of god Chandranatha at the pilgrimage Sītākuṇḍa where the inscription in Sanskrit appears as etc. ''प्रिया प्रभावती देवी · · ·'' etc.

In this way the learning and preaching of Sanskrit occupied a very significant position with the generous assistance of the Mahārājas of Tripura. The eternal appeal of the unfoathomable treasure in Sanskrit like the Vedas, Vedāṅgas, dharmaśāstras, smṛtis, purāṇas, epics, grammar, astrology, astronomy, philosophy, literature, rehtories, poeties, tantras etc. attracted the enlightened people and thus assimilated to the culture of the land. This assimilation took place since very early times. So we find in the Kharchi Puja all the fourteen gods, 'Chaudda Devatā'—Hara, Uma, Hari, Mā, Bānī, Kumāra, Gaṅeśa, Brahmā, Pṛthvī, Gaṅgā, Samudra, Himalaya, Kāmadeva and Agni are related to Brahmanical culture. The style of worshipping the fourteen gods has got an admixture of the Vedic, Tantric and other styles of worship. In the religious field, the traditional animism, as were followed by different tribal groups, had been replaced by Hindu gods, and thus ushering the cultural maturity towards a distinctive direction. Development of the other sides of life such as, the mode of behaviour, language, dress and decoration, belief and practice and also other things come under the purview of culture. In view of assimilation of two different cultures in many respects, one of the Adibashis and the other of the Vedic Brahmanas, Sri Suren Debbarma, a learned scholar of the land has rightly commented as the plathora of colours of a composite culture.

Bibliography

1. Sri Rajaratnakaram ed., Jyotish Nath, *Tripura Bangia Sahitya* (Purva vibhagah) O Sanskriti Samsad, Agartala, 2003.
2. Tripura Smriti, Samarendra Debbarma, Calcutta, 1927.
3. Shilalipi Samgraha, Chandradaya Vidyavidyavinoda, Agartala, 1904.
4. The Coinage of Tripura, N.G. Rhodes and S.K. Boase, Kolkata, 2002. M.B.B. Coliege Golden Jubilee Volume, 1997.
5. Tripura Rajye Samskrita Charcha, an Article by Sri Ramaprasad Datta, Saswata Tripura, ed. Sri Anildhan Bhattacharjee.

18

IN SEARCH OF IDENTITY: EXPLORING THE HISTORY OF THE MOGS OF TRIPURA

Satyadeo Poddar and Nirmalya Karmakar

There is a common belief that the name of Tripura has originated from "Tripura Sundari" - the presiding deity of the land which is famous as one of the fifty-one Pithas of Hindu Pilgrims. Apart from this traditional view it is believed that originally the land was known as "Tuipra" meaning a land adjoining the water. It is fact that in days of yore the boundaries of Tripura was extended up to the Bay of Bengal when its rulers held sway from Garo hills to Arakan. According to the "Rajmala', the rulers were known by the surname "Fa" which is meaning father. The rulers of Bengal helped the Tripura King in the fourteenth century when the king had to face frequent Mughal invasion. Another meaning of the Tripura has been coined from two Tripuri word "Tui" which is meaning water and "Pra" means near.

There were about nineteen different tribes living in Tripura, the *Tripuri, Jamatia, Noatia, Reang, Halam, Chakma, Mog, Garo, Munda, Lushai, Oraon, Santhal, Uchoi, Khasi, Bhil, Lepcha, Bhutia, Chaimal* and *Kuki* and they had their own cultural heritage. It is to be noted that 15 tribes out of 19 scheduled tribes in the state viz, *Tripuri, Jamatia, Reang, Noatia, Halam, Uchoi,* etc. share same linguistic chords and rich cultural identity. Tripura is the traditional home the indigenous tribals over the past decades. Tripura had beckoned and welcomed the settlement of non-tribals in the annals of history. As attested by the enumeration of the first imperial census conducted in 1872, Tripura had a non-tribal population of 30 percent which grew substantially in the succeeding decadal censuses. In accordance with the returns of 2001 census, indigenous tribals comprising altogether 19 communities constitute 31.05 per cent of the state's population while 69.95 per cent are non-tribals including a fair sprinkling of Manipuris. *Tripuri* is the big tribe in terms of population and *Bhutia* tribe being the least in the state.

Amongst the tribals, Tripuri or 'Debbarman' community form the vast majority of around fifty percent while the non-tribal population comprising by and large the Bengalis and a minuscule number of Meithei and Vishnupriya Manipuris belong to various castes and sub-castes. Tripura is largely dominated by Bengali Community, in spite of the 19 schedule tribes, that form a major chunk of the population. Fringe tribal communities, in the context of Tripura, to be precise, like the Bhils, Santhals, Mundas and Oraons who had settled in the state from the early decades of twentieth century as tea-garden labourers grace Tripura's ethnic mosaic while 'Kokborok' has emerged as Tripura's lingua franca among the tribals, fringe communities continue to speak their own languages.

There is a controversy over the origin of the word 'MOG' or 'MOGH'. According to a periodical magazine of the Burmese Research Society, this 'word' has been originated from Bengali. But in the Bengali Dictionary of Bangiya Sahitya Parishad, the origin of this word is 'unknown'. In another Dictionary this word is claimed to have originated from a Burmese word 'Mogh' which is generally used as an epithet before the name of a gentleman. Some others of course referred it to the ancient Mogadha (Magadha) Empire for its origination. But it is sad that when the domination of Hindu religion began to thrive in this ancient center of Buddha religion, a branch of Mogadha dynasty left for Chitagong and subsequently settled down in Hill Chitagong. Probably the Word 'Mogh' came from 'Mogadhi'(one who hails from Mogadha or one who is a resident of Mogadha). In English dictionary the words Mog, Mogen, Mouge have been shown as surnames to the inhabitants of Arakan in fifteenth and sixteenth centuries. Bangalees of course refer to the inhabitants of Arakan as 'Mog'. Mogs are also known as Marma in Bangladesh.

According to "Rajmala" the historical record of the royal lineage of Tripura, the Mog (Burmese origin) were the powerful Buddhist kings of Tripura. The people of 'Mog' community claimed to have come from Arakan and settled down in Tripura in 957 AD. Buddhism flourished in Tripura from second to nineth century AD. Both Theravada and Mahayana forms of Buddhism were practiced, though Theravada Buddhism have stronghold in many parts of Tripura for many centuries. The Buddhists of Tripura also had to meet the same fate. The Buddhist king of Tripura was defeated by the Hindu king and Muslim invaders. The defeated Buddhist king along with his subjects had to flee and settle in different parts of Myanmar and Bangladesh. By the eleventh century AD, Buddhism totally disappeared from Tripura. It is in the thirteenth century AD that the Mog (of Burmese origin) re-entered Tripura. With the re-entry of Mog there was revival of Buddhism in the state.

The Mogs are Buddhist by religion and almost all the people are the followers of Buddhism. The three major Buddhist communities of Tripura, viz. Mog, Chakma and Barua, have close relation with each other and observe *vassa,* Buddha Purima, Kathin Chīvara Dāna etc. in uniformity. Mog (Burmese origin), Chakma, Barua and Uchai are the followers of Buddhism in Tripura. Their cultural background and customs resemble with that of Burmese and Thai Buddhist tradition. The Mog Buddhists have close

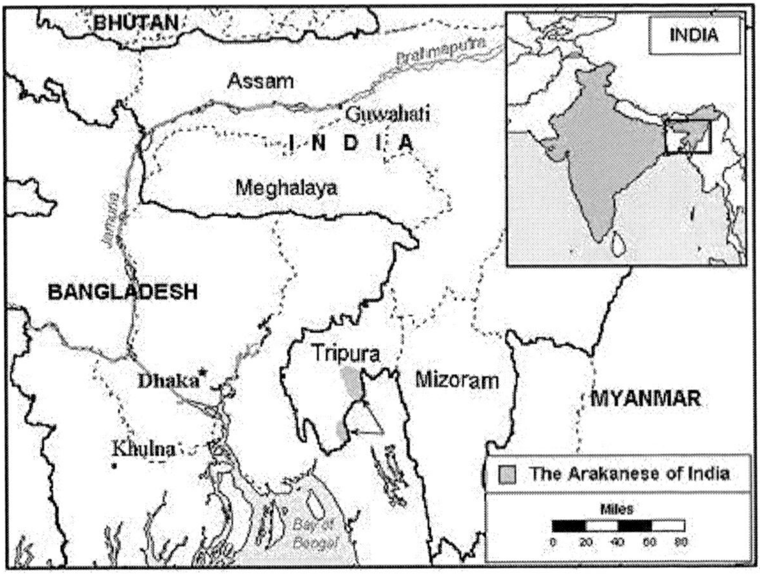

affinity with Burmese Buddhism in all socio-cultural and religious aspects. Though they live in Tripura, almost all Dhamma books such as Tripitaka, Aihakatha, Burmese [Myanmar] Translationss etc are brought from Myanmar and Dharma teaching is done in Burmese [Myanmar] script. The dialect that the Mog people speak is similar to that of Burmese [Myanmar] and Arakanese (Rakhine) language with little variation in pronunciation, but the script is the same (Burmese (Myanmar) script.

The Mogs are indigenous community of Tripura. They constitute sixth largest indigenous people of the state. Mog comprises 3.06 per cent population in total tribes of Tripura. By religion they are Buddhist. Their major concentrations are at Sabroom and Belonia in South Tripura. Their language is grouped under Tibeto-Chinese family. Mogs are depend at on Jhum cultivation. Mog's social culture and belief are centralized with Burmese culture. Mog community by tradition famous for their folk medicine. The Mogs had a dynasty in Arakan, situated in present Myanmar. There were instances and records of wars between the Arakan king and Tripura kings. They were fierce fighter, and the Mogs were inducted in the Tripura royal forces, there were many soldiers belonging to Mog community in the past. It is presumed that the Mogs started settling in Tripura since then, almost fifth to sixth centuries. The Mogs are basically agriculturist, but now a day they are found to take profession of every modern discipline. As a community the Mogs are very disciplined, self reliant, and peace loving and meek. Maintenances of internal discipline are the distinct responsibility of the head man who in the past used to lend helping hand to the king of Tripura by maintaining peace within the community.

The Mogs have a large number of manuscripts with them specially the palm leaf and manuscripts made from bark of a tree. Though many of them have already destroyed and some are about to. According to these manuscripts we have come to know few occasions, festivals and also the Mog months. *Sungrain* is the biggest festival of Mogs in Tripura. It is to rejoice for the new year. The people used to share this occasion with the fellow people by caring the olders, feeding others and enjoying the harvest. It is similar to Thingyan festival of Maynmar and is celebrated with same zeal as the Songkran of Thailand. The mythological story goes like this- once there was betting between the Sagra Maung (King of Devalok) and the Bremma Maung (King of Brahmalok), where the latter lost and as per the condition, he was beheaded. Now a big problem arose with the head. If it falls on the Earth, then the Earth will be burnt. If it is thrown to the Ocean, then the Ocean will get dried up. If it is thrown to the sky, then the universe will be set afire. So it was decided that the head will be kept hold by the princess of Devalok. Every year the carrier shall be changed. Change of guards happen when the Sun moves from Northern Hemisphere to the Southern (Sankranti). To oversee the handover activities of the princess, the King of Devalok (Sagra Maung) set out in the Universe and

Image of a Mog Calendar showed in the "Kathin Chibar Daan" ceremony at Manu Bankul Village, Sabroom, South Tripura during the Post Survey Work of Manuscripts.

descends to the Earth to look at the Manussa (The People of Martyalok).

Celebrations are aimed at welcoming the *Sagra Maung*, presenting the best behavior through various benevolent works, community feast and gaming (Daw games), Sharing and caring to fellow members of the Society, Bathing of the Buddha images as symbolic representation of cleansing the old year, Lighting the night sky with hot balloons etc. The day of Sungrain is basically penance day with strict observance of Silas (Moral discipline), Self-restraints, Strict Vegetarian foods and Dhamma discourses. The third day "Atada" is the feast day- one likes to feed others with various kinds of Pithas (Painjari, Chhay, Kdau, Kahnya), Labras (vegetable with more than 5 kinds) and others. In the neighboring Bangladesh and Arakan, the youths throw water to one another as a symbol of cleansing the old and out-dated. In as much, the festival is known as the water festival.

Wah ' festival is their annual meeting of whole community people. The name "WAH" is taken from the Pali word "vasso" meaning rain. In Thailand, it is known as pansa or phansaa. It is related to rainy retreat of Buddhist monks. Four months from June to September, the Buddhist monks are confined to a fixed temple for doing self-study, meditation and full observance of *Sila* (Moral discipline). During the intermediate period, the Buddhist monks are not allowed to leave his temple of residence. If he happens to go to nearby places, he has to come back to his temple even in the midnight as he cannot sleep elsewhere. The starting of rainy retreat is called as "Wachhu" and the end of the retreat is termed as "Wakyet". It is traditional to donate candles and other useful items to temples and monasteries on the first day of the rainy retreat. During these four months, the laymen find their monk every day in the temple. Lay Buddhists may also make special arrangements for Wah (Vassa), such as abstaining from meat, sweets, alcohol or smoking, fasting during the day or spending more time in devotional practice. After the day of hard work, they get their monk in the temple to discuss the spiritual matters. On the other hand, the monk, who is basically a wanderer but now confined in self-study in the given temple, is well equipped to answer the queries of the villagers. Such kind of system of knowledge sharing has kept alive the existence of Mog community.

The rainy retreat ends on the fullmoon day of "*Wakyet*". Legend says that Gautama Buddha preached The Abhidhamma to Maidawmi Nat (reincarnate of His Mother) in Tavatimsa Abode of celestial beings for three Lenten months and returned to the abode of men on the full-moon day of "Wakyet". The King of Celestials created gold, silver, ruby stairways for him. Buddha took the middle ruby one radiating six hues of aura. The nats came along by the right gold stairways and the brahmas by the left silver stairways. On account of that, the Mog community celebrate the full-moon day with multi-coloured illuminations. It is also called Tavatimsa Festival after the Tavatimsa Abode of the nats.

For the Sangha, it is the time for what is known as Pavarana, which means inviting, entreating, urging. In practice since the times of Buddha, it is to beg one another for forgiveness of any action that might have displeased any other among Sangha. There is also the practice among laity of paying obeisance to parents and elders.

Tenchhaungbu Lights and *Kathin Pwe* or *Kathin Chibara Daan*:

It is said that the followers were not satisfied with multi-coloured illuminations on the Wakyet full-moon night when Gautama Buddha descended from the abode of Celestial beings. In the following month i.e. Tenchhaungbu, the followers hang a high light on a bamboo Pole to illuminate the sky and to commemorate the return of Buddha. In the Mog villages the high raised lantern-like lights known as Tenchhaungbu Chhingmi are clearly visible. During the same period, every Buddhist monasteries celebrates the festival of *Kathin Chibar Dan. Kathin Chibar Dan* means difficult (Kathin) cloth (Chibar: used by monks) donation (Dan). On this day, the Buddhist devotees donate robes to the monks. These robes are woven within 24 hours starting from processing thread by spinning cotton, colouring, weaving and stitching. It is considered as the biggest merit for the Buddhist devotees. Before the system of wearing yellow robes, the Buddhist monks used to wear the

Images taken from the " Kathin Chibar Daan" ceremony at Manu Bankul Village, Sabroom, South Tripura during the Post Survey Work of Manuscripts.

abandoned old clothes in the graveyards. At this, the monks used to get attacked by diseases. Buddha then permitted the monks to accept the offerings of robes from their relatives and devotees. Ordinarily, the robes of monks are of 6 colours – Root, Stem, Bark (of trees), dry leaf, fruits and flowers. However, the monks prefer the colour of red/ yellow flowers.

The term "*Mahamuni*" is very familiar to the Mog community of Tripura. As per legend, Buddha made sojourn to Arakan when Chanda Suriya was ruling the Kingdom. At the request of the King, Buddha gave consent to cast an image of Himself on the hillock called "Selagiri" near the capital city of Dhanyawadi. The Image is said to be the exact replica of Buddha, who breathed upon to enliven the same known as the Mahamuni. To the West, Arakan is known as the land of Great Image. In 1784, the Burmese King attacked Arakan and took away the Mahamuni Image to Mandalay. Today it is revered there as "Rakhain Phya". The Mog Community of Tripura has preserved the Mahamuni tradition. Wherever are the Mog settlements, there is one Mahamuni temple in each of them. It is the extension of old Arakanese heritage and a reminiscence of the most treasured possession of the Arakanese Kings. A big fair is congregated in the precinct of Mahamuni temple in a predetermined fullmoon day. The Mog devotees offer worship to the big Mahamuni Image as a gratitude for protecting the community. Special lightings of the Mahamuni Image and of the temple are done.

In fact, the Mahamuni is an exact replica image of Lord Buddha, which was cast by the Arakanese king "Chanda Suriya" when the former visited Arakan in his lifetime. A palm leaf manuscript entitled "Sappadanapakarana" provides a detailed account of the casting of this image. Wherever are the Mog settlements, there is one Mahamuni temple in each of them. It is the extension of old Arakanese heritage and a reminiscence of the most treasured possession of the Arakanese kings. Although the Mog of

Tripura are socially, culturally and politically isolated from their counterparts of Bangladesh and Arakan, it is the Mahamuni, which trace them back to the Arakanese [Rakhaing] history.

Kawn-hmo is an individual observance for performing good "Kamma". A household or the whole village community arrange special offerings to Buddhist monks, feed them, donate essential items, listen together to the Buddhist sermon and share merits with all including the departed ancestors. It is a community festival. Some are ordained as novice monk. It is essential for a Mog to be ordained as a Buddhist monk at least once in his lifetime. Usually a novice monk called as "Sraman" has to stay in the temple for seven days. In Kawn-hmo, the various type of offerings are made, like hanging money notes in a "Wish-tree", pasting rice in pagoda like structure (Hamaung-thawn), sending hot air balloon with lightings to the sky etc. For a rich man, it is a common thing to arrange such community celebration in memory of his ancestors.

Buddhist monks and devotees go to the forest for meditation and recluse for a certain period. They express their intention beforehand, but do not reveal the place for retreat. In deep night, they leave the village temple. The next day, the villagers search them out and construct a make-shift shelter to facilitate them in doing meditation. The villagers remain in the site during the day. By the late afternoon, they come back to the village. Only those monks and devotees on vow for recluse remain and undertake meditation (Bhavana). By the morning, the villagers come to the site with foods and waters for the hermits. Offering worship in such pure and pristine precinct is considered to be meritorious. The period for such hermitage ranges from seven to fifteen days. If all hermits are monks, then the villagers are not called to the site of retreat as they may disturb the meditating monks. For food, the monks come to the border of the forest. The villagers wait for them and put the foods into the bowl carried by individual monk. On the closing day of retreat, the villagers congregate in the precinct and listen to the sermons from the monks.

Pagoda is known as "*Zadi*" also. Such pagoda is constructed in the village temple or locality with relics of Buddha or any venerable monk. Well-to-do Mog families construct pagoda in memory of departed ancestors. While dedicating the Zadi, the Buddhist monks and community members are given a grand feast and community offering of worships is arranged.

Tripura is one of the states of North East which remains the least well-known part of India, linguistically and anthropologically. At a time of great social change and also increasing interest in the region, new research is constantly being produced. However, there are many older sources which are not easy to access, either because they are out of print or because they are only available from limited outlets. This paper aim to help those interested in the region. I have tried to focus on socio-cultural as well as historical facts about the Mog people in the light of manuscripts and not all of them have any great value. Some indeed seem to be actually untrustworthy, forwarding ethnic agendas rather than any objective description. It needs more time to discover the several unwritten history of the Mog tribe. Further, a deep and serious study of the these Mog manuscripts may open a new chapter of historical research on Tripura and adjoining regions.

References

1. Das Gupta, Malabika, *Class formation among the Mogs of Tripura,* Sujan Publications, 1997.
2. Kumar Suresh Singh, *Tribal movements in India,* vol. 1, Manohar, 1982.
3. Ghose, Kamalini, *Tribal insurrection in Tripura: A Study in Relative Deprivation,* Booklinks Corp., 1984.
4. Roy, B. Datta, Tribal identity and tension in north-east India, Omsons

Publications, 1989.

5. Roychoudhury, Nalini Ranjan, *Tripura through the ages: a short history of Tripura from the earliest times to 1947 AD,* Sterling, 1983.
6. Bhattacharyya, Suchintya, Genesis of tribal extremism in Tripura, Gyan Pub. House, 1st Oct., 1991.
7. Bhargava, Gopal K, Shankarlal C. Bhatt, *Land and people of Indian States and Union Territories,* 26, Tripura, Gyan Publishing House, 2006.
8. Bhattacharya, Gayatri, "Refugee Rehabilitation and its impact on Tripura's Economy", Omsons Publication, New Delhi.
9. Chakraborty, Dipannita, "Land Question in Tripura", Akansha Publishing House, New Delhi, 2004.
10. Thakur, Somendrachandra Devvarman, " Census Bibarani," In Bengali), Tribal Research Centre, Govt. of Tripura, Agartala, 1997.
11. Bhattacharya, N.N., "Religious Culture of North-Eastern India", Manohar Publishers, New Delhi.
12. Bhaumik, D.L., "Tribal Religion of Tripura", Tribal Research Institute, Govt. of Tripura, Agartala.
13. Sen, Kaliprasanna, Sri Rajmala, Agartala: Tribal Cultural Research Institute, 2003, reprint.
14. Singha, Kailash Chandra, 1984, '*Rajmala or Tripurar Itibrityo*', ed. (Chakraborty, et al); Barnamala Prakashani, Agartala.
15. Acknowledgements for manuscripts and oral sources used in this paper, I am greatly indebted to Shri Uggya Mog, Shri Nandiya Vikhu, Shri Madhu Mog and other Mog people of the Manu Bankul Village, Sabroom, South Tripura.

19

THE HISTORY OF TRIPURA
(Ancient and Medieval Period)
A birds eye-view

SITANATH DEY

On the lap of the Noth eastern region of India, a tiny state Tripura exists along with its sister states like Arunachal, Nagaland, Manipur, Mizoram, Meghalaya, Assam and Sikkim. Since most of these states inherit common cultural heritage they are rightly recognised as sisters. If India is known as an ethnological museum to the outside world for its wide racial diversity, this term may be aptly applied for the North East also within the country. The North-Eastern region of India is bounded by four countries China, Myanmar, Bangladesh and Bhutan and thereby it is land locked. The region is strategically important and a narrow Siliguri corridor connects it by road to the rest of India.

Tripura, small but culturally developed hilly picturesque state having total area measurring 10,486 Sq. km with a population of 3.1 million only. This state with its capital at Agartala is bounded by Sylhet district of Bangladesh in the North. Cachar district of Assam in the North-East, Mizoram in the East, the districts of Noakhali and Chittagong of Bangladesh in the West No less than nineteen tribal communities belonging to different ethnic and linguistic groups are to be found in different parts of the state. The people of plains from indeterminable times have been living side by side with tribal communities of the hills resulting in cultural exchanges. This state is famous as an abode of fourteen deities of our age-long tradition; recognised as one of the fifty-one shakta peethas of India bearing the sacred shrine of the Mother Tripureswari. In the southern part a Saiva tirtha named as Unokoti, an extraordinary sculptural erection of hoary antiquity images of Hindu gods and goddesses on the body of hillocks is situated in the north district of Kailasahar. This land is also affluent with so many archeological sites specially that of Bauddha cult at Pilak in the south.

Tripura kingdom (Sanskrit: Tripura; Anglicized: Tripera) was one of the largest ancient kindoms of the Tipra people of the Bodo Kachari ethnicity in the North Eastern region of Indian subcontinent having a chronicle of nearly eighteen kings till the modern period. It is believed that after first century BC the Tipra-Kingdom was established arround the confluence of the river Brahmaputra (Twima) with the Meghna and the Surma rivers in todays Central Bangladesh area. The capital was called 'Khorongma' and was in the Syllet district of the present Bangladesh.

There is no doubt that the hoary history of Tripura is shrouded in the mist of legends and there is paucity of the historical source materials of study. Only two authentic sources, the two manuscripts—Sri Rajamala in Bengali and Rajaratnakara in Sanskrit can help reconstruct the ancient and medieval history of Tripura. Like other sources of history Sri Rajmala contains the description and legends of the kins of Tripura, origin of the royal family and their reigns etc. Rajmala was first composed during the reign of 143rd King of Tripura Dharma Manikya (1431 AD–1461 AD). The royal priest Durlabhendra Chantai recited the Rajmala in Tripuri language. After listening to that recital, two eminent Sanskrit poets of the royal court, viz. Dvija Baneswar and Dvija Sukreswar translated these stories or wrote afresh in Bengali language. The first Lahar of first part of Rajmala written in

Bengali verse is considered as one of the ancient books of Bengali language and literature. This first part of Rajmala compiled in the beginning of the fifteenth century AD and the subsequent parts were compiled in later periods. The Rajmala has four parts, written in different times and by different authors. The first part of this Rajmala treats of the traditional period of Tripura kings which is mixed up with various mythological accounts. It informs us that the ancient name of Tripura was 'Kirata' from a person of that name of the luner race, the brother of Puru who was banished to the eastern provinces by his father Yajati. This king also known as Druhya who founded a city named Tribeg on the bank of the river Brahmaputra (Turyugma). Thereafter we get the description of 133 nos. of Kings of ancient period of whom the name of the 17th King Purusena and 41st king Trilocana is worth remembering since they were associated with the period of the Ramayana and the Mahabharata respectively. It is, however, questionable whether such statement as made in the Rajaratnakara and Rajmala respectively has any historicity at all. Traditionally the ruling house of Tripura is believed to be the one of the oldest friendly dynasty of India whose rulers claim their descent from the luner race. It is surprised to note that the famous Chandra dynasty of Tripura had its 17th decendent namely king Purusena who was contemporary to the mighty kind Daśaratha of Iksaku race of Ayodhya. It is explicitly mentioned in the Rajaratnakara, the famous historical manuscript of Tripura that king Purusena of Tripura went to Ayodhya to attend the sacrifice performed by king Dasaratha. He was accompanied by Rsis and Yogis and was guarded properly by his soldiers. In that sacrifice the Tripura king was honoured duly by King Dasaratha.

(Sri Rajaratnakara, first part, 9th Sarga 86–87).

अयोध्यामगद् धीमान् स्वसैन्यैः परिवेष्टितः।
ऋषिभिर्योगिभिः सार्धं यज्ञे दशरथस्य सः।।

राज्ञा दशरथेनायं पुरुसेनः प्रपूजितः।
दृष्ट्वा वहुनि तीर्थानि प्रत्यायातः स्वकं पुरम्।।

It is mentioned in the Rajamala that Trilochana the 41st king of the ancient dynasty of Tripua attended the Rajasuya Sacrifice performed by King Yudhisthira of the Mahabharata era and was honoured by the Latter.

The above mentioned two historical documents—Rajaratnakara and Rajmala are not self sufficient and not retained also in proper condition due to the long pasage of time. Rajmala in four parts fails to throw sufficient light on the life and culture of so many kings after 159th King Gobinda manikya of royal dynasty. Manifold historical aspects such as Economics, Sociology, Anthropology, Geography, Religion, Philosophy, Political Science etc. have not been adequately dealt with due to paucity of source materials.

Among the kings of the ancient period of Tripura, the 116th King Adi Dharma fa (635–75 AD) and and 133rd King Dharmadhar (1160–1225 AD) performed great sacrifices at Sylhet. During the regime of the 137th King Dangar—fa (1280–1300 AD), the capital was shifted from sylhet to the side of river Gomati. During the eighth Century three kins namely Cheng falai (118th, 710–75 AD), Lalit Ray (119th, 745–80 AD); Mukunda—fa 9120th, 780–815 AD) reigned in Tripura. No remarkable incident took place at that period. Good political relation, however, prevailed with neighbouring rulers of Bengal at that time.

In the nineth century three kings namely Kamal Ray (121st, 815–850 AD), Krishna Das (122nd, 850–885 AD) and Yasha—fa (123rd, 885–920 AD) ruled over the State. In that period Sylhet, Kailasahar, Dharmanagar etc. were under the jurisdiction of Tripura. It may be assumed that a group of skilful sculptors were engaged by the then rulers to engrave unique statues of a number of deities on the hill sides of Kailasahar.

During the tenth Century, the following kings ruled over Tripura:

	ruling period
124th, Mucana-fa	920–55 AD
125th, Sadhu Ray	955–80 AD
126th, Pratap Ray	980–1010 AD

As a whole, peaceful situation prevailed in Tripura at that period as Tripura was free from foreign invasion.

During eleventh century the following three rulers ruled over Tripura:

127th, Bisnuprasad	1010–45 AD
128th, Baneswar	1045–76 AD
129th, Birbahu	1075–1100 AD

In the twelfth Century four kings ruled over Tripura. They were as follows:

130th, Samrat	1100–1125 AD
131st, Champa	1125–40 AD
132nd, Meghraj	1140–60 AD
133rd, Dharmadhar	1160–1225 AD

The most fatal incident of 13th century was the invasion of Bengal by Bakiyar uddin Khilji and Laksman Sen, the King of Bengal was chased away. During this period four kings namely Chengthum–fa (134th, 1225–50 AD), Achong-fa (135th, 1250–70 AD), khichong-fa (1270–80 AD), 137th Dangar-fa (1280–1300 AD) were in power. In the year 1240 AD a Turk invader named Hirabant attacked Sylhet and then though the king Chengthum-fa was afraid, his queen had shown valour and inspired the soldiers and thereby compelled the invedars to retreat. After that undesirable incident, the ruler felt unsafe to stay in sylhet and during the regime of Dangar-fa they shifted towards Southern region and finally settled by the banks of the Howrah, Gomati and

Muhuri.

Among the four number of kings who ruled Tripura during fourteenth century AD, Ratna, the Son of Dangar-fa and the brother of Raja-fa was famous. Henceforth, Tripura kings used to add this Manikya title in their names. Two successors of Ratna Manikya were Pratap Manikya (1350–75 AD), Mukut Manikya (1375–1400 AD).

The most remarkable period so to say the golden era of the medieval period in the history of Tripura of 15th century was of Dharma Manikya (143rd, 1431–62 AD).

In this glorious period of the history of Tripura, Dharma Manikya and Dhanya Manikya of Chandra race achieved name and fame owing to their multifarious activities such as extension of the boundary of the kingdom, to initiate writing of historical literature, digging of vast water ponds, to build temples, to offer Land grants, to provide good adminis-tration, to organise disciplined and powerful military forces etc. In respect of the growth and development of the history of Tripura, the name of Dharma Manikya will be ever remembered. He was pioneer in the field of writing history of the royal dynasty of Tripura. For the benifit of his subjects Dharma Manikya arranged to dig a number of big ponds named after him as Dharma Sagar in different parts of Tripura. He bestowed a vast land measuring 29 drona to the learned Brahmins in Chaitra Sankranti, 1380 Shaka era, 4561 kali era or April 1459 AD. This calculation of Time period as inscribed in a copper plate bears an authentic historical proof of that panticular period written in Sanskrit, runs as follows:

''চন্দ্র বংশোদ্ভবর স্বাপ মহামাণিক্যজঃ সুধীঃ।
শ্রীশ্রীমদ্ ধর্মমাণিক্য ভূপশ্চন্দ্র কলোদ্ভবঃ।।
শাকে শূন্যষ্ট বিশ্বাব্দে বর্ষে সোমদিনে তিষ্টৈ।
ত্রয়োদশ্যাং সিতপক্ষে মেষে সূর্যস্য সংক্রমে।।

কৌতকাদি দ্বিজাগ্রেষু পূজিতেষু চাষ্টসু
ভূমিং দদৌ শয্যপূর্নাং দ্রৌণ বিংস নবাধিকাং
জলাশয়ং দ্বিজাযে মং ধর্মসাগরমাখ্যয়া
সভূমি ফলবৃক্ষাদি ভূমিতঃ দত্তবানহং।।
মমবংশপরিক্ষাণে যঃ কশ্চিত্তু পতিভবেৎ।
তস্য দাসস্য দাসোহ হং ব্রহ্মাছাত্তংন লোপয়েৎ।।

The regime of Dhanya manikya (145th, 1490–1515 AD), the eldest son of Dharma Manikya was undoubtedly a colourful one. In a very furmoil situation he ascended the royal throne of Tripura. He succeeded to subdue the conspiracy of some generals tactfully and reformed his army with the assistance of his two faithful as well as expert generals viz. Raiekathan and Raj Kachag. The king was able to expand his territory in a remarkable way. During his administration Tripura was attacked thrice by Husen Shah of Bengal. The aforesaid heroic generals of Dhanya Manikhya led the army susccessfully and defeated the invader. Both the king Dhanya and his queen took initiative for establishing famous temples Tripura Sundari, Bhubaneswari and Bhairaba Siva temple. He introduced the Trithamukha mela during Paush Sankranti and Dambaru, declaring its status like Prayaga. Dhanya Manikya was an ardent admirer of Indian music. Sanskrit Language and Literature. He brought a group of eminent singers and dancers to Tripura from Mithila (Tribeg) the famous seat on Indian music at that time with a view to develop the standard of music in the state. After Dhanya Manikya, Dhvaja Manikya, Deva Manikya, Bijay Manikya, Ananta Manikya and Jay Manikya adorned the royal throne. Owing to constant foreign attack they had spent their ruling period in anguish. After these rulers, a significant name appeared in the medieval history of Tripura, he was Amar Manikya, the grand son or Dhanya Manikya who ruled over the state efficiently. In his initiative the second part of Sri Rajmala was composed picturing the life history of his kins from 145th to 154th in serial. This continued volume of Rajmala was written during 1577 AD by an unknown writer after listening to the oral deliberation of the then old army Chief named Rana Catur Narayan. The famous vast pond Amar Sagar reflects till date the memory of King Amar Manikya. His last period of life was spent in a sorrowful condition. Failing to combat Mog force he left his capital in secret and had to succumb a tragic death.

These are in brief the historical informations of the medieval period of Tripura in accordance with Rajmala. Many more aspecs of historical analysis are left to be explored.

In this context it is to be pointed out that Tripura if properly explored idetified and edited may usher a new light in the matter of long expected reconstruction and re-evaluation of the history of Tripura.

It is hopeful that the ministry of culture, Govt. of India has come forward with a number of concrete programme and action plans to accomplish this task of National importance.

It is expected that the mission of uneartheing the hidden treasures of manuscripts of Tripura will be fullfilled in near future through the concerted efforts of National Mission for Manuscripts and Tripura State Archives and thereby the full fledged history of Tripura eventually will come into lime light.

20

ত্রিপুরার প্রাচীন পাণ্ডুলিপি ঐতিহ্যে ভবানীনাথের রামায়ণ ঃ সমীক্ষাত্মক বিশ্লেষণ

রাজীবচন্দ্র পাল

ভারতের উত্তর-পূর্বাঞ্চলের অন্তর্গত উপজাতি ও বাঙালী সংস্কৃতির মিশ্রণে গড়ে ওঠা ছোট্ট পার্বত্য রাজ্য ত্রিপুরা। ইতিহাস অনুধাবন করলে দেখা যায় একসময় গোটা বাংলাদেশের একটা অংশ ছিল রাজন্য শাসনাধীন এই ত্রিপুরা। পরবর্তীকালে রাষ্ট্রিক, আর্থ-সামাজিক বিপর্যয়, নানা ঝঞ্ঝা-বিক্ষুব্ধ সময় অতিক্রম করে বর্তমান বাংলাদেশ থেকে বহু মানুষ এই রাজ্যে এসে নিরাপত্তাহীনতা গ্লানি ও অরাজকতার হাত থেকে রক্ষা পেতে চেয়েছেন। এই প্রেক্ষিতেও যারা এসেছেন তাদের মধ্যে এমন অনেকেই ছিলেন যারা কাঁধে করে নিয়ে এসেছেন আপন সাহিত্য সংস্কৃতির কিছু নিদর্শন। তাই বর্তমানকালে ত্রিপুরার একেবারে প্রত্যন্ত গ্রাম জনপদ থেকে আবিষ্কৃত হয়ে চলেছে বহু মূল্যবান তথ্য ও প্রাচীন পুথি, যা সাহিত্যজগতে ত্রিপুরার নামকে আরো উচ্চাঙ্গের আসনে বসিয়েছে এই অনুসন্ধিৎসার প্রয়াসেই প্রাপ্ত আলোচ্য ভবানীনাথের 'রামায়ণ'-এর পুথি। প্রসঙ্গত উল্লেখ্য যে, এখনও পর্যন্ত যে সমস্ত পুথি ত্রিপুরায় পাওয়া গেছে সেগুলি ছাড়াও পূর্ণ এবং খণ্ডিত তুলট ও পুরোনো মিলেট কাগজের বহু প্রাচীন পুথি ত্রিপুরায় রয়েছে, যা কেবল প্রচার ও প্রকাশের অপেক্ষায়।

মধ্যযুগীয় বাংলা সাহিত্য ধারায় একটি সমৃদ্ধ শাখা হল অনুবাদ সাহিত্য। পুরাণ কাহিনীকে বিভিন্ন কবিরা যুগচাহিদা অনুসারে অনুবাদ করে জাতী জাগরণ ঘটাতে চেয়েছেন। এই অনুবাদ সাহিত্যের ধারায় রামায়ণের অনুবাদ বিশেষ মাত্রা

পেয়েছে।প্রথমে কৃত্তিবাসী রামায়াণ এবং তার পরেই ভবানীনাথের 'রামায়ণ' পুথির অনুবাদ জনপ্রিয়তা লাভ করেছে।

কবি ও কাব্যের সময়কাল সংক্রান্ত সঠিক সত্যার্থ করা মধ্যযুগীয় সাহিত্যে এক জ্বলন্ত সমস্যা। এ নিয়ে পণ্ডিত মহলে বাক্ বিতণ্ডার শেষ নেই। আর ভবানীনাথের 'রামায়ণ'ও এর ব্যতিক্রম নয়। কৃত্তিবাস ও তাঁর কাব্য সংক্রান্ত সঠিক তথ্য নির্ধারণ নিয়ে যত আলোচনা, সমালোচনা দেখা যায় ভবানীনাথ ও তাঁর 'রামায়ণ' সম্বন্ধে তা ঘটতে পারে। ভবানীনাথ নিজের ও পৃষ্ঠপোষক রাজার নামটি ছাড়া আর কোনো কথাই স্পষ্ট করে বলেন নি। মধ্যযুগের বেশীরভাগ কবি বা রচয়িতা ব্যক্তিগত ব্যাপারে নীরব ছিলেন।

ভবানীনাথ রাজা জয়চন্দ্রের আদেশে তাঁর 'রামায়ণ' কাব্য লিখেছেন - এইমাত্র তথ্য কাব্য থেকে জানা যায়। কিন্তু নৃপতি জয়চন্দ্র কোন সময়ে, কোথাকার রাজা ছিলেন, কিংবা অন্যান্য আনুষঙ্গিক প্রমাণ কাব্যে উল্লিখিত হয়নি। তবে বাংলা সাহিত্যের অধ্যাপক সুকুমার সেন মহাশয় নৃপতি জয়চন্দ্রকে জগৎ মাণিক্যের নামান্তর বলেছেন। তিনি তাঁর 'বাঙ্গালা সাহিত্যের ইতিহাস' গ্রন্থের দ্বিতীয় খণ্ডের ১০৬ পৃষ্ঠায় লিখেছেন —

'দ্বিজ' অথবা 'পণ্ডিত' ভবানীনাথের রামকথা অধ্যাত্ম-রামায়ণ অনুসরণে লেখা। ভবানীনাথ সম্ভবত ভুলুয়া (নোয়াখালির প্রত্যন্ত) রাজা জয়চন্দ্রের (নামান্তরে জগৎমাণিক্যের) সভাপণ্ডিত ('সদস্য ব্রাহ্মণ') ছিলেন। তাঁহার মুখে পুরাণ কথা শুনিয়া রাজা তাহাকে গ্রন্থ লিখিতে অনুরোধ করিয়াছিলেন।'

বলাবাহুল্য যে, সুকুমার সেন মহাশয় নৃপতি জয়চন্দ্রকে জগৎ মাণিক্যের সাথে একত্রিত করেছেন। প্রকৃতপক্ষে জয়চন্দ্র নৃপতির সত্য পরিচয় কী এবং তিনি কোথাকার রাজা ছিলেন? জয়চন্দ্র কী একই ব্যক্তি না ভিন্ন? কার রাজ্যসভায় ভবানীনাথ সভাপণ্ডিত ছিলেন? কখন তিনি তাঁর কাব্য লিখেছেন? এই সমস্ত প্রশ্নচিহ্নের সমাধানকল্পে বিস্তৃত গবেষণার প্রয়োজন। সময়সাপেক্ষগবেষণাত্মক দৃষ্টিভঙ্গি থেকে এই বিষয়ে অনুসন্ধিৎসা প্রয়োজন। তবে উঠে আসবে ত্রিপুরা তথা বাংলা সাহিত্যের অন্যান্য ঐতিহাসিক দিক, সমৃদ্ধ হবে সাহিত্যের ইতিহাস। এখানে বলতে হয় যে, মাণিক্য উপাধীধারী রাজা কেবলমাত্র ত্রিপুরার রাজাদের রাজবংশে প্রচলিত ছিল। তবে ত্রিপুরার 'রাজমালা' পুথির বিভিন্ন সংকলনে জগৎমাণিক্য নামে ত্রিপুরার কোনো প্রথতযশা রাজার নামোল্লেখ নেই। রাজমালাতে কেবলমাত্র মহারাজা গোবিন্দ মাণিক্যের ছোট ভাই নক্ষত্রমাণিক্যের (ছত্রমাণিক্য) পৌত্র জগৎ মাণিক্যের উল্লেখ আছে। তবে জগৎ মাণিক্যের সভায় রামায়ণ পুথি

রচিত হতে পারে। কিন্তু প্রাপ্ত আলোচ্য ভবানীনাথের 'রামায়ণ' পুথিতে শুধুমাত্র রাজা জয়চন্দ্রের কথা বর্ণিত হয়েছে।

সুতরাং স্পষ্টতই বিষয়টি নিয়ে ঐতিহাসিক দৃষ্টিভঙ্গিতে গবেষণার প্রয়োজন। মনে হয় এই বিষয় নিয়ে সুস্পষ্ট ও সঠিক তথ্য প্রাপ্তি ঘটলে সমৃদ্ধ হবে ত্রিপুরার রাজবংশের ইতিহাস, নোয়াখালি জেলার ভুলুয়া তথা স্বাধীনতা পূর্ব অবিভক্ত দেশের ঐতিহাসিকতা। সেইসঙ্গে অবিভক্ত ত্রিপুরা এবং বাংলাদেশের সাংস্কৃতিক রাষ্ট্রনৈতিক ঐতিহাসিক তথ্যাদিও সমৃদ্ধ হবে।

কাব্যের কোথাও জগৎ মাণিক্যের নাম পাওয়া যায়নি, জয়চন্দ্র নৃপতি ছাড়া। কাব্যে প্রাপ্ত ভণিতাগুলোতে তার প্রমাণ রয়েছে। যেমন কয়েকটি ভণিতা হল —

১। 'জয়চন্দ্র নরপতি রসিক সুজন অতি
সভাসদ ভবানী ব্রাহ্মণ।'

২. 'জয়চন্দ্র নরপতি আদেশ পাইয়া'
রচিলা ভবানীনাথ ব্যাস পুথি চাইয়া।'

প্রাচীন ভারতীয় আর্যভাষার সময়কালে যখন সংস্কৃত ভাষায় রামায়ণ, মহাভারত প্রভৃতি ধর্মগ্রন্থগুলো রচিত হয়েছে তখন থেকেই পুরাণকাহিনীর প্রতি মানুষের সহজাত আকর্ষণবোধ উত্তরোত্তর বৃদ্ধি পেতে থাকে। রামায়ণ কাহিনীর ক্ষেত্রেও তার ব্যতিক্রম ঘটেনি। যুগান্তর কাল থেকে কবিকুলতিলক বাল্মীকির রামায়ণ কাহিনীর জনপ্রিয়তা আজকের এই একবিংশ শতাব্দীর দ্বিতীয় দশকেও কোনো অংশেই হ্রাস পায়নি। বলাবাহুল্য যে, যুগান্তর অতিক্রম করে রামায়ণ কাহিনী এখনো জন মানসচিত্তে সমান মর্যাদার অধিষ্ঠিত। আর ভবানীনাথের 'রামায়ণ'-এর ক্ষেত্রেও এই জনপ্রিয়তা ক্রিয়াশীল।

মুদ্রণোত্তর সময়কালে সমস্ত বিদ্যাচর্চা হস্তলিখিত পুথির মধ্যেই সীমাবদ্ধ ছিল। তাই তখনকার সময় জনপ্রিয় কোনো কবির রচনা বহুজনসমাদৃত হয়ে জনসংযোগ ও জনমনোরঞ্জনের মাধ্যম হিসাবে অনুকৃত হতো। যে রচনা যতবেশি আস্বাদ্য ছিল সেই রচনা তত বেশিই অনুলিপিকারদের মাধ্যমে লিপিকৃত হতো। লিপিকারের দ্বারা গুণগ্রাহী রাজা কিংবা অমাত্য, বা পৃষ্ঠপোষক সেই মুলপুথির অনুলিপি করিয়ে নিতেন, ভবানীনাথের 'রামায়ণ' পুথির ক্ষেত্রেও এর ব্যতিক্রম ঘটেনি। পুথির বিভিন্ন অংশ বিভিন্ন লিপিকারের দ্বারা জনপ্রিয়তা অনুযায়ী লিপিকৃত হয়ে অসংখ্য পালাকাব্যের উদ্ভব ঘটিয়েছে। সুতরাং জয়চন্দ্র রাজার রাজসভায় রচিত

কাব্য ত্রিপুরার সঙ্গে সঙ্গে গোটা দেশে জনপ্রিয় হয়ে উঠেছিল।
সাহিত্য, সমাজ ও সংস্কৃতি এই শব্দগুলো একে অপরের সাথে ওতপ্রোতভাবে জড়িত। প্রখ্যাত পাশ্চাত্য দার্শনিক অ্যারিস্টটল তাঁর 'Poetics' গ্রন্থে বলেছিলেন 'Art is imitation' অর্থাৎ সাহিত্য হল অনুকরণ, এই অনুকরণ সমাজের, এই অনুকরণ জীবনের। আর সে কারণে কোনো সাহিত্যে রচনাকারের সমসাময়িক সমাজ জীবনধারার পরিচয় স্বাভাবিকভাবে উঠে আসে। আলোচ্য রামায়ণ পুথিতে সপ্তদশ শতাব্দীর রাজনৈতিক বিধ্বংসী পরিস্থিতিকেই পাওয়া যায়। ভবানীনাথ রাম, লক্ষ্মণ, ভরত ও শত্রুঘ্ন এই চার ভ্রাতার যুদ্ধজয়ের কাহিনীর মাধ্যমে পরাধীন দেশের চিত্রকেই তুলে ধরেছেন।

সপ্তদশ-অষ্টাদশ শতাব্দীতে বিদেশীর শাসনে পর্যুদস্ত সমাজপ্রেক্ষিতে জাতীয় জাগরণ ঘটানোর প্রয়াস থেকেই ভবানীনাথ তাঁর বীররসাত্মক কাব্য রচনা করেছেন। চৈতন্য পরবর্তীযুগের এই কবি রামায়ণের অসংখ্য কবির মধ্যে নিঃসন্দেহে বাঙালী জনমানবচিত্তে স্থায়ী আসনের দাবীদার। সুতরাং তিনি যে রাজার রাজসভা আলোকিত করেছেন সেই 'জয়চন্দ্র নরপতি' সপ্তদশ শতাব্দীর কোনো এক সময়ে বর্তমান ছিলেন। কিন্তু নক্ষত্র মাণিক্যের সঙ্গে জয়চন্দ্রের সাদৃশ্য এখানে নেই বলেই মনে হয়। রামকথার নবকাব্য নির্মাণের মাধ্যমে ভবানীনাথ গোটা বঙ্গদেশে জনপ্রিয় হয়ে উঠেছিলেন।

উপনিবেশোত্তর কালের প্রবহমানতায় মানব জীবন যখন বিপর্যস্ত তখন আলোচ্য পুথির যুগ চাহিদা একান্ত কাম্য। রাম-লক্ষ্মণ এখানে দৈব অবতার নন; আর্থ-সামাজিক প্রেক্ষিতে হয়ে উঠেছেন রাষ্ট্রনৈতিক নেতৃত্ব। পৌরাণিক অঙ্গন ছাড়িয়ে প্রতিটি চরিত্র স্বমহিমায় একান্ত বাস্তব যুগপ্রভাবিত হয়ে উঠেছে গ্রন্থকারের সৃষ্টির কুশলতায়।

সুতরাং ভবানীনাথের 'রামায়ণ'পুথিতে প্রাপ্ত নৃপতি জয়চন্দ্র ও সুকুমার সেন মহাশয় কথিত জগৎমাণিক্য সম্পূর্ণ স্বতন্ত্র ব্যক্তি। তবে জয়চন্দ্রের অন্য নাম জগৎ মাণিক্য কিনা তা কাব্যে কোথাও পাওয়া যায় না। তাই উল্লিখিত এই বিষয় নিয়ে মধ্যযুগীয় ধোঁয়াশা থেকেই যাবে। উপযুক্ত ঐতিহাসিক তথ্য ছাড়া এই সমস্যার নিরসন অবান্তর বলেই উল্লেখ করা চলে। সমাজ পরিবর্তনশীল। সময় চলমান। তাই কালের আবর্তে কোনো এক মুহূর্তে উন্মোচিত হবে উল্লিখিত সমস্যাগুলোর রহস্যাবরণ। সমাজ-ইতিহাসাশ্রিত সমালোচনাত্মক বিচার বিশ্লেষণ ও কাব্য বিচারাত্মক সাহিত্য সমীক্ষণ এখানে অত্যন্ত প্রাসঙ্গিক।

21

ত্রিপুরার ইতিহাসের উপাদানে বিভিন্ন পুঁথি

জহর আচার্জী

ত্রিপুরার প্রকৃত ইতিহাস আলোচনা করতে গেলে 'রাজমালা' নামক পুঁথি অপরিহার্য। সেইসঙ্গে ইতিহাসাশ্রয়ী বিভিন্ন পাণ্ডুলিপি (manuscript) চর্চা করতে গেলে শিলালিপি (stone inscription) তাম্রলিপি (Coper plate inscription), মুদ্রা (Coin inscription) ইত্যাদির কথা অবশ্যই এসে যায়। এসব ছাড়া শুধু রাজমালার উপর নির্ভর করে ত্রিপুরার ইতিহাস লেখা সম্ভব নয়। ত্রিপুরায় রয়েছে বিভিন্ন লেখক দ্বারা রচিত বিভিন্ন ধরণের রাজমালা এবং এর পাণ্ডুলিপি। এসব পাণ্ডুলিপি এখন খুব একটা পাওয়া যায় না। প্রাচীন রাজমালার পাণ্ডুলিপির মধ্যে অষ্টাদশ শতাব্দীর মধ্যভাগে রচিত একটা পাণ্ডুলিপি কলকাতার বঙ্গীয় সাহিত্য পরিষদ-এ সংরক্ষণ রয়েছে। অবশ্য সেটি বই আকারে ১৯৬৮ খ্রীষ্টাব্দে ত্রিপুরা সরকার কর্তৃক প্রকাশিত হয়েছিল।

রামনারায়ণ দেব কর্তৃক কপি করা সেই রাজমালায় তৃতীয় বিজয় মাণিক্যের (১৭৪৮ খ্রীঃ) নাম উল্লেখ রয়েছে। সুতরাং বলা যায় যে, সে রাজমালা লেখা হয়েছিল দ্বিতীয় ইন্দ্র মাণিক্য কিংবা তৃতীয় বিজয় মাণিক্যের সমসাময়িক কালে। এতে রাজমালার প্রাচীনত্ব লক্ষ্য করা যায়। তাছাড়া রয়েছে 'রাজরত্নাকর' এবং 'রাজরত্নাকরম্' নামক কিছু সংস্কৃত পাণ্ডুলিপি। 'রাজরত্নাকর' কবে বা কোন রাজার আমলে লেখা হয়েছিল তা এখনও জানা যায়নি।

ত্রিপুরার প্রায় প্রত্যেক রাজাই যার যার মতো করে রাজ পণ্ডিতদের দ্বারা নতুনভাবে রাজকাহিনী লিখতে সচেষ্ট ছিলেন। মহারাজ বীরচন্দ্র ও (১৮৬২-

৯৬ খ্রীঃ) 'রাজরত্নাকর' লিখিয়েছিলেন। এমন কী ত্রিপুরার শেষ দুইজন মহারাজও এ ব্যাপারে পিছিয়ে ছিলেন না। নতুন করে রাজমালা লেখার কাজ অব্যাহত ছিল। তাঁর সময়ে কালীপ্রসন্ন সেন রাজআজ্ঞায় 'শ্রীরাজমালা' গ্রন্থ নতুনভাবে সম্পাদনা করেছিলেন। তবে সেন মহাশয়ের শ্রীরাজমালার 'মধ্যমণি' বিশেষভাবে উল্লেখযোগ্য। ভুপেন্দ্র চন্দ্র চক্রবর্তী মহাশয়ও স্কুলের ছাত্রদের জন্য দ্রুত পঠন হিসেবে নতুনভাবে 'রাজমালা' গ্রন্থ রচনা করেন। এসব ব্যাপারে রাজকুমার নবদ্বীপ চন্দ্র বাহাদুর তাঁর 'আবর্জনার ঝুড়ি' নামক এক প্রবন্ধে বলেছিলেন, 'রাজবাড়িতে দুই এখন পুঁথি লেখক ব্রাহ্মণ পণ্ডিত নিয়ত পুঁথি লিখিতেন এবং তাহারা যন্ত্রের মতো লেখার খাটুনি খাটিতেন... এই পুঁথিগুলির পোনর আনাই ঐতিহাসিক কালের পূর্বেকার তথ্য।'

দুর্গামণি উজির কর্তৃক ১৮২৮ খ্রীষ্টাব্দে সংশোধিত এক রাজমালার পাণ্ডুলিপির কথা জানা যায়। দুর্গামণি উজির রাজমালা সংশোধন করতে গিয়ে বললেন —

'পুরাতন রাজমালা আছিল রচিত।
প্রসঙ্গেতে অলগ্নিক ভাষা যে কুৎসিত।।
পূর্ব্ব প্রসঙ্গ পরে পর পূর্ব্বে কত।
সেই কারণে লোকে নাহি বুঝে যত।।
ত্রিপুরা রাজ্যের নাম ত্রিপুর যে মতে।
ত্রিপুর রাজার প্রমাণ না লিখিছে তাতে।।
বারশ আটত্রিশ মন ত্রিপুরা যখনি।
তাহাকে সুধিল পুনি উজীর দুর্গামণি।'

সে পাণ্ডুলিপি বই আকারে প্রকাশিত হয়েছিল ১৮৯৬ খ্রীষ্টাব্দে। কালীপ্রসন্ন সেন কর্তৃক রচিত চার খণ্ডে 'শ্রীরাজমালা' রচিত হয়েছিল ১৯২৬ থেকে ১৯৩৪ খ্রীষ্টাব্দের মধ্যে। সে রাজমালার অনৈতিহাসিক বিবরণ মোটেই গ্রহণযোগ্য নয়।

কালীপ্রসন্ন সেন মহাশয় নতুনভাবে রাজমালা রচনা করতে গিয়ে পৌরাণিক অংশ বিশেষভাবে সংশোধন করলেন। অন্যদিকে তিনি ত্রিপুরার উপজাতি রাজগণকে মহাভারতের সমসাময়িক বলে প্রতিপন্ন করার বৃথা চেষ্টাও করেছিলেন। মধ্য ভারতের ত্রিপুরা নামক রাজ্যের সঙ্গে পূর্ব ভারতের বর্তমান ত্রিপুরা রাজ্যের

তালগোল পাকিয়ে ফেলেছিলেন। তাঁর রাজমালায় অনৈতিহাসিক বিবরণ বিজ্ঞান সম্মত নয়। তিনি ছিলেন রাজকর্মচারী। তাঁর পক্ষে রাজাকে সন্তুষ্ট করা কিছু অসম্ভব ছিল না। যাই হোক, এসব ছাড়া ত্রিপুরার ইতিহাস বিষয়ক যে সব পাণ্ডুলিপির কথা জানা যায় সেগুলো হল, 'শ্রেণীমালা' 'চম্পকবিজয়', 'গাজীনামা', 'কৃষ্ণমালা', 'রাজমালিকা', 'যোগিনী মলিকা', 'লক্ষণমালিকা', 'বাল্যকানিম্ময়', 'হরগৌরীসংবাদ', ইত্যাদি।

'শ্রেণীমালা' দুর্গামণি উজির কর্তৃক রচিত। সেটি সম্ভবত ঊনবিংশ শতাব্দীর প্রথম ভাগে রচিত। শ্রেণীমালার পাণ্ডুলিপি কখনো বই আকারে প্রকাশিত হয়নি। সে পাণ্ডুলিপিটি উজির বাড়ি থেকেই পাওয়া গিয়েছিল। এটাও রাজমালারই নামান্তর। অন্যদিকে শেখ মনোহর কর্তৃক রচিত 'গাজীনামা' সমশের গাজী এবং কৃষ্ণ মাণিক্যের যুদ্ধ বিগ্রহ ইত্যাদি নিয়ে রচিত। সেটির রচনাকাল কৃষ্ণ মাণিক্যের সমসাময়িক। প্রকৃতপক্ষে কৃষ্ণ মাণিক্যকে সমশের গাজীর ভয়ে জঙ্গলে বেশ কিছুকাল অবস্থান করতে হয়েছিল। 'কৃষ্ণমালায়' মহারাজ কৃষ্ণ মাণিক্যের রাজত্ব সম্বন্ধে বিবরণ রয়েছে। সেটিরও রচনাকাল কৃষ্ণ মাণিক্যের সময়। 'হর গৌরী সংবাদ'এবং 'রাজমালিকা' সম্ভবত সপ্তদশ শতাব্দীর প্রথমভাগে রচিত। কারণ সেখানে কল্যাণ মাণিক্যের (১৬২৬ থেকে ১৬৬০ খ্রীঃ) কথা বর্ণনা করা হয়েছে। কল্যাণ মাণিক্য যে 'গুণের সাগর' হয়ে জন্ম গ্রহণ করবেন সে কথা প্রথম ধর্ম মাণিক্যকে রাজ পণ্ডিতগণ বলেছিলেন রাজমালিকায় হরগৌরী সংবাদে শঙ্কর নিজের মুখে নাকি বলেছেন যে এমন রাজা ভবিষ্যতে রাজকুলে জন্মগ্রহণ করবেন। সেখানে নাকি লেখা ছিল

'ই বলিয়া দই দ্বিজে পুস্তক আনিল।
হরগৌরী সম্বাদেত প্রমাণ জানাইল।।'

তাছাড়া ১৮৪৫ খ্রীঃ দ্বিজবঙ্গ চন্দ্র কর্তৃক রচিত 'ত্রিপুর বংশাবলী' নামক হস্তলিখিত পুঁথি রয়েছে। এই 'ত্রিপুর বংশাবলী' পুঁথি রাজমালারই নামান্তর। সে পুঁথির কয়েকটি লাইন এখানে উপস্থাপন করা হল,

'বিজয় মাণিক্য রাজা এমত করিয়া সজ্জা,
দিগ্বিজয়ে গমন করিল।
গোমতী নদী দিয়া, চলে নৌকা ভাটি বাইয়া।" ইত্যাদি

অবশ্য এর মধ্যে কিছু পুঁথি বই আকারে প্রকাশিত হয়েছে। বিভিন্ন সময় ত্রিপুরার রাজগণ বিভিন্ন 'রাজমালা'গ্রন্থ রচনার জন্য সর্বদা লোক নিয়োগ করতেন।

সে সব রাজমালা রচনার ক্ষেত্রে মহারাজগণ পরিবর্তন, পরিবর্ধনও নিজেদের ইচ্ছেমত রাজপণ্ডিতদের মাধ্যমে সংশোধন করে নিতেন। উক্ত আলোচনা থেকে স্পষ্ট প্রতীয়মান হয় যে, প্রথম রাজমালার রচনাকাল পঞ্চদশ শতাব্দী না হয়ে আরো পরবর্তী সময়ে হওয়া খুবই স্বাভাবিক।

ত্রিপুরার ইতিহাস সংক্রান্ত আরো কিছু মূল্যবান পুঁথির মধ্যে রয়েছে রত্নকুন্দলী এবং অর্জুনদাস বর্ণিত ত্রিপুরা দেশের কথা। রত্নকুন্দলী এবং অর্জুনদাস অষ্টাদশ শতাব্দীর প্রারম্ভে ত্রিপুরায় অবস্থান করেছিলেন। তাঁরা দুজন মূলতঃ ছিলেন আসাম রাজার রাষ্ট্রদূত। দেশে ফিরে দিয়ে তাঁরা তখনকার ত্রিপুরা রাজ্যের মোটামুটি বর্ণনা লিপিবদ্ধ করে গেছেন। তাছাড়া আবুলফজল রচিত আইন-ই-আকবরী, মির্জানাথন রচিত বাহারিস্তান-ই-গায়েবি ইত্যাদি উল্লেখযোগ্য। অন্যদিকে মগ সম্প্রদায়ের কিছু পাণ্ডুলিপি আবিষ্কৃত হয়েছে। যতটুকু জানা যায় চকমা সম্প্রদায়েরও কিছু পাণ্ডুলিপি রয়েছে।

তবে চকমা সম্প্রদায়ের যেসব পাণ্ডুলিপি এখন পর্যন্ত পাওয়া গেছে সেগুলি ত্রিপুরার ইতিহাস সম্মত নয়। সেগুলি মূলত আয়ুর্বেদ, তন্ত্র-মন্ত্র ইত্যাদি নিয়ে রচিত। মগদের পাণ্ডুলিপি পাঠোদ্ধার হলে ত্রিপুরার ইতিহাস সম্বন্ধে নতুনভাবে কিছু জানা যেতে পারে। আধুনিক গবেষণায় প্রমাণিত হয়েছে যে, আরাকানের সঙ্গে কুমিল্লার 'পট্টিকেরা' রাজ্যের বৈবাহিক, রাজনীতি এবং বাণিজ্যিক সম্পর্ক ছিল। হরিকেলের মুদ্রায় আরাকান রাজদের পুরোপুরি প্রভাব লক্ষ্য করা যায়। তখন ত্রিপুরা হরিকেল রাজ্যের অধীনে ছিল। পাশাপাশি এও বলা যায় যে, 'তিপ্রা' সম্প্রদায়ের পূর্বেই মগরা এদেশে এসেছিলেন। সুতরাং মগদেরকেই 'ভূমিপুত্র' বলা যেতে পারে। এ ব্যাপারে প্রত্নতাত্ত্বিক নিদর্শন যথা পিলাক সভ্যতা, হরিকেল মুদ্রা, পট্টিকেরা রাজ্যের সঙ্গে ঘনিষ্ঠ যোগাযোগ ইত্যাদি রয়েছে। পিলাক সভ্যতায় মগদের যে অবদান ছিল তাতে কোন সন্দেহ নেই। 'পিল্লাক' শব্দটি মগজাত শব্দ। যার অর্থ হল লুক্কায়িত সম্পদ। এসব ছাড়া ব্রজেন্দ্র দত্ত রচিত 'উদয়পুর বিবরণ, 'ধর্মনগর বিবরণ', 'খোয়াই বিবরণ', 'সোনামুড়া বিবরণ', পুঁথিগুলিও ত্রিপুরার ইতিহাস রচনায় সহায়ক। অবশ্য এসব পুঁথি বই আকারে প্রকাশিত হয়েছে।

১৮৯৬ খ্রীষ্টাব্দে কৈলাস চন্দ্র সিংহ মহাসয় গদ্যে রাজমালা (ত্রিপুরার ইতিবৃত্ত) নামক গ্রন্থ লিখে ত্রিপুরার ইতিহাসকে অনেকটা বিজ্ঞান ভিত্তির উপর দাঁড় করাতে সচেষ্ট ছিলেন। অবশ্য সেজন্য তাঁকে রাজরোষে পড়তে হয়েছিল।

তিনি ত্রিপুরার রাজন্যবর্গের ইতিহাসকে কাঠগড়ায় দাঁড় করিয়ে লিখেছিলেন 'বৌদ্ধ বিপ্লব সময়ে ব্রাহ্মণগণ ভারতের দিকদিগন্তে তাহাদের আধিপত্য বিস্তারের জন্য যত্নবান হইয়াছিলেন। ভারতের যে সব ক্ষত্রিয় নরপতি বৌদ্ধধর্ম গ্রহণ পূর্বক ব্রাহ্মণদের অসীম অধিপত্যের মূলে কুঠারঘাত করিতে সমুদ্যত হইয়াছিলেন, ব্রাহ্মণগণ সেই ক্ষত্রিয়বর্গকে ব্রাত্য শ্রেণীতে সন্নিবিষ্ট করিয়া আপন আশ্রয়দাতা নরপতিবর্গকে 'চন্দ্র-সূর্য বংশীয়' প্রচার করতঃ তাঁহাদের শ্রেষ্ঠত্ব প্রতিপাদন মানসে বদ্ধপরিকর হইয়াছিলেন।'

এখানে উল্লেখযোগ্য যে ত্রিপুরার ইতিহাস সম্বন্ধীয় পাণ্ডুলিপি বেশি একটা পাওয়া যায় না। এর মধ্যে দুটো পাণ্ডুলিপির কথা বিশেষভাবে উল্লেখযোগ্য এবং সে দুটো পাণ্ডুলিপিই রয়েছে ত্রিপুরার সরকারি সংগ্রহশালায়। কিন্তু সেই সংগ্রহশালার অবজ্ঞায় এবং অদক্ষতায় আজ তা জীর্ণ অবস্থায় পড়ে আছে। এর একটি হল 'রাজরত্নাকর' নামক সংস্কৃত রাজমালা। অবশ্য সেটি কবেকার রচিত কিংবা তার ঐতিহাসিক মূল্য কতটুকু তা ত্রিপুরাবাসী জানেন না। অন্যটি হল 'সূর্য ফুজা খেলাই মণি' নামক কক্ বরক্ ভাষায় এবং বাংলা হরফে লিখিত চৌদ্দদেবতার মন্ত্র সমন্ধীয় পুঁথি। সেটা লেখা হয়েছিল মহারাজ মহেন্দ্র মাণিক্যের আমলে ১৬২১ শকাব্দে তথা ১৬৯৯ খ্রীষ্টাব্দে। সেটি চৌদ্দদেবতার মন্ত্র সমন্ধীয় হলেও এর সঙ্গে ত্রিপুরার ইতিহাস জড়িয়ে রয়েছে। এর অন্যতম গুরুত্ব হল কক্-বরক্ ভাষার আদিতম লিখিত পুঁথি। সে মূল্যবান পুঁথিটি সম্বন্ধেও সরকারি সংগ্রহশালায় লোকেরা পুরোপুরি উদাসীন।

বঙ্গীয় সাহিত্য পরিষদে রক্ষিত রাজমালা নামক পুঁথিটির অনুলেখক হলেন বাংলাদেশের বিদ্যাকট নিবাসী রামনারায়ণ দেব। সেই কপি করা পুঁথিটির মুল কবি সম্বন্ধে কোনো কিছুই জানা যায় না। সেটি পূর্ণাঙ্গ পুঁথি। এর ভাষা স্বচ্ছ ও সরল। অবশ্য বানানে প্রচুর ভুল রয়েছে। তিনি যে খুব বিদ্বান লোক ছিলেন না তার প্রমাণ পাওয়া যায় সেই পুঁথি থেকে। তা সত্ত্বেও সেটিকে প্রাপ্ত বাংলার রাজমালার মধ্যে প্রাচীনতম পুঁথি বলা যায়। তাই ত্রিপুরার ইতিহাস রচনায় এ পুঁথিটির খুব গুরুত্ব রয়েছে। কারণ, পরবর্তী সময়ে রচিত সম্পাদিত, পরিমার্জিত কিংবা পরিবর্ধিত ভাবে লিখিত রাজমালাগুলোর মধ্যে স্বেচ্ছাচারিতা বা মর্জিমাফিকতা এবং অনেক কাল্পনিক ব্যাপার স্থান পেয়েছিল।

পরবর্তী সময়ে রচিত পুঁথিগুলোর মাধ্যমে ত্রিপুরা রাজ্যের প্রকৃত ইতিহাস বিকৃত হয়েছিল এবং পাশাপাশি ইতিহাস চাপা দেবার চেষ্টাও হয়েছিল। সেক্ষেত্রে

রামানারায়ণ দেবের রাজমালাকে বেশি গুরুত্ব দেওয়া উচিত বলে আমরা মনে করি। বিভিন্ন সংস্কৃত রাজমালা কবে রচিত হয়েছিল এবং এগুলোর মূল পাণ্ডুলিপিগুলি কোথায় তা সঠিকভাবে জানা যায় না। একথা বলছি এ কারণে যে, বীরচন্দ্র মাণিক্যের আমলে এবং মহারাজ বীরেন্দ্র কিশোর মাণিক্য ও বীর বিক্রমের আমলেও রাজমালা রচনার উদ্যোগ লক্ষ্য করা যায়।

ত্রিপুরার ইতিহাস বিশেষজ্ঞ এবং সুপণ্ডিত ড. দীনেশ চন্দ্র সরকার মহাশয় রাজমালা সম্বন্ধে মন্তব্য করে বলেছিলেন, 'ত্রিপুরার ইতিহাস লেখকেরা 'রাজমালা' প্রভৃতি গ্রন্থের দ্বারা প্রভাবিত। কিন্তু ত্রিপুরারাজ্যবিষয়ক ঐ ধরণের গ্রন্থের প্রথমাংশ সম্পূর্ণ নির্ভরযোগ্য নহে।' তিনি আরো বলেন, 'রাজমালা'-র প্রথম লহর খ্রীষ্টিয় পঞ্চদশ শতাব্দীতে রচিত বলিয়া বিশ্বাস করা হয়, ইহা 'অষ্টাদশ শতাব্দীর মধ্যভাগের পর (সম্ভবতঃ ঊনবিংশ শতাব্দীতে) লিখিত হইয়াছিল কারণ,ইহাতে ১৭৫২ খ্রীষ্টাব্দে রচিত 'অন্নদমাঙ্গল' এবং অষ্টাদশ শতাব্দীর প্রথম ভাগের পর রচিত একান্নপীঠ বিষয়ক একখানি আধুনিক তান্ত্রিক গ্রন্থের প্রভাব রহিয়াছে।' ড. দীনেশ চন্দ্র সরকার মহাশয় আরো বলেছিলেন, 'আমি সন্দেহ করিয়াছিলাম যে, প্রাচীন ও মধ্যযুগ সম্পর্কে 'রাজমালা'তে যাহা বলা হইয়াছে, তাহা সর্বদা গ্রহণযোগ্য হইতে পারে না।' অন্য এক ত্রিপুরার ইতিহাস বিশেষজ্ঞ অধ্যাপক অমরেন্দ্র নাথ লাহিড়ী বলেন, 'বিভিন্ন সময়ে রচিত এই (রাজমালার) গ্রন্থের ছাপানো যে কয়টি খণ্ড আছে, কোনো কোনো পণ্ডিতের মতে সেগুলি সংকলিত হয়েছে উনবিংশ শতাব্দীর প্রথমদিকে। ফলে রাজমালায় ত্রিপুরার ১৮৪ জন রাজার যে তালিকা আছে, তাঁদের মধ্যে তথাকথিত প্রথম নৃপতি 'চন্দ্রের' পরবর্তী ধর্মধর বা ছেংফাছাগ পর্যন্ত ১৩৯ জনই ছিলেন প্রায় অনৈতিহাসিক ব্যক্তিত্ব। পরবর্তী ১৪০ থেকে ১৮৪ সংখ্যক ব্যক্তিরা ইতিহাসের গণ্ডিতে আসেন।'

উক্ত আলোচনা থেকে স্পষ্ট প্রতীয়মান হয় যে রাজআজ্ঞায় রচিত রাজমালায় ত্রিপুরার প্রকৃত ইতিহাস প্রতিফলিত হয়নি। তাই ত্রিপুরার ইতিহাস লেখার জন্য বিজ্ঞান সম্মত বিচার বিশ্লেষণ অত্যন্ত প্রয়োজন। সে সঙ্গে ত্রিপুরার মুদ্রা, তাম্রলিপি, শিলালিপি, টেরাকোটা, পটারী ইত্যাদি বিশ্লেষণের প্রয়োজন রয়েছে।

22

প্রাচীন ত্রিপুরার পুঁথি-লিখনে রাজানুকূল্য ও সংস্কৃতি-সংবর্ধন

সংহিতা দাস

আলোচ্য গবেষণা-নিবন্ধে আমি সংস্কৃত পুঁথি সম্পর্কেই কিছু আলোচনা করার জন্য মনস্থ করেছি, তবে যেসব বাংলা পুঁথিতে প্রাচীন ত্রিপুরার চির সংস্কৃতিমনস্ক রাজরাজড়াদের কথা সংস্কৃত ভাষায় পুষ্পিকাতে ব্যবহৃত হয়েছে, তাও আমাদের বিশ্লেষণের বহির্ভূত হবে না।

সাম্প্রতিককালে কবিগুরু রবীন্দ্রনাথ ঠাকুরের (১৮৬১-১৯৪১) ১৫০তম জন্মজয়ন্তী উৎসব উপলক্ষ্যে ভারত তথা বিশ্বব্যাপী কবিগুরুর অনন্য অবদানের কথা স্মরণ বরণ ও মনন করছে, তাই মনে রেখে পুঁথিসংক্রান্ত আলোচনার সূত্রপাত করছি। উল্লেখ্য, কবিগুরু রবীন্দ্রনাথ মহারাজ বীর বিক্রম কিশোর মাণিক্য বাহাদুরের আমলে (১৯২৩-১৯৪৭) সপ্তমবার বা শেষবার ১৯২৬ খ্রীষ্টাব্দের ১০ই ফাল্গুন ত্রিপুরায় শুভ পদার্পণ করেন এবং কুঞ্জবনের 'পুষ্পবন্ত প্রাসাদে' (অধুনা রাজ্যপাল-নিবাস) অবস্থান করেন। তখন ১৩ই ফাল্গুন ত্রিপুরার সাহিত্যিক প্রেক্ষাপট সম্পর্কে কবিগুরু সাহিত্যিক ও রাজকীয় ব্যক্তিবর্গের সঙ্গে আলোচনায় প্রবৃত্ত হন। সেখানে রাজসভাভূষণ হরিদাস ভট্টাচার্য্যও উপস্থিত ছিলেন। ভট্টাচার্য্য মহোদয় লিখলেন — তখন রাজমালা — সম্পাদক কালীপ্রসন্ন সেন বিদ্যাভূষণ, মহারাজকুমার ব্রজেন্দ্রকিশোর দেববর্মণের উপস্থিতিতে কালীপ্রসন্ন বাবু তার লিখিত রাজমালার পাণ্ডুলিপির ও গীতচন্দ্রোদয়ের পুঁথি কবিগুরুকে দেখালেন।..

গীতচন্দ্রোদয়ের পুঁথিখানা নিয়ে কবি প্রথমেই হস্তাক্ষরের বিশেষ প্রশংসা করলেন এবং কাব্য রসের মাধুর্যে মুগ্ধ হয়ে বলেছিলেন 'এই পুস্তকখানা অতি সত্তরই যাহাতে স্থানীয় কিশোর সাহিত্য সমাজ প্রকাশ করেন তদ্বিষয়ে সচেষ্ট হওয়া কর্তব্য। পুস্তকখানা যাহাতে পরহস্তগত না হয় তদ্বিষয়েও সাবধানতা অবলম্বন করিয়ে বারম্বার বলিলেন'। (রবি, ত্রৈমাসিক, ২য় বর্ষ, ৪র্থ সংখ্যা, আগরতলা ১৩৩৫ ত্রিপুরাব্দ)।

আজ থেকে ৩৫৬ বৎসর পূর্বের একখানা গাছের বাকলের পুঁথি আমাদের দৃষ্টিগোচর হয়েছে। ১৫৭৭ শকাব্দের ১০ই আষাঢ়, পুঁথিটি মহারাজ কল্যাণ মাণিক্যের রাজত্বকালে (১৬২৫-১৬৬০ খ্রীঃ) লিখিত হয়েছিল। পুষ্পিকাতে লিপিকার গোপীনাথ শর্মা লিখলেন — 'শ্রীরস্তু লেখকে সদা।' এর ভাষা সংস্কৃত। উক্ত পুঁথিতে দশকর্ম বিধানের উপনয়ন পদ্ধতি সম্পর্কে বলা হয়েছে। এই 'রাজসনেয়ি উপনয়নপদ্ধতিঃ' শীর্ষক পুঁথির বিষয়বস্তুতে আছে — গর্ভাধান, সীমন্তোন্নয়ন, নামকরণ, নিষ্ক্রমণ, অন্নপ্রাশন, চূড়াকরণ তথা সমাবর্তন।

সমাজে নিত্যকর্মপদ্ধতি সংক্রান্ত পুঁথিটি অত্যন্ত প্রয়োজনীয় ও গুরুত্বপূর্ণ পুঁথি বলে এটি সর্বজনগ্রাহ্য।

২০৪ বৎসর পূর্বে মহারাজ দুর্গা মাণিক্যের পৃষ্ঠপোষকতায় লিপিকার রামশরণ শর্মা বিষ্ণুপুরাণের পুঁথি নির্মাণ করেন। মহারাজের অর্থানুকুল্যে রামশরণ শুধু যে পুঁথিটি প্রস্তুত করেন এমন নয়। পুঁথিটি মহারাজের সংগ্রহে স্থান পেয়েছিল। (১৭২৯ শকাব্দে)। এই সংস্কৃত পুঁথির পুষ্পিকাতে উল্লেখ করা হয়েছে — 'শ্রী দুর্গামণিদেবস্য স্বকীয়পুস্তকমিদং।' এতে বৈষ্ণবধর্মের উৎকর্ষ চোখে পড়ে। ত্রিপুরার বৈষ্ণবী সংস্কৃতির প্রাচীনকালীন প্রতিষ্ঠা এতে প্রমাণিত। রাজারা বৈষ্ণবধর্মের প্রতি সর্বদা আনুকূল্য প্রদর্শন করেছেন।

'সংসার তারণের' জন্য তথা 'ভবভয় নিবারণের' জন্য অধ্যাত্মরামায়ণ পাঠ প্রয়োজন তাই মহারাজ রামগঙ্গা মাণিক্যের (১৮১৪-১৮২৫) আদেশানুসারে ১৭৪০ শকাব্দে সংস্কৃত অধ্যাত্ম রামায়ণের পুঁথি নির্মিত হয়। লিপিকার হচ্ছেন শিবেশ দ্বিজ। আজ থেকে ১৯৪ বৎসর পূর্বে রামগঙ্গা মাণিক্যের পৃষ্ঠপোষকতায় রচিত উক্ত পুঁথিটি মহারাজের ধর্ম ও সংস্কৃত প্রীতি প্রমাণ করেছে। এই দুই বিষয়ের প্রতি মহারাজার আকর্ষণ ছিল উচ্চাঙ্গীন।

মহারাজ কৃষণকিশোর মাণিক্যের আদেশে ১৮৩৫ খ্রীষ্টাব্দে লিপিকার সংস্কৃত

পুঁথি পদকল্পতরু লিখলেন। প্রসিদ্ধ মূল গ্রন্থ সম্পর্কে ডঃ সুকুমার সেনের মন্তব্য হল, সতীশচন্দ্র রায় সম্পাদিত ৫ খণ্ডে রচিত গ্রন্থই শ্রেষ্ঠ। (বাংলা সাহিত্যের ইতিহাস, প্রথম খণ্ড, অপরার্ধ, কলি - ১৯৭৮)। কিন্তু বৈষ্ণব শিরোমণি হরিদাস দাস (১৮৯৮-১৯৫৭) শ্রীশ্রী গৌড়ীয় বৈষ্ণব অভিধানে লিখলেন এতে পদকর্তার সংখ্যা ১৩০। তবে সব পদ এই পুঁথিতে স্থান পায়নি।

লিপিকার তাঁর পৃষ্ঠপোষক মহারাজ কৃষ্ণকিশোরের গুণজ্ঞান ও মহত্ত্ব বিবৃত করে দীর্ঘ প্রশস্তি বাক্য সংযোজন করেছেন পুষ্পিকাতে। তাতে রয়েছে —

'যো ভূপালশিরোমণিঃ ক্ষিতিতলে শ্রীমন্ মহাধার্মিকো ধীমান্ কৃষ্ণকিশোরঃ ভূপতি-রনেক-জ্ঞানার্ণবঃ শীলবান্।' ইত্যাদি।

মহারাজ কৃষ্ণকিশোর মাণিক্যের (১৮৩০-১৮৯) রাজত্বকালে ললিতমাধব নাট্যের পুঁথি তৈরি করলেন স্বরূপ গোস্বামী। এটি ১৮৩৮ খ্রীষ্টাব্দের সংস্কৃত পুঁথি মহারাজ কৃষ্ণ কিশোরের পৃষ্ঠপোষকতায় লিখিত লিপিকার পুষ্পিকাতে — শ্রীহরিঃ পাতু নৃপতিং' লিখে রাজার প্রতি কৃতজ্ঞতা প্রকাশ করেছেন।

শ্রী গোস্বামী উক্ত গ্রন্থের দশমাঙ্কের অনুবাদ পুঁথি দুই-ই করেছেন। এখানে শ্রীহরি সর্বনিয়ন্ত্রক শক্তির নিকট লিপিকার তার পৃষ্ঠপোষক নৃপতির সার্বিক কল্যাণ কামনা করেছেন। প্রসঙ্গত দার্শনিক ডঃ রাধাকৃষ্ণাণের মন্তব্য স্মর্তব্য—

"Life remain unfulfilled until there is a vision of the Supreme'

পূর্বোক্ত মহারাজ কৃষ্ণকিশোর ছিলেন ঐতিহ্যশালী উন্নত সংস্কৃতির প্রতি শ্রদ্ধাবান ব্যক্তিত্ব। তারই অনুজ্ঞায় পণ্ডিত পশুপতি-প্রণীত দশর্মদীপিকার অন্তর্গত বিবাহ পদ্ধতি' গ্রন্থখানার পুঁথি রচনা করলেন লিপিকার গৌরাকান্ত শর্মা।

এটি সংস্কৃতে লেখা তালপাতার পুঁথি। পুষ্পিকায় পুঁথি। পুষ্পিকায় পুঁথি লেখার তারিখ চিহ্নিত হয়েছে— ১৭৬৭ শকাব্দ (১৮৪৫ খ্রীঃ)। লিপিকারের কোন অভিপ্রায় এতে সংযোজিত হয়নি। তবে, পণ্ডিত পশুপতি কৃষ্ণকিশোর আমলের রাজপণ্ডিত। আর আজ থেকে ১৬৬ বৎসর পূর্বে সমাজের উন্নতিকল্পে রাজপণ্ডিতের অস্তিত্ব অবশ্যই ঐতিহাসিক ঘটনা।

প্রসঙ্গতঃ ঐতিহাসিক তথা লিপিতাত্ত্বিক ডঃ দীনেশ চন্দ্র সরকারের একটি কথা স্বভাবতঃ মনে আসছে, যাতে রয়েছে —

'যেসব তথ্য যখন কোন পরিচিত রাষ্ট্রীয় তথ্যের সঙ্গে যুক্ত হয় তখনই তা দেশ কালের আশ্রয় পায় এবং যথার্থ ঐতিহাসিক উপাদান বলে গণ্য হয়।" (শিলালেখ তাম্রশাসনাদির প্রসঙ্গ, পৃঃ ৮)। এই পুঁথিতে রাজ্যের ঐতিহাসিক তথ্য

বিদ্যমান।

কৃত্তিবাসী রামায়ণ হচ্ছে — মহর্ষি বাল্মীকিকৃত রামায়ণের বাংলা ভাষায় অনূদিত গ্রন্থ। তারই পুঁথি লিখলেন— ত্রিপুরার মনিয়ন্দের হরিচন্দ্র বর্মণ। তাতে লিপিকার হরিচন্দ্র পুষ্পিকা লিখেছেন — সংস্কৃতে। পুঁথিটির প্রাচীনত্ব হচ্ছে ১৭৪ বৎসরে (১২৪৭ ত্রিপুরাব্দে লিখিত)। এতকাল পূর্বেও ত্রিপুরা জন জীবনে রামায়ণে প্রভাব দেখা যায়। এটিও মহারাজ কৃষ্ণকিশোর মাণিক্যের আমলেই তারই সদিচ্ছায় লিখিত। রামায়ণের অসাধারণ রস মাধুর্য্য প্রজাবর্গের নিকট এতে প্রকাশিত হয়েছে।

অধুনাতন কালেও ত্রিপুরায় রামায়ণের প্রভাব সম্যক্ দৃষ্ট হয়। বস্তুতঃ ত্রিপুরার মানসচিত্রে রামায়ণের সমাদর ও ব্যপ্তি বিষয়ে ডঃ সীতানাথ দে যথার্থ বলেছেন, ত্রিপুরার জাতি জনজাতির মধ্যে এখনো রামায়ণের প্রচুর প্রভাব বিদ্যমান।

আসলে সংস্কৃত থেকে বাংলা ভাষায় ছন্দো মাধুর্যে, বোধকরি, এটাই সর্বপ্রথম অনূদিত বাংলা রামায়ণ। আর কৃত্তিবাসী রামায়ণ ৫০০ শত বৎসরের অধিক কাল ধরে দেশে সম্পূজিত হয়ে আসছে। এর ভাবধারা নানা ভাষার মধ্যে, নাট্যে, গল্পে, গানে ছন্দে পরিবেশিত হয়ে আসছে ত্রিপুরার ঐতিহ্যবাহী রামায়ণ পুঁথির প্রভাবে।

মহারাজ ঈশানচন্দ্র মাণিক্যের (১৮৪৯-১৮৬২) অনুজ্ঞায় ও অর্থানুকূল্যে লিপিকার অপূর্ব কিশোর শর্মা বিশাল কলেবর শ্রীমদ্ভাগবতের পুঁথি নির্মাণ করেন। ৫২৫ পৃষ্ঠায় পুঁথিটির গাত্রে লেখা রয়েছে —

'শ্রীকৃষ্ণঃ শরণম্।
শ্রীহরিঃ শরণম্।

শ্রীরামঃ শরণম্।' আগরতলা শ্রীপাটের শ্রদ্ধেয় কর্তাপ্রভু শ্রীল দোল গোবিন্দ গোস্বামীর শুভেচ্ছায় গ্রন্থটি দেখার সৌভাগ্য হয়েছিল ১৯৯৫ খৃষ্টাব্দে। পুঁথিটি বৈষ্ণবধর্মের প্রচার ও প্রসারে ত্রিপুরায় গুরুত্বপূর্ণ ভূমিকা পালন করে চলেছে। পুঁথিটি প্রভু বাড়ির শ্রীশ্রী নীলকান্ত মণি জিউর মন্দিরে পূজিত হচ্ছে।

বিশেষ বিশেষ পর্ব উপলক্ষ্যে শ্রীপাঠের প্রভুরা তা পাঠ করে থাকেন। ত্রিপুরা পাহাড় অঞ্চলে প্রভুদের যেসব শিষ্যবর্গ রয়েছেন তাদের কাছে উক্ত পুঁথির ভাবধারার উপর বক্তব্য রেখে থাকেন প্রভু গোস্বামীরা। তাতে ভক্তবৃন্দ বৈষ্ণব

ধর্ম বিষয়ে প্রকৃষ্ট জ্ঞান লাভ করতে পারেন।

(পুঁথিটি বহু রং-এর সূতা দিয়ে হাতে সেলাই করা কাঁথা দিয়ে সুন্দর ভাবে মুড়িয়ে রাখা হয়েছে। তাতে আরো বিশেষ গুরুত্বপূর্ণ বিষয় হচ্ছে — মহারাজ বীরচন্দ্র মাণিক্যের বিষয় নিয়ে একটি বাংলা কবিতা সূচীকর্মে তুলে ধরা হয়েছে। এটি সূচী শিল্পেরও চমৎকারিত্বের নিদর্শন।)

উক্ত পুঁথির প্রায় আর একটি সংখ্যা আগরতলার শ্রীশ্রী লক্ষ্মী নারায়ণ মন্দিরে সযত্নে রক্ষিত আছে। তাকে ফুল, চন্দন, তুলসী, বেলপাতা দিয়ে নিত্য পূজা করা হচ্ছে।

এসব ভক্তিগ্রন্থের পাশাপাশি অন্যান্য যৌগিক তন্ত্র গ্রন্থের পুঁথিও রচিত হয়েছিল রাজার রাজত্বে। ত্রিপুরার নুর নগরের অধিবাসী লিপিকার লক্ষ্মী নারায়ণ দাস মহারাজ ঈশানচন্দ্র মাণিক্যের (১৮৪৯-১৮৬২ খ্রীঃ) রাজত্বকালে তারই আনুকূল্যে শ্রীশ্রী গোরক্ষমুনিরচিত শ্রীগোরক্ষ পুরাণের পুঁথি রচনা করেন ১২৭১ ত্রিপুরাব্দে (১৮৬১ খ্রীঃ)। তাতে রাজার উদার চারিত্রিক বৈশিষ্ট্যই প্রকটিত হচ্ছে।

বৈষ্ণব ধর্মের বিখ্যাত গ্রন্থ বৃন্দাবনলীলামৃতের নকলকারী হলেন রামমণি শর্মা।

এই পুঁথিটিও মহারাজ ঈশানচন্দ্র মাণিক্যের পৃষ্ঠপোষকতায় রচিত হয়। লিপিকার তার পৃষ্ঠপোষক মহারাজ ঈশানচন্দ্রের উদ্দেশ্যে দীর্ঘ প্রশস্তি সংস্কৃতে সংযোজন করেছেন। তাতে রয়েছে —

> ‘নিখিলগুণনিধি — রাজরাজেন্দ্রকল্পঃ।
> শ্রীরাধাকৃষ্ণ-পদাম্বুজ-গলিত-সুধারাশি-সংসিক্ত-চিত্তে
> দীনানাং ত্রাণকারী রিপুকুলদমন—
> ধার্মিকো দীনবন্ধুঃ’ ইত্যাদি।

পুষ্পিকাটি ত্রিপুরার রাজার কৃতিত্বের ইতিহাস সংকলনের ও সংরক্ষণের পক্ষে খুবই মূল্যবান।

মহারাজ ঈশান চন্দ্র মাণিক্যের উত্তরপুরুষ কীর্ত্তিধর বীরচন্দ্র যুবরাজ — যুবরাজী আমলেই সংস্কৃতির প্রতি বিশেষ আগ্রহী ছিলেন। প্রকাশ থাকে যে — কৌটালী পাড়ার নিবাসী শ্রীরামজয় তর্ক বাগীশের প্রদৌহিত্র শ্রীবিশ্বম্বর দেবশর্ম্মা কূর্ম্মপুরাণের পুঁথি বিক্রয়ার্থে ত্রিপুরায় প্রেরিত হলে ১৭৮৮ শকাব্দের শ্রাবণ

মাসের নবন দিনে ঐ পুঁথি উনিশ টাকা দিয়ে কিনে রাখলেন যুবরাজ মহারাজ বীরচন্দ্র মাণিক্য (১৮৬২-১৮৯৬ খ্রীঃ)। তিনি পুঁথির তথা বৈদিক সংস্কৃতিবাহী শিক্ষা-দীক্ষার প্রতি যে সমাদর ও অর্থানুকুল্য প্রদর্শন করেছেন তা ১৪৬ বৎসর আগের ত্রিপুরা ইতিহাসের এক অনন্য দলিল।

রামজয় শুধু লিপিকারই নন, তিনি ঐকান্তিক হরিভক্তিপরায়ণও। আর মহারাজ বীরচন্দ্র যথার্থ পুঁথিপ্রেমী এবং পুঁথির পৃষ্ঠপোষক।

মহারাজ বীরচন্দ্র মাণিক্যের (১৮৬২-১৮৯৬ খ্রীঃ) অর্থানুকূল্যে ও পৃষ্ঠপোষকতায় লিপিকার ভারত চন্দ্র ব্রাহ্মণ বৃহন্নারদীয় পুরাণের পুঁথি লিখলেন। নকলকারী ভারতচন্দ্র তাঁর পৃষ্ঠপোষক শ্রীযুক্ত বীরচন্দ্র নরপতির আজ্ঞানুসারে পুঁথিখানা লিখলেন তা পুষ্পিকায় জানিয়েছেন।

রাজন্য ত্রিপুরায় পুঁথি-লিখনে মহারাজদের আন্তরিক আনুকূল্য ও পৃষ্ঠপোষকতার তথ্য পাওয়া যায় মহারাজকুমার নবদ্বীপচন্দ্র দেববর্মণের 'আবর্জনার ঝুড়ি' নামক প্রবন্ধ থেকে। প্রবন্ধটি ১৯২৮ খ্রীষ্টাব্দে লিখিত— তাতে আছে 'রাজবাড়িতে দুই একজন পুঁথিলেখক ব্রাহ্মণ পণ্ডিত নিয়ত পুঁথি লিখিতেন এবং তাঁহারা মন্ত্রের মত লেখার খাটুনি খাটিতেন। প্রাচীন নিয়মে তাহারা কর্ম পাইতেন। চাকুরীর মত না হইয়া উত্তরাধিকার মত, অবশ্য লিপিকুশলতা তাহাতে ছাড় পড়িত না।'

১৯৪৭ খ্রীষ্টাব্দে কলিকাতার বঙ্গীয় সাহিত্য পরিষদ সংগ্রহশালা থেকে রাজমালার একটি পুঁথি আবিষ্কৃত হয়েছে। এর আবিষ্কর্তা হলেন — ত্রিপুরারাজ অবসরসচিব দ্বিজেন্দ্র চন্দ্র দত্ত (১৯০১-১৯৭৭ খ্রীঃ)। পুঁথিটি চারটি ভাগে বিভক্ত। লিপিকার হিসাবে রামনারায়ণ দেবের নাম পাওয়া যাচ্ছে। তবে, এই দুষ্প্রাপ্য পুঁথিটি কালীপ্রসন্ন সেন বিদ্যাভূষণের (১৮৬২-১৯৩৪ খ্রীঃ) সম্পাদিত চার লহর রাজমালার ইতিহাসে আর একটি নব সংযোজন এই বাংলা পুঁথির মাঝে মাঝে বহু সংখ্যক শ্লোকে উদ্ধৃত ইতিহাসের বহু তত্ত্ব ও তথ্য চোখে পড়ে।

এতে মহারাজ গোবিন্দ মাণিক্য, মহারাজ বিজয় মাণিক্য, মহারাজ ধর্ম মাণিক্য সংক্রান্ত বহু সংস্কৃত শ্লোক এতে লিপিকার সংযোজন করেছেন।

গোবিন্দ মাণিক্য খণ্ডে লিপিকার মহারাজ গোবিন্দ মাণিক্যের (১৬৬০, ১৬৬৭-১৬৭৬ খ্রীঃ) প্রাচীন বৈদিক সাহিত্যের প্রতি প্রীতির কথা ব্যক্ত করেছেন। গোবিন্দ মাণিক্য এত কালপূর্বে বৈদিক সাহিত্যের বিবৃত আধ্যাত্মিক ও বৈষয়িক বিষয় বস্তুর উপরে খুবই আস্থাবান ত্রিপুরধিপতি ছিলেন।

সর্বশেষে এক বিশেষ বার্তা পরিবেশন করেই বক্তব্যের সমাপ্তি করছি। তা হল, ডঃ মোহম্মদ আব্দুল কাইউম তাঁর বিখ্যাত গ্রন্থে ১৯৮৬ সালে লিখলেন যে —

আবদু হামিদ রচিত 'দুররে মজলিশ' কাব্যের পুঁথিতে লিপিকার দৌলত আগরতলা সম্পর্কে একটা চমৎকার তথ্য দিয়েছেন যাতে আছে —

'এবেঁ কহি মোর স্থান নিবাস কথন।
যাহাতে লিখিনুঁ এই পাঁচালী বিবরণ।।
আগরতলা সহর জান অতি দিব্যস্থান।
ত্রিপুরা বংশে ত বৈসত্র প্রধান।।'

তাতে বোধ হল, এক একটি পুঁথি একটা রাজ্যের ইতিহাস ও মর্দাদাকে এভাবে আলোকিত করতে পারে।

23

প্রাচীন লিখনে প্রতিফলিত ঊনকোটি - অসম্পূর্ণতা ও সম্পূরণ প্রয়াস

প্রিয়ঙ্কু চক্রবর্তী

ঊনকোটির ইতিহাস রচনায় ভাস্কর্যশৈলীর তুলনাত্মক ও বিজ্ঞানসম্মত অধ্যয়ন, তাম্রলিপি, শিলালেখ ইত্যাদির সহায়ক ভূমিকার পাশাপাশি প্রাচীন লিখিত উপাদানের গুরুত্ব অনস্বীকার্য। কিন্তু এক্ষেত্রে লিখিত উপাদানের পরিমাণ প্রয়োজনের তুলনায় নিতান্তই ন্যূন। তাছাড়া এ যাবৎ লব্ধ লিখিত সব উপাদানই প্রাচীনত্বের নিরিখে ঊনকোটির নির্মাণকালের থেকে কম করে সাড়ে চার থেকে পাঁচশ বছর পরবর্তী। এই সমস্যা ঊনকোটির ইতিহাস নির্ণয়ে নিঃসন্দেহে গুরুতর।

'রাজমালা'য় ত্রিপুরার রাজকীর্তি ও প্রশস্তির মুখরতার পরম্পরা হঠাৎই যেন মৌন হয়ে যায় - ঊনকোটির বিষয়ে। প্রশ্নটা স্বাভাবিক - কেন?

সংস্কৃতি ও বাংলা রাজমালায় বলা হয়েছে — বিমারতনয় কুমার মনু তীরে 'ছাম্বুলনগর' নামক স্থানে শিবসাধনা করেন এবং 'শিবলিঙ্গং সমাদ্রাক্ষীৎ সুবড়াই কৃতে মঠে।' এখন প্রশ্ন হলো - কে এই 'সুবড়াই'? 'ছাম্বুলনগর'-ই কি কৈলাসহর? ঊনকোটিই যদি সেই স্থান হয় তবে সেখানকার বিশাল ও প্রধান প্রধান ভাস্কর্যের কথা না বলে শুধু শিবলিঙ্গের উল্লেখ কেন হলো? না কি এ ঊনকোটি-ব্যতীত অন্য কোন স্থান, যেখানে শিবলিঙ্গ বিদ্যমান? - যেমন, ঊনকোটির অদূরবর্তী নূনছড়ার বিশালাকার শিবলিঙ্গ। নয়তো কি এ নিছকই তীর্থস্থানের সঙ্গে জড়িয়ে রাজমাহাত্ম্য বৃদ্ধির প্রয়াস - যেমনটা করা হয় মহাভারত ও পুরাণের সঙ্গে রাজাদের জুড়ে দেবার কৌশল? এই সকল প্রশ্ন এখনো অমীমাংসিত। সুবড়াই উপজাতিদের দেবতা। অনেকে আবার সুবড়াই ও রাজা ত্রিলোচনকে অভিন্ন দায়ী

করে এবং তাঁকে 'অষ্ট্রিক জাতীয়' চিহ্নিত করে ভিন্নতর ব্যাখ্যাদানের প্রচেষ্টা করেছেন। যাইহোক আমরা পূর্বোক্ত 'মঠ' কথাটি স্মরণে রাখব নিবন্ধের পরবর্তী অংশের দাবীতে।

বস্তুত, ত্রিপুরার রাজমালার ১৪শ-১৫শ শতাব্দীর পূর্ববর্তী ইতিবৃত্ত কল্পনাশ্রয়ী অতিশয়োক্তির ধোঁয়াশা আচ্ছন্ন। রাজ্যসভাকবিগণ বিরচিত এই তথাকথিত ইতিহাসরচনার (চাটুকারিতায়?) পশ্চাতে ছিল রাজানুগ্রহ লাভের লিপ্সা।

অথচ উনকোটির বিস্তৃত এলাকা জুড়ে গড়ে ওঠা বিশাল 'ভাস্কর্য সাম্রাজ্য' রাজানুকল্য বা তৎতুল্য ব্যক্তির পৃষ্ঠপোষকতা ব্যতীত তৈরি হতে পারে না, দশম-একাদশ শতকে তো আর গণতন্ত্র ছিল না। কিন্তু ত্রিপুরার ইতিহাস সম্মত 'মাণিক্য' উপাধিধারী রাজাদের সাথে ঊনকোটি নির্মাণের প্রত্যক্ষ বা পরোক্ষ যোগাযোগ দৃষ্ট হয় না কোনও প্রামাণ্য দলিলে। তীর্থদর্শন মানসে কোনও কোনও রাজপুরুষ ঊনকোটি ভ্রমণ করেছেন মাত্র। যেমন রাজমালায় বর্ণিত আছে বিজয়মাণিক্য (ষোড়শ শতাব্দীতে) ঊনকোটিতে গিয়েছিলেন —

'কতদিন পরে রাজা ঊনকোটি গেল।
এক ঊনকোটি লিঙ্গ তথা দেখিল।।"

তারপর এসেছেন রাজধরমাণিক্য (১৫৮৫-১৬০০ খ্রীঃ) —

'রাজধর চলিল দুলালী গ্রামপথে।
ইটাগ্রাম হৈয়ে চলে ঊনকোটি তীর্থে।।"

তারপর এসেছেন রাধাকিশোর মাণিক্য, বীরবিক্রম কিশোর মাণিক্য প্রমুখ।

অন্যদিকে, মাণিক্যযুগে কুকি-অধ্যুষিত এই রাজপ্রভাব যে জোরদার ছিল না, তার একাধিক প্রমাণ পাওয়া যাচ্ছে রাজমালায়। মহারাজ ধন্যমাণিক্যের আমলে (আনুমানিক ১৪শ শতাব্দী) এতদঞ্চলের ওপর মাণিক্য আধিপত্য কায়েম হয়েছে। তার আগে এই অঞ্চল স্বাধীন কুকি রাজ্য, প্রাচীন দলিলে যা 'খানাংচি' নামে পরিচিত বলে সুরেন দেব্বর্মা 'ত্রিপুরারর আদিবাসী জীবন ও সংস্কৃতি' গ্রন্থে উল্লেখ করেছেন।আবার ড. পুরঞ্জন প্রসাদ চক্রবর্তী সম্পাদিত রাজমালায় এই অঞ্চল 'কিরাতভূমি' নামে উক্ত হয়েছে। অবশ্য এর অবস্থান নিয়ে বিতর্ক রয়েছে।

সমরেন্দ্র চন্দ্র দেব্বর্মণ মাণিক্য রাজপরিবারের সদস্য হয়েও ঊনকোটি নির্মাণ বিষয়ে অজ্ঞতা প্রকাশ করেছেন তাঁর 'ত্রিপুরার স্মৃতি' গ্রন্থে (প্রকাশকাল ১৯২৭ খ্রীঃ)। আর প্রত্নতাত্ত্বিক অনুসন্ধান ও ভাস্কর্য-গঠন শৈলীর বিশ্লেষণে একথা মোটামুটিভাবে প্রতিষ্ঠিত যে ঊনকোটির নির্মাণকাল নবম থেকে একাদশ শতাব্দী।

সুতরাং ঊনকোটি নির্মাণে ত্রিপুরার মাণিক্য রাজবংশের যোগদানের সম্ভাবনা নেই বললেই চলে।

১৮৯৩ সালে মহারাজ বীরচন্দ্রের মন্ত্রী ধনঞ্জয় 'দেব্বর্মার 'কৈলাসহরের বিবরণ', ১৯০৩ এ প্রকাশিত পণ্ডিত চন্দ্রোদয় বিদ্যাবিনোদের 'শ্রীশ্রীযুতের কৈলাসহর পরিভ্রমণ', ১৯২১ সালে প্রকাশিত প্যারীমোহন দেব্বর্মার 'ঊনকোটি তীর্থ', 'ত্রিপুরার স্মৃতি' ইত্যাদি গ্রন্থে প্রাচীন হস্ত লিখিত সংস্কৃত পুঁথির উল্লেখ ও উদ্ধৃতি পাওয়া যায়। পুঁথিটির নাম - 'ঊনকোটি তীর্থমাহাত্ম্য'। শ্রীরাজমালার সম্পাদক কালীপ্রসন্ন সেন 'মধ্যমণি' টীকার (রাজমালার দ্বিতীয় লহরের) আকারগ্রন্থের সূচীতে এই হস্তলিখিত গ্রন্থটির উল্লেখ করেছেন। কিন্তু এই পুঁথি থেকে উদ্ধৃতি সর্বত্রই এক। এর কারণ বলা বাহুল্য, উদ্ধৃতিটি এরূপ -

'বিন্ধ্যাদ্রেঃ পাদসম্ভূতো বরবক্রঃ সুপুণ্যদঃ।
দক্ষিণস্যাং নদস্যাস্য পুণ্যা মনুনদীস্মৃতা।।
অনয়োরন্তরা রাজন্ ঊনকোটিগিরির্মহান্।
যত্র তোপে তপঃ পূর্বং সুমহৎ কপিলো মুনিঃ।।
তত্র বৈ কাপিলং তীর্থং কপিলেন প্রকাশিতম্।
লিঙ্গঞ্চ কপিলং তত্র সর্বসিদ্ধিপ্রদং নৃণাম্।।"

পৌরাণিক-ধাঁচের প্রশস্তি। বাংলা অনুবাদ করলে সারার্থ এই দাঁড়ায় - বিন্ধ্যশৈলের পাদদেশজাত পুণ্যপ্রদ বরাক নদী ও দক্ষিণে পুণ্যতোয় মনু নদী - এই দুয়ের মধ্যে মহান ঊনকোটি পর্বত স্থিত। সুমহান কপিলমুনি এখানে তপস্যা করে এই সর্বসিদ্ধপ্রদ তীর্থকে প্রকাশিত করেছিলেন।

পুঁথি থেকে উদ্ধৃতাংশ ঊনকোটির ভৌগোলিক অবস্থানসূচক যে বর্ণনা পাওয়া যাচ্ছে তাতে অসঙ্গতি এই - বরাক কীভাবে বিন্ধ্যশৈলীর পাদোদ্ভুত হবে? কিন্তু পুরাণের অতিশয়োক্তির আবরণ সরিয়ে বিন্ধ্যপর্বতের মতো মহিমময় পর্বতজাত বললে আপাত অর্থসঙ্গতি এলেও আপত্তির সুযোগ থেকেই যাচ্ছে। না বললেও চলে, যদি পুঁথিটি পাওয়া যেত তাহলে তা ঊনকোটির ইতিবৃত্তে হয়তো নতুন আলোকসম্পাত হতো। কেউ কেউ মনে করেন, কামাখ্যার পাণ্ডাদের বা মন্দির ট্রাস্টের কাছে এই পুঁথি থাকতে পারে, তবে সম্ভাবনা অত্যন্ত ক্ষীণ (স্বর্গীয় রমাপ্রসাদ দত্তের অভিমত)।

বিশিষ্ট গবেষক নীহাররঞ্জন রায় ত্রিপুরার পার্বত্য প্রদেশকে প্রাচীন বঙ্গের অংশবিশেষ বলে মনে করেন। ভৌগোলিক বিচারে উত্তর ত্রিপুরার ধর্মনগর,

কৈলাসহর সহ ঊনকোটি অঞ্চল প্রাচীন বঙ্গের পৌণ্ড্রবর্ধনভুক্তির শ্রীহট্টমন্ডলের অন্তর্ভূক্ত ছিল। বিষয়টি আরও সুস্পষ্ট হয় 'বৃহত্তর সিলেটের ইতিহাস' গ্রন্থে কমলাকান্ত গুপ্ত মহাশয়ের লিখিত প্রবন্ধে প্রকাশিত তথ্যের আলোচনায় (এ বিষয়ে ঐতিহাসিক দীনেশ চন্দ্র সরকারও আলোকপাত করেছেন)। শ্রীহট্টের মৌলভী বাজারের অন্তর্গত রাজনগর থানার পশ্চিমভাগ গ্রামে প্রাপ্ত বিক্রমপুরের মহারাজা, আনুমানিক ১০ম শতাব্দীর চন্দ্র শাসক শ্রীচন্দ্র পশ্চিমভাগ তাম্র শাসন প্রবর্তন করেন। এতে উল্লেখিত রয়েছে - পৌণ্ড্রবর্ধনভূক্তির অন্তর্গত গরলা, পগার ও চন্দ্রপুর - এই তিন বিষয়ে বিশাল এলাকা ব্রাহ্মণ ও বৌদ্ধধর্মাবলম্বীদের স্বার্থে শ্রীচন্দ্র দান করেন। তাম্রলিপি বর্ণিত সীমা বেশ খাপ খায় ঊনকোটির ভৌগোলিক অবস্থানের সাথে[১]। বিদ্বৎমণ্ডলীর অনুমান মনু নদীর অববাহিকায়[২] গড়ে উঠা ঊনকোটি সভ্যতা তাম্রশাসন বর্ণিত ধর্মস্থান নির্মাণ প্রকল্পেরই অংশবিশেষ। খ্রীষ্টিয় ১০ম শতকের প্রথমার্ধে গড়ে ওঠা এই মঠ বা প্রকল্পে, তৎকালীন সমাজজীবন, ধর্ম-সংস্কৃতির যে পরিচয়, তার নিদর্শন ঊনকোটির ধ্বংসস্তূপে পরিলক্ষিত। সেইসময়, পাল-চন্দ্র যুগের বঙ্গে, ধর্মীয় সহনশীলতার যে আবহাওয়া ছিল তার পরিণতিস্বরূপ ঊনকোটিতে ব্রাহ্মণ্য তথা বৌদ্ধধর্মের সহবস্থান (বা, মিশ্রণজনিত অবস্থান) লক্ষণীয়। অথবা এমনও হতে পারে বৌদ্ধ বজ্রযান ও শৈবতন্ত্রের মিশ্রণোদ্ভুত শৈবনাথপন্থীর তীর্থে কালের বিবর্তনে পরবর্তীতে সংযোজিত হয়েছে ব্রাহ্মণ্য দেবদেবীগণ। হয়তো তাই পৃথক প্রস্তরখণ্ডে খোদিত ভাস্কর্য পর্বতগাত্রাপেক্ষা অপেক্ষাকৃত উন্নত কারুকার্যময় অর্থাৎ পরবর্তীকালের। অবশ্য ড. নন্দী প্রমুখ এক্ষেত্রে ভিন্নমত পোষণ করেন।

রাজা শ্রীচন্দ্র বৌদ্ধধর্মাবলম্বী হওয়া সত্ত্বেও ব্রাহ্মণ ও হিন্দু তীর্থস্থানের উন্নতির জন্য এই ভূমি প্রদান করেছিলেন। 'বাঙালীর ইতিহাস' অনুসারে শ্রীচন্দ্রের পিতা ত্রৈলোক্য চন্দ্র ঊনকোটি, ধর্মনগর সহ শ্রীহট্ট অঞ্চলও অধিকারভুক্ত করেছিলেন। কাজেই, শ্রীহট্ট সংলগ্ন এলাকাগুলিও চন্দ্রশাসকদের অধীন ছিল।

শ্রীচন্দ্রের পৌত্র লহড়চন্দ্র হিন্দুধর্মে উৎসাহী ছিলেন। কিংবদন্তী অনুসারে ১১শ শতাব্দীতে তাঁর পুত্র গোবিন্দচন্দ্র স্বীয়মাতা ময়নামতী ও নাথসিদ্ধের দ্বারা বিশেষভাবে প্রভাবিত হয়ে নাথ পন্থীতে রূপান্তরিত হন। খুব সম্ভবত ঊনকোটির নির্মাণে গোবিন্দচন্দ্রের যোগদান ছিল - যে অঞ্চলটি ইতিপূর্বেই তাঁর পূর্বপুরুষ দ্বারা ধর্মীয় উদ্দেশ্যে দানকৃত।

পাশাপাশি ড. দীনেশচন্দ্রের 'বৃহৎবঙ্গ' থেকে আমরা জানতে পারি গোবিন্দ

চন্দ্র (আ. ১০২০-১০৫৫ খ্রীঃ) নাথধর্মে দীক্ষিত হন এবং ত্রিপুরার উত্তরাংশ ও সিলেট হয়ে উঠে নাথধর্মের মুখ্য কেন্দ্র।

সুতরাং ১০ম-১২শ শতাব্দীতে চন্দ্র শাসকরাই বর্তমান উত্তর ত্রিপুরায় রাজত্ব করেছিলেন। সম্ভবত সেই সময় কুকিরা সেখানে ছিল রায়ত হিসাবে। তাম্রশাসন থেকে জানা যায় চন্দ্রপুর বিষয়ে আটটি মঠ ছিল - চারটি বাঙালীদের জন্য, চারটি অবাঙালীর জন্য। এই অবাঙালী বলতে কুকিদেরই নির্দেশ করছে। এ বিষয়ে সিদ্ধান্ত আরও বলবতী হয় ধর্মনগরের হুরুয়া অঞ্চলে প্রত্নতাত্ত্বিক নিদর্শন প্রাপ্তিতে। মন্টু দাস প্রমুখরা মনে করেন প্রকল্পোক্ত বাঙালী মঠের মধ্যে এটি একটি। আর অবাঙালী মঠের গণনায় উনকোটি, নূনছড়াকে ধরা হয়। চন্দ্রপুরবিষয়ের অন্যতম আরাধ্য দেবতা ছিলেন মহাকাল শিব, যিনি বজ্রযানি তান্ত্রিকদের আরাধ্য বৌদ্ধ প্রভাবিত রূপকল্প বিশেষ। উনকোটির ভয়ঙ্কর কালভৈরব ভাস্কর্য এই সিদ্ধান্তকে সমর্থন করে। তবে এ বিষয়ে সিদ্ধান্ত আরও নিবিড় অনুধ্যান ও গভীর গবেষণার দাবী রাখে।

১৯৭২ সালে প্রকাশিত 'ত্রিপুরা রাজ্যে ত্রিশ বৎসর ঃ ধর্মনগর বিভাগ' পুস্তিকার পরিসংখ্যান অনুযায়ী উনকোটি সংলগ্ন অঞ্চলে বহু নাথ, দেবনাথ, নমশুদ্র, ঢুলি, মুচি প্রভৃতি জনগোষ্ঠী রয়েছে। এরা মূলতঃ বৌদ্ধধর্মাবলম্বী। অধ্যাপক বিনয়তোষ ভট্টাচার্যের অনুসরণে বলতে গেলে — এরা পরবর্তীতে বৌদ্ধ বজ্রযান ও শৈবধর্মের মিশ্রণোদ্ভূত শৈবনাথপন্থী। এ অঞ্চলে বহু নাথ যুগীরা বাস করেন। ধর্মঠাকুর ছিলেন তাঁদের আরাধ্য দেবতা। এ প্রসঙ্গে ঊনকোটির কূর্মমূর্তিটি স্মরণ করছি।

ঊনকোটির কর্ণকুণ্ডলযুক্ত মৎস্যমূর্তিটিও এ প্রসঙ্গে প্রণিধেয়। নাথধর্মীয় পুঁথি 'গোরক্ষবিজয়'-এ উল্লেখ রয়েছে - শিব-পার্বতীর গোপন তন্ত্রালোচনা লুকিয়ে শুনছেন নাথগুরু মৎস্যেন্দ্রনাথ - 'মৎস্যরূপ ধরি ততা মীন মোসান্দর /টাঙ্গির লামাতে রহে বগল সুন্দর।' প্রাচীন তিব্বতী চিত্রে কুণ্ডল পরিহিত মৎস্যেন্দ্রনাথের প্রতিকৃতি দেখা যায়। ঊনকোটির মৎস্যমূর্তির কর্ণকুণ্ডল নাথ যোগীদের (কনফন্ট) কুণ্ডলধারণের প্রথা মনে করিয়ে দেয়।

ঊনকোটির ভাস্কর্যে বৌদ্ধ বজ্রযান[৩] তথা নাথপন্থার প্রভাবের সমান্তরালে স্থানীয় আদিবাসী উপজাতীয় প্রভাবও রয়েছে। প্রসঙ্গত, বিশেষ করে পৃথক প্রস্তরে খোদিত ভাস্কর্যে বঙ্গপ্রভাব সুস্পষ্ট। তাছাড়া পর্বতে খোদিত ভাস্কর্যের পরিধেয়, অলঙ্কারে বঙ্গপ্রভাব বিদ্যমান। আরও, উনকোটির ঘোড়ামুখ সিংহ দুটি

বাংলার চিরাচরিত ঘোড়ামুখো সিংহের প্রাচীনতম অনুকরণ যেন।

শবরীপার চর্যাপদে শবরশ্রেণীর (কিরাত বা মঙ্গোলয়েড) মানুষের জীবনযাত্রার চিত্র দেখা যায়। যেমন - 'উঁচা উঁচা পাত তাহি বসাই শবরি বলি.../ এ কেলি শবরি এবন হিন্দাই কর্ণকুণ্ডল বজ্রধারী।' ঊনকোটির কেন্দ্রীয়মূর্তির ডানপাশে শবর-দম্পতির ছবির সাথে এর মিল আশ্চর্যজনক। এর সঙ্গেই গভীর রেখায় খোদিত রয়েছে মদ্যপাত্র। শিকারিজাতি শবরের মদ্যপানেরও উল্লেখ রয়েছে চর্যায়।

এযাবৎ বিভিন্ন প্রাচীন পুঁথি, গ্রন্থ, তাম্রশাসন ইত্যাদিতে প্রতিফলিত ঊনকোটির আলোচনা অসম্পূর্ণ থেকে যাবে ১৯১৩ খ্রীঃ ত্রিপুরা রাজ্যে ব্রিটিশ নিযুক্ত পলিটিক্যাল এজেন্ট Captain R.C.B. Williams সাহেবের তদানীন্তন ASI-এর পূর্বাঞ্চলীয় প্রধানের কাছে লিখিত প্রতিবেদনটির উল্লেখ না করলে। শ্রী বিকচ চৌধুরীর সৌজন্যে প্রাপ্ত প্রতিবেদনটি থেকে সামান্য অংশ উদ্ধৃত করছি - "my knowledge of Hindu Mythology was too inocmplete for me to make out the identity of the majority but I noticed fairly well defined representation of Hanuman & Ganesh, while the foot prints of Bishnu are in an excellent state of preservation." ইত্যাদি আরও অনেক কথা। অ-ভারতীয়দের দৃষ্টিতে উনকোটি।

১৯২১-১৯২২ সালের প্রতিবেদনে একটি চাঞ্চল্যকর তথ্য রয়েছে যে উনকোটিতে আবিষ্কৃত চতুর্মুখ লিঙ্গের পাদদেশে 'শ্রীজয়দেব' নামের উল্লেখ ছিল। এটি ১১শ-১২শ শতকের বাংলা হস্তলিপির নমুনা বলে উল্লেখ উক্ত প্রতিবেদনে। তবে বর্তমানে প্রাপ্ত 'চতুর্মুখ লিঙ্গ' অভিহিত ভাস্কর্যদ্বয়ের কোনটির পাদদেশে এটা উৎকীর্ণ ছিল তা জানবার উপায় নেই। তথাপি এই তথ্য নিঃসন্দেহে মূল্যবান।

পূর্ব প্রসঙ্গের জের টেনে বলছি, গোবিন্দ চন্দ্রের রাজত্বের শেষে সেন যুগে বাংলায় ব্রাহ্মণ্য ধর্মের অভ্যুদয় ঘটে। বৌদ্ধতান্ত্রিকরা বিতাড়িত হয়ে চীন, তিব্বতে আশ্রয় নেন। নইলে 'চর্যাচর্য বিনিশ্চয়' নেপালের রাজদরবারে আবিষ্কৃত হতোনা। সাধারণ মানুষের জীবনযাত্রার পরিচয় উনকোটির ভাস্কর্যে বিদ্যমান, যা চর্যা যুগের ধর্মীয় উদারতার পরিচায়ক। কিন্তু পরবর্তীকালে তা চক্ষুঃশূল হয়েছে ব্রাহ্মণ্যবাদীদের। কালক্রমে উনকোটি পরিত্যক্ত ধর্মস্থানে পরিত্যাক্ত হয়। হয়তো তাই উনকোটির উল্লেখ তথাকথিত প্রাচীন হিন্দু সাহিত্যে নেই। এবং আজও ব্রাহ্মণ্যপ্রথায় পূজাবিধান নেই উনকোটিতে।

হাজার বৎসরাধিক প্রাচীন উনকোটির ভাস্কর্য সাম্রাজ্যের পরিচয় বহুকালীন, বহুমাত্রিক। বিচিত্র মিশ্র ধর্ম-সংস্কৃতির প্রকাশ সুপ্রাচীন এই প্রত্নরত্নভূমিতে। বহির্বিশ্ব অর্থাৎ কম্বোডিয়া, তিব্বত, চীন, নেপাল ইত্যাদির ভাস্কর্যের সাথে ভাস্কর্যের সাদৃশ্য ও তুলনামূলক অনুসন্ধান গবেষণার বিশাল দিগন্তের উন্মোচন করে, সময়াভাবে বিরত রইলাম।

প্রসঙ্গত, ঊনকোটিতে এক কম কোটি মূর্তি না থাকলেও বহু মূর্তি ছিল — একথা ইতিহাস সম্মত। কিন্তু বর্তমান নিবন্ধকারের রিসার্চে বর্তমানে উনকোটির মূর্তির যে পরিসংখ্যানটি পাওয়া গেছে সেটি হলো ১১৮। বিশেষভাবে বলা প্রয়োজন, তিনটি বিশেষ ভাস্কর্য উনকোটিতে আমি খুঁজে পেয়েছি বিগত পাঁচ বছরের অনুসন্ধানে - একটি আবক্ষবিস্তৃত নারী মূর্তি (পর্বতগাত্রে খোদিত), দ্বিতীয় ও তৃতীয়টি গিরগিটি বা কুমারী জাতীয় প্রাণীর মূর্তি। প্রাচীন বা আধুনিক কোনও লিখনেই ভাস্কর্যগুলির উল্লেখ নেই। অভিজ্ঞতাপ্রসূত সিদ্ধান্ত এই যে, উপযুক্ত খননকার্যের ফলে উনকোটিতে আবিষ্কৃত হবে নতুন ভাস্কর্যসম্পদ। এই সমস্ত অনুসন্ধান পূরণ করবে উনকোটি সম্বন্ধিত পুঁথি বা লিখিত উপাদানের ন্যূনতাকে। সেইসঙ্গে গভীর পরিতাপের বিষয় - ১৯৬১ এর ১লা আগস্ট প্রত্নতত্ত্ব বিভাগ ঊনকোটির অধিগ্রহণ করলেও চূড়ান্ত অবহেলায় ঊনকোটি ধ্বংসোন্মুখ।

গ্রন্থপঞ্জি

১। অচ্যুত চরণ চৌধুরী 'শ্রীহট্টের ইতিবৃত্ত'

২। দীপক ভট্টাচার্য্য, 'ঊনকোটি'।

৩। কালীপ্রসন্ন সেন সম্পাদিত 'শ্রীরাজামালা'।

৪। সুরেন দেববর্মা, 'ত্রিপুরার আদিবাসী জীবন ও সংস্কৃতি'।

৫। মন্টু দাস সম্পাদিত 'বহ্নি শিখা' পত্রিকা।

৬। পুররঞ্জন প্রসাদ চক্রবর্তী সম্পাদিত 'ত্রিপুরার রাজমালা'।

৭। সমরেন্দ্র চন্দ্র দেববর্মন, 'ত্রিপুরার স্মৃতি'।

৮। প্যারিমোহন দেববর্মা, 'ঊনকোটি তীর্থ'।

৯। নীহার রঞ্জন রায়, 'বাঙালীর ইতিহাস'।
১০। দীনেশ চন্দ্র সেন, 'বৃহৎবঙ্গ'।
১১। ব্রজেন্দ্র চন্দ্র দত্ত, 'ত্রিপুরা রাজ্যে ত্রিশ বৎসর ঃ ধর্মনগর বিভাগ'।
১২। আশিস কুমার নৈবদ্য, 'ঊনকোটি ও দেবতামুড়া ভাস্কর্যের রূপরেখা।'
১৩। শীতলচন্দ্র চক্রবর্তী, 'ত্রিপুরার প্রাচীন ইতিহাস'।
১৪। Biswadip Nandi, 'Rockcut and sculptures of Tripura'.
১৫। জয়ন্তনাথ চৌধুরী, 'আবৃত ঊনকোটি ইতিহাস'।
১৬। রঞ্জিত দে, 'ত্রিপুরার লোকজীবন ও সংস্কৃতি'।
১৭। Goutam Sengupta, 'Early Sculptures of Tripura' published in 'Studies in the History of North-East India'.
১৮। এল.সি. নাথ, 'নাথ সম্প্রদায়ের ইতিহাস'
১৯। বিকচ চৌধুরী, 'ত্রিপুরার প্রত্নতাত্ত্বিক অনুসন্ধানে অ-ভারতীয় প্রয়াস', 'ত্রিপুরায় শতাব্দীর প্রবন্ধ চর্চায় প্রকাশিত
২০। Ratna Das, 'Art and Architecture of Tripura'.

১। দানকৃত ভূমির চতুঃসীমা তাম্রপটে এইরূপ বলা হয়েছে — উত্তরে কুশিয়ারা নদী, দক্ষিণে মনু নদী, পূর্বে বৃহৎ কোট্টালি অর্থাৎ আসমাইল ও পাথরিয়া পাহাড়, পশ্চিমে বেত্রযুঙ্গী নদী ও যুজ্জন খাতক।

২। পূর্বে মসু নদী ঊনকোটি পর্বতের আরোও সন্নিহিত ছিল। কালীপ্রসন্ন সেনও তাঁর রাজ্যমালায় বিষয়টির উল্লেখ করেছেন।

৩। 'সাধনামালায়' উক্ত বজ্রযানের চারটি কেন্দ্রের মধ্যে একটি হল শ্রীহট্ট। 'সাধনামালা' ও 'নিস্পন্নযোগাবলী' গ্রন্থে বহু ভয়ঙ্কর দেবতার বর্ণনা দেখা যায়, যার সাথে ঊনকোটির ভাস্কর্যের সাদৃশ্য রয়েছে।

24

পাণ্ডুলিপি আশ্রয়ে অতীত ত্রিপুরার সন্ধান এবং করণীয়

হরেকৃষ্ণ আচার্য

পাণ্ডুলিপি আশ্রয়ে ত্রিপুরার সামগ্রিক ইতিহাস খুঁজতে গেলে আগে ত্রিপুরার ভৌগোলিক অবস্থান এবং রাজনৈতিক ইতিহাসের একটা রূপরেখা চোখের সামনে থাকা দরকার।

উত্তর পূর্ব ভারতের সীমান্ত ক্ষুদ্ররাজ্যে ত্রিপুরা একটি প্রাচীন রাজ্য। ১৯৪৯ সনে ভারতের সঙ্গে যোগ দেবার পূর্ব পর্যন্ত ত্রিপুরা ছিল স্বাধীনরাজ্য। ভারতীয় জনগোষ্ঠীর জাতিগত বৈশিষ্ট্য অনুসারে ত্রিপুরার জনগোষ্ঠী মোঙ্গলয়েড গোষ্ঠীর অন্তর্গত। এদের বাস আসাম, ভারত-ব্রহ্মদেশের সীমান্ত অঞ্চল, চট্টগ্রামের পার্বত্য অঞ্চল, সিকিম, ভুটান প্রভৃতি অঞ্চলে। ত্রিপুরার রাজবংশও এই জনগোষ্ঠীর অন্তর্গত। ব্রহ্মদেশের উত্তর অংশের শ্যামবংশীয় রাজাদের এক শাখা যারা 'ফা' উপাধি ব্যবহার করতেন, তারা কামরূপের পূর্বাংশে একটি স্বাধীনরাজ্য স্থাপন করেন। এইরাজ্যের ছোট রাজকুমার ত্রিপুর কাছাড়ের উত্তরাংশে যে রাজ্য স্থাপন করেন তাই প্রাচীন ত্রিপুরা (তৃপুরা, ত্রীপুরা)। এই রাজ্য ক্রমশঃ দক্ষিণে সরতে থাকে এবং ক্রমশঃ বর্তমান ত্রিপুরা রাজ্যের জন্ম হয়।

ত্রিপুরা প্রায় আঠারশো থেকে দু হাজার বছর পুরানো রাজ্য।এই দীর্ঘ সময়ের ইতিহাসে বারবার পরিবর্তিত হয়েছে রাজধানী। রাজ্যের সীমা কখনো বেড়েছে তো কখনো কমেছে। উত্থান-পতন ঘটেছে রাজনীতি ও অর্থনীতির। মিশ্রণ ঘটেছে জাতিগত দিক থেকে। বিবর্তিত হয়েছে সমাজ, ধর্ম, শিক্ষা, চিকিৎসা, কৃষি প্রভৃতির ইতিহাস। এই বিবর্তন পথ বেয়েই আজকের ত্রিপুরা।

এই বিবর্তনের ধারায় যে বিস্তৃত রোড ম্যাপ পাওয়া যায় তার অঙ্গ হলো

কাছাড়, আসাম, মণিপুর, উড়িষ্যা, পশ্চিমবঙ্গ, বর্তমান বাংলাদেশ প্রভৃতি। তাই ত্রিপুরার ইতিহাস খুঁজতে গিয়ে আভ্যন্তরীণ অনুসন্ধানের সঙ্গে এই রোডম্যাপ ধোরেও ঘুরতে এবং খুঁজতে হবে।

ত্রিপুরার রাজবংশের রাজাদের উপাধির দিক থেকে 'ফা এবং মাণিক্য'-এই দুরকম উপাধি পাওয়া যায়। 'ফা' উপাধিক রাজা রাজত্ব করেছেন আনুমানিক নিরানব্বই জন। আর ভারত ভুক্তির পূর্ব পর্যন্ত 'মাণিক্য' উপাধিক রাজা রাজত্ব করেছেন ৪৫ জন। ত্রিপুরার ইতিহাসে প্রাচীন যুগ ধরতে হবে 'ফা' উপাধিক রাজাদের কালকে। এসময়ে লিখিত কোন তথ্য পাওয়া যায়নি। তাই এ সময়ের ইতিহাস পুরোটাই ধোঁয়াচ্ছন্ন। কোন কোন বিশেষ রাজ্য সম্বন্ধে যতটুকু জানা যায় তার উৎস হলো পরম্পরাগত লোকশ্রুতি।

১০০তম রাজা রত্ন ফা-র আমল থেকে ত্রিপুর রাজারা মামিক্য উপাধি ধারণ করে। এসময় থেকেই নির্দিষ্ট সন তারিখ পাওয়া যায়। রত্ন ফা সিংহাসনে বসেন আনুমানিক ১২৮৮ খ্রীষ্টাব্দে। এসময় থেকে ত্রিপুরা এবং ত্রিপুরার রাজবংশের সঙ্গে বাইরের যোগাযোগ স্থাপিত হয়। এবং ত্রিপুরায় রাজনীতি হোতে শুরু করে দেন জীবনের সকল স্তরের পরিবর্তনও শুরু হয় এসময় থেকেই। তাই এসময়কেই ত্রিপুরার ইতিহাসে মধ্যযুগ আখ্যা দেওয়া যেতে পারে।

তারপর ১৩২-তম রাজা কৃষ্ণমাণিক্যের কাল থেকে ত্রিপুরার আধুনিক যুগ ধরা যায়। এসময় থেকেই ত্রিপুরায় ইংরেজ শাসন প্রণালীর আদল প্রচলন হতে থাকে। ত্রিপুরায় মধ্যযুগে অনেক রীতি-নীতি এবং সংস্কারেরও পরিবর্তন ঘটতে থাকে। আধুনিক যুগকে দু'ভাগ করতে হবে। প্রথম অর্ধ ১৩২তম রাজা থেকে ১৪৪তম রাজা কিরীটবিক্রম কিশোর মাণিক্যের কাল পর্যন্ত। ১৯৪৯ সনে ত্রিপুরার ভারতভুক্তি থেকে আধুনিক যুগের দ্বিতীয় অর্ধের শুরু।

ত্রিপুরা রাজ্যের এই দীর্ঘ ইতিহাসের পাণ্ডুলিপি কেন্দ্রিক তথ্য খুঁজতে গেলে বলতে হয় প্রাচীনযুগের কোনো পাণ্ডুলিপি পাওয়া যায়নি। মধ্যযুগের ক্ষেত্রে ১৩২৯ শক বা ১৪০৭ খ্রীষ্টাব্দে ১০৪তম রাজা ধর্মমাণিক্য 'শুক্রেশ্বর এবং বাণেশ্বর' নামের দুজন পুরোহিত দ্বারা পদ্যে যে রাজমালা লিখেছেন তা এক মূল্যবান দলিল ছিলো। কিন্তু এখন সেই রাজমালা পাওয়া যায় না। এটা ত্রিপুরার ইতিহাসের ক্ষেত্রে খুবই দুর্ভাগ্যজনক। এর ১৯০ বছর পরে ১১৪তম রাজা অমরমাণিক্য উজীর দুর্গা মাণিক্যকে দিয়ে রাজমালা পরিবর্ধিত করেছিলেন-এ গ্রন্থ

মূল্যবানদলিল হিসেবে এখনো আছে।

দ্বিতীয়তঃ ত্রিপুরার ঐতিহাসিক দলিল হিসেবে আর যে পাণ্ডুলিপিগুলোর নাম শোনা যায় তার একটি হলো শেখ মনোহর রচিত সমসের গাজীর জীবনীগ্রন্থ গাজীনামা এবং অন্যটি হলো চম্পকবিজয় নামক গ্রন্থ। শুনেছি ঢাকা বিশ্ববিদ্যালয়ের পুঁথিশালায় দুখানা পাণ্ডুলিপি আছে।

তৃতীয়তঃ মোঘল সম্রাট সাজাহানের পুত্রদের বিবাদের প্রেক্ষাপটে ত্রিপুরার রাজাকে লেখা সম্রাট ঔরঙ্গজেবের একখানা চিঠি রক্ষিত আছে ত্রিপুরা আর্কাইভস্-এ। কিন্তু একটা রাজ্যের চলমান জীবনের নানা তথ্য খুঁজতে গেলে নামতে হবে ক্ষেত্রানুসন্ধানে। এই বিশ্বাস বুকে নিয়েই আমি ১৯৮০ সনে (এম.এ. পরীক্ষার পরেই) ত্রিপুরায় ক্ষেত্রানুসন্ধান শুরু করি। বিশেষ কিছু পাবো এমন ভরসা কমই ছিলো। কিন্তু খুঁজতে খুঁজতে আজ পর্যন্ত আড়াইশোর উপর পাণ্ডুলিপি পেয়ে গেছি। সাধারণ মানুষের নিকট অযত্নে পতিত এসব পাণ্ডুলিপি সংগ্রহের নেশা আমায় ঘুরিয়েছে সমগ্র ত্রিপুরা, শিলচর, কলকাতা, বাংলাদেশ প্রভৃতি রাজ্য এবং দেশ। এসব পাণ্ডুলিপি মূলতঃ ত্রিপুরার মধ্যযুগের নানা ইতিহাসের প্রমাণ বহন করে। এবার আমার আবিষ্কৃত পাণ্ডুলিপিগুলোর প্রেক্ষাপটে ত্রিপুরার ইতিহাসের বিষয়টি সূত্রাকারে নির্দেশ করছি। তাই এই প্রবন্ধকে গবেষণার রূপরেখা বলা যাবে — ঠিক গবেষণা সন্দর্ভ নয়।

একসময় সমতল ত্রিপুরা এবং পার্বত্য ত্রিপুরা নামে সমগ্র ত্রিপুরা দুভাগে বিভক্ত ছিল। ১০৬তম রাজা ধন্যমাণিক্য, ১১০তম রাজা বিজয় মাণিক্য প্রমুখদের চেষ্টায় পশ্চিমদিকে বর্তমান বাংলাদেশের অনেকটা ভূমিই ত্রিপুরার অন্তর্ভুক্ত হয়। যেমন শ্রীহট্টের কিছু অংশ, ব্রাহ্মণবাড়িয়া, আখাউড়া, জাজীনগর, কুমিল্লা, ফেনী, নোয়াখালি প্রভৃতি অঞ্চল নিয়ে ছিলো সমগ্র ত্রিপুরা। আবার কখনো কখনো তা ত্রিপুরার হাতছাড়াও হয়ে যায়। বর্তমানে এসব অঞ্চল তো বাংলাদেশ রাষ্ট্রের অংশ। ভারতভাগের প্রেক্ষাপটে ত্রিপুরার পার্শ্ববর্তী এসব অঞ্চলের হিন্দুদের যারা ত্রিপুরায় উঠে এসেছেন, তাদের নিয়ে আসা পাণ্ডুলিপিগুলোকে ত্রিপুরার নাকি বাংলাদেশের বলা হবে তাও গবেষণা সাপেক্ষ। (২০১১ সনের ১৭ থেকে ২১ ডিসেম্বর ঢাকা বিশ্ববিদ্যালয়ে ২য় আন্তর্জাতিক বঙ্গবিদ্যা সম্মেলনে আমন্ত্রিত সদস্য হিসেবে গিয়ে আমি বাংলাদেশ এবং ত্রিপুরা মিলিয়ে যৌথ গবেষণার বিষয়টি পণ্ডিতমহলে উপস্থাপনও করে এসেছি। আমার মনে হয় এই যৌথ প্রচেষ্টা একান্ত জরুরী।) বর্তমানে আমি সে বিচারে না গিয়ে ত্রিপুরায়

আবিষ্কৃত আমার পাণ্ডুলিপিগুলোকে অখণ্ড ত্রিপুরার ধোরেই বিভিন্ন দিক থেকে ত্রিপুরার বিবর্তনের পরিচয় দেবার চেষ্টা করছি।

আগেই উল্লেখ করেছি যে, ১০০তম রাজা রত্ন ফা (মাণিক্য) থেকেই ত্রিপুরায় মধ্যযুগের শুরু। এসময় ত্রিপুরার সনাতনী রাজ্যশাসন পদ্ধতি, ধর্মবোধ, সমাজনীতি, শিক্ষা - সংস্কৃতি সব কিছুতেই নবজাগরণ আসে। কারণ এসময় থেকে রাজ্যশাসন, জাতিগত অভিন্নতা, ধর্ম, সমাজ সব ক্ষেত্রেই একটা মিশ্রণ ঘটে যায়। ত্রিপুরায় আগমন ঘটে হিন্দু-বাঙালী এবং মুসলমানদের। কারণ রত্ন ফা (মাণিক্য) লক্ষণাবতীর মালিক তুঘ্রলখাঁর সাহায্য নিয়ে ভাইদের পরাজিত করে ত্রিপুরার সিংহাসন দখল করেন। এর আগে ত্রিপুরার ইতিহাসে এমন প্রমাণ নাই যে, বিদেশীর সাহায্য নিয়ে কেউ রাজ্য দখল করছেন। ফলে ত্রিপুরার সঙ্গে সম্পর্ক স্থাপিত হয় বাংলার মুসলমান শাসকদের।

ভাইদের দ্বারা বিতাড়িত হয়ে গৌড়ে অবস্থানকালে তিনজন হিন্দু বাঙালীর সঙ্গে রত্নফার বন্ধুত্ব হয়। প্রথম দুজন বড় খাণ্ডব ঘোষ এবং পণ্ডিত রাজ ছিলেন লিপি ব্যবসায়ী এবং তৃতীয় নারায়ণ সেন ছিলেন চিকিৎসক। রাজা হয়ে রত্ন মাণিক্য এদের ত্রিপুরায় নিয়ে আসেন। শুরু হয় ত্রিপুরার সঙ্গে হিন্দু বাঙালীদের সম্পর্ক। তারপর থেকে রাজকাজ, সেনাবিভাগ, শিক্ষা, স্বাস্থ্য সব ক্ষেত্রেই হিন্দু বাঙালীরা উচ্চপদে আসীন হতে থাকে। রত্ন মাণিক্যের আমলেই হিন্দু ব্রাহ্মণদেরও আগমন ঘটে ত্রিপুরায়। কথিত আছে যে, ক্রমশঃ স্থানীয় ব্রাহ্মণদের স্থলাভিষিক্ত হতে থাকেন হিন্দু ব্রাহ্মণরাই। মোটকথা এই যে, রত্ন মাণিক্যের আমল থেকেই ত্রিপুরার সনাতনী রাজ্য শাসন প্রণালী, জাতিগত শুদ্ধতা, ধর্মনীতি, সমাজনীতি, চিকিৎসা প্রভৃতি নতুন পথে প্রবাহিত হয় এবং মিশ্র সংস্কৃতির জন্ম হয়। ত্রিপুরার পাণ্ডুলিপিগুলো এই মিশ্র ইতিহাসেরই পরিচায়ক। আমার আবিষ্কৃত পাণ্ডুলিপির অধিকাংশই ধর্ম বিষয়ক। তাই ধর্ম প্রসঙ্গ দিয়েই শুরু করা যাক ঃ

ত্রিপুরায় ধর্মের ক্ষেত্রে ঐতিহাসিক বিবর্তন অনুধাবন করলে পাওয়া যায় ঃ

১। ৯৯তম রাজা পর্যন্ত ভেজালহীন জাতীয় ধর্ম। প্রধান ছিলেন চৌদ্দ দেবতা।

২। ১০০তম রাজা থেকে হিন্দুধর্ম তথা ব্রাহ্মণ্য প্রভাব। (এ সময় ত্রিপুরার রাজারা মূলতঃ শাক্ত এবং শৈব)।

৩। দ্বাদশ-ত্রয়োদশের দিকে ত্রিপুরা বৌদ্ধধর্মের প্রবেশ ঘটে। কিন্তু এই ধর্ম রাজা-প্রজা কারো ওপরই তেমন প্রভাব বিস্তার করতে পারেনি।

৪। ১১৫তম রাজধর মাণিক্যের আমলে নিত্যানন্দ বংশজ গোস্বামীগণ রাজপরিবারে কৃষ্ণমন্ত্রের বীজ বোনেন। ফলে রাজ্যবাসীর মধ্যেও তা বিস্তৃত হয়। তবে, রাজপরিবার বৈষ্ণব হলেও দেশীয় সংস্কার, শাক্ত-শৈব সংস্কার কখনো বর্জিত হয়নি। তাই ত্রিপুরায় রাজা-প্রজা সবাই মিলে যে ধর্মের জন্ম দিয়েছেন তা হলো মিশ্রধর্ম।

মিশ্র সংস্কৃতি হলেও মাণিক্য আমলের রাজারা হিন্দুতথা বৈদিক সংস্কৃতি গ্রহণ ও পৃষ্ঠপোষণ করেছেন বলে এই সংস্কৃতি আশ্রিত পাণ্ডুলিপির সংখ্যাই বেশী এবং এগুলো বিভিন্নরকম পূজাবিধি এবং মন্ত্রের। যেমন -

১। সন্ধ্যাপদ্ধতি, ২। গন্ধবিধি, ৩। হরিপূজন বিধি ৪। শিবপূজা বিধি ৫। অনন্ত ব্রতবিধি ৬। যজুর্বেদিয় কুশণ্ডিকা হোমবিধি, ৭) মহিযোৎসর্গ বিধি ৮) দোলপূজা বিধি ৯) বলিদান বিধি ১০) মন্ত্র পুনশ্চরণ বিধি ১১) পিপিতক দ্বাদশ ব্রতবিধি ১২। হরিহরের পূজাবিধি, প্রভৃতি। এছাড়া এক্ষেত্রে আছে ১৩। পুর বর্গ ১৪। পাতাল বর্গ ১৫। পৃথিবী বর্গ, ১৬। শিলা বর্গ নামের পাণ্ডুলিপি। সব দেশের সব সমাজের জন্ম এবং মৃত্যুর পরে মানুষ কিছু আচার অনুষ্ঠান, ক্রিয়াকর্ম করে থাকে। মৃত্যুর পরে ক্রিয়াকর্মের যে পাণ্ডুলিপিগুলো পেয়েছি তার মধ্যে অন্ত্যেষ্টি বিধি, অশৌচ বিধি, শ্রাদ্ধ বিধি, দশকর্ম বিধি প্রভৃতি বিশেষ উল্লেখযোগ্য।

ত্রিপুরায় প্রাচীনকাল থেকেই তন্ত্রসাধনার একটা ধারা প্রবাহিত ছিল। পরে মন্ত্র শাখার মতো তন্ত্র শাখাও ত্রিপুরার জনজীবনকে বিশেষবাবে প্রভাবিত করেছিল। এ শাখার আবিষ্কৃত পাণ্ডুলিপিগুলো হলো ঃ শ্রীশ্রীচণ্ডী, দুর্গাপূজা বিধি, ত্রিপুরা সুন্দরী পূজাবিধি, দুর্গাষষ্ঠি পূজাবিধি, শীতলা পূজাবিধি, চণ্ডিকা পূজাবিধি প্রভৃতি।

মধ্যযুগ থেকে ত্রিপুরায় জ্যোতিষ শাস্ত্রের চর্চাও ছিল। এ বিষয়ে কয়েকটি পাণ্ডুলিপি পাওয়া গেছে।

আয়ুর্বেদ হলো চিকিৎসা শাস্ত্র। 'শরীরং রোগমন্দিরম্'। প্রাণী মাত্রেরই রোগ ব্যাধি আছে এবং তা থেকে রক্ষা পাওয়ার চেষ্টাও চিরকালই ছিল, আছে এবং থাকবে। আধুনিক চিকিৎসা বিজ্ঞানের আবিষ্কারের পূর্বে রোগ থেকে বাঁচার উপায় ছিল ভেষজ চিকিৎসা এবং বিভিন্ন দেবদেবীর পূজার্চনা। ত্রিপুরাও এর ব্যতিক্রম নয়। প্রাচীনকালের ত্রিপুরায়ও ভেষজ এবং দেবদেবীর পূজার মাধ্যমে রোগমুক্তির চেষ্টা হতো। ত্রিপুরার চৌদ্দজন কুল দেবতার মধ্যে বূড়াচ্ছা এবং বুড়াচ্ছার দুই পুত্র বনিরাও এবং ধনিরাও ছিলেন রোগমুক্তির দেবতা।

ব্রাহ্মণ সংস্কৃতি প্রবেশের পরে ত্রিপুরায় আয়ুর্বেদ শাস্ত্রের প্রচলন ঘটে। আয়ুর্বেদ শাস্ত্রের বেশ কিছু পাণ্ডুলিপি পেয়েছি আমি। এই পাণ্ডুলিপিগুলো তিনভাগে বিভক্ত। কিছু রোগ নির্ণয়ের, কিছু হলো রোগ চিকিৎসার এবং কিছু হলো ঔষধ বানানোর পদ্ধতি বিষয়ক। ত্রিপুরার দক্ষিণে আরাকান রাজ্যের মগ রাজারা বৌদ্ধধর্মাবলম্বী। আরাকানের সঙ্গে ত্রিপুরার রাজনৈতিক টানাপোড়েন ঐতিহাসিক ঘটনা। মগ রাজারা একবার ত্রিপুরার রাজধানী উদয়পুরও লুঠ করেছিল। ত্রিপুরার লোকসমাজ এবং সমাজজীবনে বৌদ্ধধর্ম প্রভাব বিস্তার করতে না পারলেও মগ সম্প্রদায়ের কিছু লোক ক্রমশ ফেনী নদী পেরিয়ে এসে ত্রিপুরায় বসতি স্থাপন করে। এসূত্রেই বর্তমান দক্ষিণ ত্রিপুরায় মগ সম্প্রদায়ের বৌদ্ধধর্মালম্বী কিছু বসতি আছে। এঁদের নিকট বৌদ্ধধর্মের অনেক পাণ্ডুলিপি আছে। আমি একখানা সংগ্রহ করতে পেরেছি। পুঁথিখানা বার্মিজ ভাষায় লেখা।

রাজপরিবারে কৃষ্ণমন্ত্রের বীজ বোনা হলো। তাই রাজ পরিবার এবং ত্রিপুরার সমাজ জীবনেও বৈষ্ণবধর্মের প্রভাব ছড়িয়ে পড়ে। ফলে বৈষ্ণব ধর্মের চর্চাসূত্রে এই ধর্মের অনেক পাণ্ডুলিপি রচিত হয়। আমি বেশ কিছু পাণ্ডুলিপি পেয়েছি। কিছু উদাহরণ ঃ

১। বৈষ্ণব পদাবলী ও কৃষ্ণ লীলা ২) অষ্টপ্রকার শক্তিসঞ্চারণ ৩। হরিনামের বিচার ৪। সাধক চূড়ামণি

৫। জ্ঞান চৌতিযা ৬। জ্ঞান প্রদীপ ৭। জ্ঞান রত্নমালা ৮। আশ্রয় তত্ত্ব ৯। বৃন্দাবন তত্ত্ব প্রভৃতি। এগুলোর মধ্যে একখানা বিশেষ পাণ্ডুলিপি আছে। এতে বৃন্দাবন তত্ত্ব লিখতে গিয়ে লেখক আরবী রীতির প্রয়োগ করেছেন। অর্থাৎ কাহিনী শেষ পৃষ্ঠা থেকে প্রথম পৃষ্ঠার দিকে এগিয়েছে। পৃষ্ঠা সংখ্যাও এগিয়ে বামদিকে কিন্তু পৃষ্ঠার চরণগুলো বাংলা ভাষার রীতিতেই বাম থেকে ডানে।

শিক্ষা, সংস্কার, ধর্ম যতই থাকনা কেন, সমাজের তৃণমূল স্তরে তাবিজ-কবজ, জলপড়া, তেলপড়া প্রভৃতির প্রচলন দেখা যায় সবসময়ই। ত্রিপুরাতে এরূপ দুখানা পাণ্ডুলিপি পেয়েছি।

ত্রিপুরায় প্রত্যক্ষভাবে শিক্ষার বিস্তার শুরু হয়েছিল সংস্কৃত সাহিত্য এবং সংস্কৃত ব্যাকরণ শিক্ষার মাধ্যমে। কালিদাসের শৃঙ্গার তিলক ও স্বপ্নাধায় নামক পাণ্ডুলিপি এবং খ্যাত বৃদ্ধি ও কলাপ ব্যাকরণের পাণ্ডুলিপিগুলো তার প্রমাণবহ।

তাছাড়া নবজাগরণের কালে জ্ঞানের পিপাসা মেটাতে গড়ে ওঠে অনুবাদ সাহিত্য শাখা। ভারতের ঐতিহ্যবহ সংস্কৃত ভাষার রামায়ণ, মহাভারত প্রভৃতি

মহাকাব্যগুলো ত্রিপুরাতে বাংলা ভাষায় অনূদিত হয়েছিল। আমার সংগ্রহে আছে অনূদিত রামায়ণ - মহাভারতের পাণ্ডুলিপি। এ শাখার প্রাকৃতভাষা থেকে অনূদিত একখানা পাণ্ডুলিপিও পেয়েছি। নাম, বৈশাখ মাহাত্ম্য। পুঁথির পুষ্পিকা অংশ থেকে জানা যায় যে, পুঁথির উৎস উৎকল তথা উড়িয্যা। প্রমাণ ঃ

নরসিংহ উৎকলেতে বিরচিলা পরাকৃতে
শ্রবণেতে অতি মনোহর।
ঠাকুর শ্রীদিগম্বর শরণ তার অন্তর
হরিনাম গান নিরন্তর।।
তাহার হইল আজ্ঞা না করিলাম অবিজ্ঞা
ঐ বাণী দৃঢ়করি মানি।
বঙ্গবাক্যে বিরচিল সেবি সাধু ধর্মশীল
লক্ষণেরে যা কর আপনি।।

বিষয় বিচারে পাণ্ডুলিপিখানা ব্যক্তিক্রমধর্মী। বৈশাখ মাসে গরমে খাদ্যাখাদ্য নির্ণয়, আগত অতিথির প্রতি কর্তব্য নির্ণয় প্রভৃতি বর্ণিত হয়েছে। তাছাড়া গ্রীষ্মকালে পুকুর খনন, গাছ লাগানো, গাছের গোড়ায় জল দেয়া, জলসত্র স্থাপন করা প্রভৃতি কাজকে খুব পুণ্যকাজ বলে বর্ণনা করা হয়েছে। কাহিনী বর্ণিত হয়েছে মূল গল্পের সঙ্গে ছোট ছোট গল্প জুড়ে। সবটা প্রায় ১৬টি গল্পের একটি মালা। এই পুঁথিখানা গবেষণার অপেক্ষা রাখে। প্রথম প্রয়োজন উৎকলের প্রাকৃত গ্রন্থখানার সন্ধান করা। আমার পক্ষে তা এখনো সম্ভব হয়ে ওঠেনি।

অনুবাদের মাধ্যমে জ্ঞানচর্চার ক্ষেত্রে এরপরে উল্লেখ করতে হয় বিভিন্ন সংস্কৃত পুরাণ থেকে কথা-কাহিনী অনুবাদের বিষয়। বেশকিছু পাণ্ডুলিপি পেয়েছি এক্ষেত্রে।

পালাগানের মাধ্যমেও রামায়ণ-মহাভারতের কথা সমাজে প্রচার হতো। রামায়ণের পালাগানের পাণ্ডুলিপি পাওয়া গেছে পিতা-পুত্র পরিচয়, মহাভারতের কথা আশ্রিত পালাগানের পাণ্ডুলিপি পাওয়া গেছে প্রহ্লাদ চরিত্র এবং নল-দময়ন্তী কথা। বৈষ্ণব ধর্মাশ্রিত পালা কীর্তনের পাণ্ডুলিপি পাওয়া গেছে মানভঞ্জন এবং রাইউন্মাদিনী প্রভৃতি।

বাংলা সাহিত্যের মধ্যযুগে অনুবাদ শাখার পাশে গড়ে ওঠে লোকসাহিত্য শাখা। লোকসাহিত্য,যা জনগণের, জনগণের দ্বারা এবং জনগণের জন্য রচিত। এরূপ সাহিত্যের একটি শাখা হলো পাঁচালি সাহিত্য। পাঁচালির আবিষ্কৃত

পাণ্ডুলিপিগুলোর মধ্যে কিছু হলো — সত্যদেব নারায়ণের পাঁচালি সাহিত্য। পাঁচালির আবিষ্কৃত পাণ্ডুলিপিগুলোর মধ্যে কিছু হলোঃ সত্যদেব নারায়ণের পাঁচালি, শনির পাঁচালি, অনন্ত ব্রতকথা পাঁচালি, অক্ষয় তৃতীয়া ব্রতকথা পাঁচালি, হরিহরের ব্রতকথা পাঁচালি, মাঘিব্রত পাঁচালি, গঙ্গামাহাত্ম্য পাঁচালি প্রভৃতি।

'Individual product' থেকে 'Group product'-এর দিকে গতি হলো লোকসাহিত্যের একটা প্রধান বৈশিষ্ট্য। এই সূত্রে পাঁচালিকে বুকে ধরে মঙ্গলকাব্যের জন্ম। এক্ষেত্রে পণ্ডিত জানকীনাথের পদ্মাপুরাণের পুঁথি পেয়েছি সাড়ে দশখানা। সুকবি বল্লভ নারায়ণ দেবের মনসামঙ্গলের পুঁথি একখানা এবং দ্বিজরামদেবের অভয়ামঙ্গলের পুঁথি দুখানা। মঙ্গলকাব্যের পাণ্ডুলিপিগুলো সমাজ বিবর্তনের ইতিহাসে খুবই গুরুত্বপূর্ণ। সমাজের আচার-বিচার, সংকার-কুসংস্কার, খাদ্যতালিকা, রন্ধনপ্রণালী সবকিছুরই ইতিহাস বহন করে মঙ্গলকাব্যগুলো। বিশেষতঃ মনসামঙ্গলের কাব্যগুলোতে ত্রয়োদশ শতক থেকে অষ্টাদশ শতক পর্যন্ত সমাজ বিবর্তনের দ্বারা প্রবাহিত। ত্রিপুরা রাজ্যে পুরো শ্রাবণমাস মনসামঙ্গল পাঠ করা হয়। হিন্দু বাঙালীদের প্রতি ঘরে অন্ততঃ একদিন পুঁথি পাঠের রীতি প্রচলিত। বিশেষত রমণীরাই দলবদ্ধভাবে পুঁথি-পাঠ-কীর্তন করে। সমস্ত শ্রাবণ মাসে মনসার পুঁথি পাঠ তো উৎসবের রূপ নেয়। এ অঞ্চলে মূল গায়ককে বলা হয় ওঝা। তাই এখানে মনসা পুঁথি পাঠের আরেক নাম ওঝার গান। শ্রাবণ সংক্রান্তির মনসা পুজোর অনুষ্ঠান ও অঞ্চলে দুর্গোৎসবের সমতুল্য।

অবসর বিনোদনে বিশেষত বর্ষাকালে ঘরে আবদ্ধ মানুষজন ঘরে নানারকম খেলার সৃষ্টি করে। এক্ষেত্রে নারী মহলে বর্তমান কালে বিশেষ প্রচলিত হলো 'লুডু খেলা'। দুরকম লুডু আছে। একটি হলো ছকলুডু এবং অন্যটি হলো সাপলুডু। আমি সাপলুডু মতে ওঠা - পড়ার রীতিতে খেলার এক রকম লুডুর পাণ্ডুলিপি পেয়েছি। নাম-গোলাকধাম লুডু। বর্তমান লুডু শুধুই খেলার বিষয়ক। কিন্তু গোলকধাম লুডুর সঙ্গে ধর্মীয় শিক্ষা যুক্ত আছে। অর্থাৎ সবার উপরে আছে গোলকধাম। গোলকধামে পৌঁছতে গেলে নানা বাধা অতিক্রম করতে হয়। যেমন সাপের মাথায় পোড়লে আবার লেজে চোলে আসতে হয় তেমনি গোলকধামে পৌঁছার পথে অনভিপ্রেত স্থানে পোড়লে জীবনে যে আবার পতন ঘটে তারই ইঙ্গিতবহ হলো গোলকধাম লুডু।

রাজশাসিত রাজ্যে নানা উপলক্ষেই প্রজারা রাজা, রাণী, রাজকুমার, রাজকুমারীদের বন্দনা নামে একখানা পাণ্ডুলিপি পেয়েছি।

বৈষ্ণব ধর্মের মূলে আছে প্রেম। প্রেমের সঙ্গে কামের সম্পর্ক। তাই

একসময় বৈষ্ণবধর্মে কামাচার আশ্রিত তন্ত্রাচার ঢুকে পড়ে। বলার অপেক্ষা রাখে না যে, তন্ত্রাচার ঢোকায় শুদ্ধপ্রেমের বৈষ্ণবধর্মে অশুদ্ধতা দেখা দেয়। মহারাজ বীরচন্দ্র মাণিক্য বাহাদুর বৈষ্ণবধর্মের শুদ্ধাচার রক্ষায় সচেষ্ট হয়েছিলেন। তিনি বৈষ্ণবদেরকে চার দফায় ভাগ করেছিলেন এবং 'একরানামা' প্রদান করেছিলেন। এরূপ একখানা 'একরানামা' পেয়েছি। দাতা উদয়পুর তুলামুড়ার শ্রী যুক্তহরি মুড়াসিং মহাশয়। তাঁর সম্প্রদায়ের প্রাচীন ব্যক্তিটি মূল পাণ্ডুলিপিখানা দেননি বোলে যুক্তহরি বাবু ফটোকপি করে এনে আমায় দিয়েছেন।

মহারাজা বীরচন্দ্রমাণিক্য বাহাদুরের আমলে বৈষ্ণবদেরকে রাজকোষাগারে বার্ষিক কিছু টাকা জমা দিতে হত। টাকা জমা দেওয়ার একখানা রসিদও ফটোকপি করে এনে দিয়েছেন শ্রদ্ধেয় শ্রীযুক্তহরি মুড়াসিং মহাশয়। রসিদ পত্রটিতে স্বাক্ষর করেছেন রাজগুরু শ্রীল শ্রীযুক্ত মানিকলাল প্রভু।

ত্রিপুরায় জমির সংক্রান্ত বিষয়গুলোর মধ্যে আছে রাজাদের দ্বারা নিষ্কর ভূমিদান, জমিবিক্রি, পাট্টানামাদান, জমিবন্ধক দেয়া প্রভৃতি। নিষ্কর ভূমিদানের বিষয় তাম্রপত্র প্রভৃতিতে হলেও অন্যবিষয়গুলো সাধারণ কাগজে হাতে লিখেই কাজ চালনো হতো মহারাজ বীরচন্দ্র মাণিক্যের দেওয়ান নীলমণি দাস কর্তৃক ১২৮৩ ত্রিং থেকে স্ট্যাম্পে দলিল রেজিস্টারির নিয়ম প্রচলনের পূর্ব পর্যন্ত।

ত্রিপুরার রাজারা ব্রাহ্মণদেরকে ব্রহ্মোত্তর সম্পদ দান করতেন-তা ঐতিহাসিক সত্য। বিশেষ বিশেষ কীর্তিমান প্রজাদেরকেও ভূমিদান করতেন। এরূপ একখানা তাম্রপত্র পেয়েছি। তাছাড়া, সাধারণ দরিদ্র প্রজারাও যে রাজার নিকটে খোরপোসের আবেদন করতো অনুরূপ একখানা আবেদনপত্রও পেয়েছি।

ত্রিপুরায় মহাজনী ব্যবসা ছিলো প্রাচীনকাল থেকেই। মানুষ প্রয়োজনে জমি বন্ধক রেখে মহাজনদের নিকট থেকে টাকা ঋণ নিতো। স্ট্যাম্পের ব্যবহার শুরু হলে মহাজনদের নিকট জমি বন্ধক রেখে ঋণ নেওয়ার বিষয়টিও স্ট্যাম্পের মাধ্যমে প্রচলিত হয়। এরূপ একখানা দলিল পেয়েছি ১৮০০ শকাব্দ তথা ১৮৭৮ খৃষ্টাব্দেব। এ দলিল দেখে বোঝা যায় যে, মহাজনীপ্রথা সরকারী স্বীকৃত ছিল।

ত্রিপুরায় পাট্টাদান প্রথাও প্রচলিত ছিল। জমিদার জমিদারীরা যে কোন অংশ নির্ধারিত খাজনায় অন্যের সহিত পুরুষানুক্রমে ভোগদখল করার শর্তে চিরস্থায়ী যে বন্দোবস্ত করেন তার নাম পত্তনি বা পত্তনি তালুক। পত্তনির লিখিত দলিলকে বলা হয় পাট্টানামা। সরকারী স্ট্যাম্পে লিখিত এরূপ কয়েকখানা পাট্টানামা পেয়েছি।

জমি সংক্রান্ত বাদ বিবাদের আরো বেশ কয়েকখানা দলিল পেয়েছি। দলিলগুলো পড়ে একথা বলা যায় যে, ত্রিপুরায় রাজ আমলের বিচার ব্যবস্থা ছিল নিরপেক্ষ।

রাজারা অনেকসময় রাণীদের নামে ভূমিদান করতেন এবং পরে এসব ভূমি নিয়েও নানা জটিলতা সৃষ্টি হয়েছে। শ্রী শ্রীমতি মহারাণী প্রভাবতী দেবীর নামাঙ্কিত অনুরূপ একখানা দলিল পেয়েছি। ক্রমশঃ রাজপরিবরের জমি যে, সাধারণ মানুষের নিকট বিক্রি হওয়া শুরু হয়েছে তার প্রমাণ মূলক একটি দলিলের সূচনা এরূপ ঃ

শ্রী শ্রীমতি যষ্ঠ মহারাণী চন্দ্রতারা দেবী পতি স্বর্গীয় মহারাজা বীরেন্দ্র কিশোর মাণিক্য বাহাদুর পক্ষে আমমোক্তার মহারাজ কুমার শ্রীদুর্জ্জয় কিশোর দেববর্মা পিতা স্বর্গীয় মহারাজ বীরেন্দ্র কিশোর মাণিক্য বাহাদূর সাকিন নুতন হাবেলী পরগণে আগরতলা থানা ও সাবরেজিস্ট্রি সদর জিলা ত্রিপুরা। জাতি ক্ষত্রিয় ব্যবসা তালুকদারী আদি।

সাফ কাবালা দলিল দাত্রী পক্ষে আমমোক্তারদাতা

শ্রীমতি সুষমাদেবী পতি শ্রীগোবন্দিচন্দ্র দে সাকিন নতুন হাবেলী টাউন কৃষ্ণনগর পরগনে আগরতলা থানা ও সাবরেজিস্ট্রি সদর জিলা ত্রিপুরা। জাতি হিন্দু ব্যবসা তেজারতি আদি। সাফ কাবালা দলিল গ্রহিত্রী।

আরেকখানা দলিল পেয়েছি যা পাকিস্তান এবং ত্রিপুরায় মোধ্যে জমি বিনিময়ের প্রমাণ। পাকিস্তান থেকে এসেছিলেন জমিদার লালমোহন ভৌমিক এবং এখান থেকে গিয়েছেন শিবনগরের আবদুল কায়ুম খান। (দলিল বিষয়ে বলার তাৎপর্য এই যে, এগুলো আরো ভালো করে পর্যালোচনা করতে হবে। তাহলে ত্রিপুরার এবং আগরতলার ভূমি এবং রাজস্ব সংক্রান্ত অনেক পুরানো তথ্য আবিষ্কৃত হবে)।

সমাজ এবং সমাজের গতি নদীর মতো নিত্য গতিশীল এবং পরিবর্তনশীল। চলার পথে রাজনীতি, অর্থনীতি, সমাজনীতি পরিবর্তিত হতে থাকে এবং রচিত হতে থাকে ইতিহাস। আবার সৃষ্টির উল্লাসে উন্মত্ত মানুষ নিজের কালের সমাজের ছবি এবং চিন্তা চেতনা প্রকাশ করতে থাকে নানা উপায়ে। প্রকাশের মাধ্যম যখন যেমন তার সাহায্যই আশ্রয় করা হতো। লেখার সূত্রে পাণ্ডুলিপির সৃষ্টি। তাই কেবল পাণ্ডুলিপির আশ্রয়ে কোনো দেশ বা জাতির বিকাশের পূর্ণাঙ্গ ইতিহাস রচনা করা সম্ভব নয়। শিলালিপি হতে শুরু করে সব কিছুর সাহায্যই নিতে হয়। তবে সব উপকরণের চেয়ে পাণ্ডুলিপির ভূমিকা যে প্রধান তা অনস্বীকার্য।

পাণ্ডুলিপির কাগজ বানানোর ক্ষেত্রে গ্রামীণ অর্থনীতির একটা ধারা প্রচলিত

থাকতো গ্রামে। এসূত্রেই গ্রামে থাকতো 'কাগজী পাড়া'। ত্রিপুরাতে এরূপ পাড়ার পরিচয় আজও পাওয়া যায়নি। তবে শোলা, বেত, তালপাতা, তেরেট পাতা-পাণ্ডুলিপি লেখার এসব উপাদান ব্যক্তিগত চেষ্টায় হয়েছে মানা গেলেও নানাধরনের তুলোট কাগজ এবং তার বহুল ব্যবহার দেখে অনুমান করা যায় যে, কাগজ তৈরির ক্ষেত্রে অর্থনৈতিক সম্পর্ক ছিল।

ত্রিপুরার ক্ষেত্রে পাণ্ডুলিপি সংগ্রহ এবং সরক্ষণের চেষ্টা হয়নি সচেতনভাবে। তাই পণ্ডুলিপির আশ্রয়ে ত্রিপুরার পূর্ণাঙ্গ ইতিহাস রচনার আগে জোর দিতে হবে আরো পাণ্ডুলিপি সংগ্রহের দিকে। প্রশ্ন হলো ত্রিপুরায় এখনো প্রাচীন এবং মধ্যযুগীয় পাণ্ডুলিপি পাওয়ার সম্ভাবনা আছে কতটুকু।

এক্ষেত্রে দীর্ঘদিনের অনুসন্ধানী হিসেবে আমার অভিজ্ঞতা এই যে, প্রাচীনযুগের পাণ্ডুলিপি পাওয়াটা সন্দেহ যুক্ত। মধ্যযুগের পাণ্ডুলিপি এখনো কিছু মানুষ রক্ষা করছে ঐতিহ্যের প্রতি শ্রদ্ধাসূত্রে। রাজনৈতিক দাঙ্গা, প্রাকৃতিক বিপর্যয়, আগুন এবং উইপোকার আক্রমণে দিনে দিনে কমছে রক্ষিত পাণ্ডুলিপি। তাই প্রথম কাজ সুনির্দিষ্ঠ ব্যবস্থাপনায় রাজ্যের ভিতরে পাণ্ডুলিপি সন্ধান করা। এই সন্ধানের জন্যে ত্রিপুরায় আগত বিভিন্ন জাতির ঐতিহাসিক রোডম্যাপ ধরে অনুসন্ধান করতে হবে। যেমন ত্রিপুরার উত্তর দিকে বাঙালী ছাড়া ঢুকেছে মণিপুরিরা, দক্ষিণে আরাকান থেকে আগত মগসম্প্রদায়ের উপজাতিরা, পূর্বদিকে কুকি, এবং অন্য অন্য উপজাতিরা। সবচেয়ে বেশি সংযোগ ছিলো পশ্চিম দক্ষিণের হিন্দু মুসলানদের সঙ্গে। এই রোডম্যাপ অনুসরণ করলে মণিপুরী, মগ প্রভৃতি জাতির পাণ্ডুলিপি পাবার সম্ভাবনা এখনো প্রবল। এটা আমার বাস্তব অভিজ্ঞতা। দ্বিতীয়তঃ পাশ্ববর্তী রাজ্যের গুরুত্ব বিচার করে এইসব রাজ্যের সংগৃহিত পাণ্ডুলিপির ভান্ডারে অনুসন্ধানকাজ চালাতে হবে গবেষকের দৃষ্টি নিয়ে। এই ক্ষেত্রে উল্লেখযোগ্য সাহায্য পাওয়া যাবে ঢাকা বিশ্ববিদ্যালয়ের পাণ্ডুলিপি সংগ্রহশালা থেকে। ত্রিপুরা বাংলাদেশের কোলের ভেতর বসে আছে এবং ঐতিহাসিক দিক থেকে বাংলাদেশের সঙ্গে ত্রিপুরার রাজনৈতিক, ভৌগোলিক, সাংস্কৃতিক সম্পর্ক সহোদরের মতো। তাই বাংলাদেশের বাংলা একাডেমি, জাদুঘর, ঢাকা বিশ্ববিদ্যালয়ের পাণ্ডুলিপি সংগ্রহশালা প্রভৃতিতে যে সব পাণ্ডুলিপি সংগৃহিত অবস্থায় আছে সেগুলো অনুসন্ধানের মাধ্যমে ত্রিপুরার ইতিহাস ররচনার অনেক উপাদান পাওয়া যাবে। দক্ষিণে খোঁজ করা যেতে পারে চট্টগ্রামে। পশ্চিমবঙ্গের সঙ্গেও ত্রিপুরার যোগাযোগ দীর্ঘদিনের। তাই পশ্চিমবঙ্গে কোলকাতা বিশ্ববিদ্যালয়, বঙ্গীয় সাহিত্য পরিষদ, প্রভৃতি সংগ্রহশালায় রক্ষিত পাণ্ডুলিপি সন্ধান করা যেতে পারে। উত্তরে কাছাড়েও

চলতে পারে খোঁজাখুঁজি।

বৈশাখ মাহাত্ম্য নামে আমার আবিষ্কৃত পাণ্ডুলিপির কথা আগেই উল্লেখ করেছি। তার উৎস উৎকল এবং তা প্রাকৃত ভাষা থেকে বাংলা ভাষা অনুদিত গ্রন্থ। ফলে রোডম্যাপ আরো এগিয়ে চলে গেল উড়িষ্যা পর্যন্ত এবং প্রমাণ হলো যে, উড়িষ্যার সঙ্গেও ত্রিপুরার সাংস্কৃতিক যোগ ছিল।

Contributors

1. Jahar Acharjee, Eminent Numismatist, owner of Rajendra Kirtishala Private Museum, Joynagar, Agartala.
2. Dr. Harekrishna Acharjee, Ex-Headmaster, Ramesh Higher Secondary School, Udaipur, Gomati.
3. Dr. Nirmal Bhadra, Assistant Professor (Sr. Grade), Govt. Degree College, Khumulwng, West Tripura.
4. Dr. Soma Basu, Associate Professor, School of Vedic Studies, Rabindra Bharati University, Kolkata.
5. Dr. Juthika Basu Bhowmik, Former Publication Officer, Department of Education, Government of Tripura.
6. Bikach Chaudhuri, Tripura's renowned intellectual, writer and scholar on Rabindranath Tagore.
7. Priyanku Chakraborty, Dept. of Sanskrit, Tripura University.
8. Chiranjivi Chaubey, Assistant Professor, Bihar.
9. Dr. Chandan Kumar Chakraborty, Associate Professor, Dept. of Sanskrit, Tripura University.
10. Rupak Debnath, Assistant Director, Directorate of Distance Education, Tripura University
11. Samhita Das Assistant Professor, Govt. Degree College, Amarpur, South Tripura.
12. Dr. Rabindranath Das Shastri is the Retd. Principal, Tripura Govt. Sanskrit College.
13. Pradeep Kumar Deepak, Assistant Professor, Dept. of History, Tripura Government College.
14. Naresh Ch. Dev Varma, Eminent Kokborok writer and researcher of Tripura.
15. Professor Sitanath Dey, (Retd.), Dept. of Sanskrit, Tripura University.

16. Dr. Kalpana Haldar Bhowmik, Deputy Librarian (Research), Dhaka University Library, Bangladesh.
17. Bihari Jha, Research Scholar, Dept. of Political Science, Tripura University.
18. Ng. Kangiia Mangang, Former Principal, Presidency College, Manipur.
19. Nirmalya Karmakar, Research Scholar, Dept. of History, Tripura University.
20. Sanjukta Mandal, Senior Principal Officer, Agrani, Bank, Dhaka.
21. Ashok Kumar Nath, Library and Information Officer, National Library, Kolkatta.
22. Rajibchandra Paul, Researcher, Dept. of Bengali, Tripura University.
23. Professor Satyadeo Poddar, teaches at the Dept. of History, Tripura University. He obtained his Master and Doctoral Degree from Banaras Hindu University, Varanasi. He is engaged in teaching and research in the Dept. of History, Tripura University for the last 27 years and at present he is Dean, Faculty of Arts and Commerce, Tripura University.
24. Professor I. Sarkar, Department of History, University of North Bengal, West Bengal
25. Neeru Wahal, Teacher, Kendriya Vidyalaya, Varanasi.